Mathematical Methods for Economists

Third Edition

Mathematical Methods for Economists

Stephen Glaister

Third Edition

Basil Blackwell

First edition 1972
Second edition 1978
Reprinted 1980
Third edition 1984
Reprinted 1985

Basil Blackwell Publisher Limited
108 Cowley Road, Oxford OX4 1JF, England

Basil Blackwell Inc.
432 Park Avenue South, Suite 1505
New York, NY 10016, USA

British Library Cataloguing in Publication Data

Glaister, Stephen
Mathematical methods for economists.—3rd ed.
1. Economics, Mathematical
I. Title
510'.2433 HB135

ISBN 0-631-13712-2

Typeset by Unicus Graphics Ltd, Horsham, West Sussex
Printed in Great Britain by Bell & Bain, Glasgow

Contents

Preface to this edition

Mathematical Methods for Economists proved to be sufficiently popular to justify the production of a second edition, and now a third edition, because it is concise. In preparing this edition I have preserved this. Apart from a few editorial alterations and an extension of the last chapter, the text is largely unaltered. However, I have made one major change. This is the addition of simple computer programs in the BASIC language to help explain points of principle and to provide further practical illustrations of the uses to which the techniques may be put.

Two things have led me to do this. One is a growing awareness that it is not uncommon for able students to work through a mathematics text such as this with apparent success, only to reveal at a later stage that they have a poor feel for what numbers and quantities really are. The second factor is the dramatic fall in the cost of calculators and small computers that has occurred since the earlier editions appeared. A number of readers will now be able to have access to such equipment. I hope to encourage students to experiment with numbers so as to confirm their understanding of the mathematical principles. They may also learn a little about how problems can be formulated so as to be amenable to exploration by numerical methods. Some of the routines presented have value as tools in themselves. They include simple matrix operations, curve plotting, differentiation, integration, numerical solution of first-order simultaneous difference and differential equations, and simple spectral analysis through the use of fast Fourier transforms.

The reader who has no interest in the new material will be able to use the text much as it was in the earlier editions by ignoring the sections on the computer programs. Readers who wish to try some of the programs should make a point of reading section 1.2.

Preface to the first edition

A course of twenty-five weekly lectures which have been given each year for a number of years at the London School of Economics constitute the origins of this book. Its purpose is to provide students with the knowledge of mathematics they will need during the course of their studies for the MSc in Economics which they will normally be taking the following year.

My intention in the lectures is to provide a working knowledge of certain fields of mathematics which are useful to economists, statisticians and other social scientists. I aim to give an understanding of the principles involved rather than simply providing a string of 'cook-book' recipes. At the same time I feel that it is important that the student sees some application of what he is learning at an early stage and that he quickly learns to apply it correctly for himself. Otherwise he is often discouraged by having to plough through a great deal of abstract material of no obvious relevance to his interests. This has to be accomplished within the limited lecturing time available and assuming that the students have little prior knowledge of the subject.

The resulting book is somewhere in between a set of terse lecture notes and a fully explanatory text—which would have filled a volume several times the size of this one. Definitions and theorems are stated formally so that it is easy to identify the precise formal content of what is being said. Formal proofs of many results are also given because many people find that it is only by working through proofs that the full meaning and significance of a result can be understood. However, there is some informal explanation and discussion and at each stage liberal use is made of applications and illustrations from various fields of economics.

Although I have attempted to make the whole book accessible to a reader starting with little knowledge of mathematics the rate of progress is high. A reader in difficulty might be well advised to refer to a more leisurely text before returning to this one. Suggested references appear elsewhere. The meaning of certain undefined words should become clear through their usage.

A system of asterisks is introduced: * appended to a section number indicates that the material was not a vital part of the course; ** mean that the section is difficult, was not mentioned in the lectures and may be omitted. Formal proofs are terminated thus: ∎

The problems at the end of each chapter are those constructed for use in the seminar classes associated with the course and in examinations. They should be regarded as an integral part of the text and the reader is urged to test his understanding by working them. In several instances material appears only in the problems and occasionally the reader is asked to develop important concepts for himself in problems which anticipate the relevant portion of the text. It is also recommended that as many problems as possible be worked from other texts. This will insure against the possibility of overconfidence which might otherwise result from the necessarily brief and superficial nature of some parts of this book.

The order in which the two halves, linear algebra and analysis, are presented corresponds with that of the lectures but is not critical. The reader wishing to learn some calculus without all of the linear algebra could well proceed to Chapter 11 after the short Chapters 1 and 2.

I am grateful for advice from colleagues Tony Shorrocks and Steve Nickell and to many of the students on the courses for their valuable comments and assistance.

1 Introduction

Many problems in economic science involve complex relationships. Mathematical methods provide a flexible and convenient way of representing and analysing them. They provide techniques for making logical deductions which involve more variables than can be easily handled in other ways. They encourage rigour and force one to expose assumptions. The subject is becoming much more quantitative and the use of statistical analysis dictates the development of economic theory in mathematical form.

1.1 The topics in this book

The topics included in this book are of particular importance to anyone wishing to read or contribute to the quantitative economics literature. It is a narrow selection from the field of mathematics. It is not the selection that a physicist, engineer or mathematician would make.

Most economic theory concerns hypotheses about agents who cannot take decisions independently of one another and who are maximizers with limited resources. Hence we need to be able to analyse what happens in complex interdependent systems when something changes, for which the techniques of linear algebra are useful; and we need to be able to deal with rates of change and maximizing behaviour, for which the techniques of the calculus are useful. These are the two main fields chosen.

1.2 Computing

It is important to understand at every stage that the mathematics in this book is a way of making general statements about numbers. It is easy to lose sight of this simple fact when one is struggling with new concepts which are expressed symbolically. Calculators, programmable calculators and small computers have now become readily available and so, where it is appropriate, computer programs are introduced to encourage the reader to experiment with numbers in order to deepen his understanding. The programs are written in the BASIC language, but they are simple and can be translated into an alternative without difficulty. BASIC is used because it is the most commonly available language on small machines and because, as its name suggests, it is extremely simple for the beginner to pick up. It will generally be obvious on inspection what a program does. It will therefore be easy to implement it on a programmable calculator or to execute it by hand on a simple calculator in some cases. These exercises are not essential to the text and the reader may wish to ignore some, or all, of them.

Whilst the reader who carries out these exercises may learn some of the rudiments of computing he should be aware that they are not designed to demonstrate good programming practice. Computer science and numerical analysis are important subjects in their own right and the intending economics specialist would do well to give them some careful attention. A minimal familiarity with the computing equipment that you intend to use is assumed. Implementations of BASIC vary a little in detail, as do the capabilities of the machines on which they run. You may well find that you will have to make small changes in the programs to make them work on your particular machine. You will have to contend with the inevitable errors that will occur in keying the programs into the machine and also with the possibility that errors have crept into the printed text. Although long variable names are used for intelligibility only the first two characters are significant on the machines on which the programs were developed and tested, so you may wish to save effort by only using the first two. There should be no problem in translating these simple programs into an alternative language such as PASCAL or FORTRAN. It should also be easy to implement them on a programmable calculator with the exception of the graphics routines. There are many self-teaching books available on the elements of computing specifically for the commonly available machines. Kemeny and Kurtz (1971) provide an excellent and authoritative introduction to serious BASIC programming techniques.

1.3 Linearity

A 'unifying principle' running through this book is the principle of linearity. The following example illustrates it.

Suppose that consumption C is related to income Y and to the rate of interest r:

$$C = \alpha r + \beta Y,$$

where α is a negative constant and β is a constant between 0 and 1. This is a simple consumption function, α being the effect on income of a one-point change in the rate of interest holding income constant and β being the marginal propensity to consume, that is the effect on consumption of a £1 change in income holding the interest rate constant. The following program illustrates this.

```
100  LET ALPHA = 0 : REM SET VALUES OF THE CONSTANTS
110  LET BETA = 0.75
120  INPUT "RATE OF INTEREST"; R : REM INPUT VALUES FOR
                                    INDEPENDENT VARIABLES
130  INPUT "INCOME"; Y
140  LET C = ALPHA*R + BETA*Y : REM CALCULATE
                                 CONSUMPTION
150  PRINT "CONSUMPTION = ", C : REM PRINT THE RESULT
160  PRINT : REM PRINT A BLANK LINE FOR READABILITY OF
             RESULTS
170  GOTO 120 : REM GO BACK FOR ANOTHER SET OF INPUTS
```

In a BASIC program the colon is used to separate one instruction or statement from another if more than one occurs on the same line. The statements which begin with 'REM' are REMarks which are ignored by the computer. Lines 100, 110 and 140 are assignment statements. These give a new value to the quantity on the left-hand side of the = sign; the word 'LET' makes this clear but in most versions of BASIC the word is optional. Line 140 contains the actual consumption function.

By trying a few values of interest rate and income with this program you will find that the interest rate has no effect and that consumption is always three-quarters of income. This, of course, is because the interest rate coefficient is set at zero in line 100 and the marginal propensity to consume is set at three-quarters in line 110. Note that in this case the marginal and the average propensities to consume are the same. Another way of saying this is to say that consumption is directly proportional to income; multiplying income by any constant causes consumption to be multiplied by that same constant. By changing the value of 0.75 in line 110 you can confirm that this property holds whatever value you use there.

Now change line 100 to give a non-zero value to the interest rate coefficient. You will again find that if you multiply both the interest rate and income by the same constant, then consumption will also be multiplied by that constant. For example, doubling the interest rate and doubling income doubles consumption. This is the property of homogeneity. This is expressed symbolically as

$$\begin{aligned}\alpha(\lambda r) + \beta(\lambda Y) &= \alpha\lambda r + \beta\lambda Y \\ &= \lambda(\alpha r + \beta Y) \\ &= \lambda C\end{aligned}$$

for any value of λ.

There is a second requirement for linearity, that of additivity. Suppose that we observe two countries with the same consumption function (that is, the same values of α and β) but differing rates of interest and incomes, given by r_1, r_2, Y_1 and Y_2. Then we can obtain total consumption in one of two ways. We can either calculate consumption in each country individually, to give

C_1 and C_2, and then add them, or we can add the rates of interest and incomes in the two countries and then apply these totals to the common consumption function. The two methods will give the same result, as the following modification of the above program will illustrate.

```
100  LET ALPHA = −100
110  LET BETA = 0.75
120  INPUT "RATE OF INTEREST IN COUNTRY 1"; R(1)
125  INPUT "RATE OF INTEREST IN COUNTRY 2"; R(2)
130  INPUT "INCOME IN COUNTRY 1"; Y(1)
135  INPUT "INCOME IN COUNTRY 2"; Y(2)
140  LET C(1) = ALPHA*R(1) + BETA*Y(1)
145  LET C(2) = ALPHA*R(2) + BETA*Y(2)
147  LET C(3) = ALPHA*(R(1) + R(2)) + BETA*(Y(1) + Y(2))
150  PRINT "CONSUMPTION IN COUNTRY 1 = ", C(1)
155  PRINT "CONSUMPTION IN COUNTRY 2 = ", C(2)
156  PRINT "THE SUM OF THE TWO = ", C(1) + C(2)
158  PRINT "CONSUMPTION EVALUATED AT THE SUM OF THE
     INDEPENDENT VARIABLES = ", C(3)
160  PRINT
170  GOTO 120
```

Symbolically the property of additivity can be represented as follows. We have

$$C_1 = \alpha r_1 + \beta Y_1$$
$$C_2 = \alpha r_2 + \beta Y_2.$$

So adding,

$$\begin{aligned} C = C_1 + C_2 &= \alpha r_1 + \alpha r_2 + \beta Y_1 + \beta Y_2 \\ &= \alpha(r_1 + r_2) + \beta(Y_1 + Y_2) \end{aligned}$$

and so we see that the total consumption is obtained by adding together the values of r and Y in the two countries, and then applying our original formula to these two aggregates. This is the property of additivity. As an example of a relationship which is not linear, put $\alpha = 0$ and consider

$$C = \beta Y^2.$$

Now,

$$\begin{aligned} \beta(\lambda Y)^2 &= \lambda^2 \beta Y^2 \\ &= \lambda^2 C \neq \lambda C \quad \text{(unless } \lambda = 1) \end{aligned}$$

and if

$$C_1 = \beta Y_1^2$$

and

$$C_2 = \beta Y_2^2,$$

then

$$\begin{aligned} C &= C_1 + C_2 \\ &= \beta Y_1^2 + \beta Y_2^2 \\ &\neq \beta(Y_1 + Y_2)^2 \end{aligned}$$

so this relationship exhibits neither proportionality nor additivity.

These properties may be confirmed by replacing line 140 in the first program by

```
140  LET C = BETA * Y * Y
```

If we fix r at some value, we can plot our linear function on a *graph* as in Figure 1.1, and we see that the result is a family of parallel *straight* lines, each line being identified by the particular value fixed for αr. The *slope* of each line is β, and the *intercept*, being the value of C when $Y = 0$, is αr (see Problem 2.3.2). If r is held constant the relationship becomes

$$C = a + \beta Y$$

where $a = \alpha r$ is a constant, the familiar simple linear consumption function.

It would be a useful exercise to use the output from the first program to construct a graph similar to Figure 1.1. Note that if Y varies but r does not then the relationship no longer satisfies the requirement of homogeneity (unless α is zero, in which case the graph passes through the origin): it is linear in r and Y but not in Y alone. Further, in this case there is a difference between the marginal and the average propensities to consume.

Models containing linear relationships only are said to be linear models. They have the great advantage that if a solution exists then it is always possible to find it by techniques which are both routine and simple in principle. This is not necessarily the case with nonlinear models. Even if it is not reasonable to assume that a particular piece of economic behaviour is linear the techniques of linear models can be useful in several ways. For example, it is often possible to use a mathematical device to transform a nonlinear

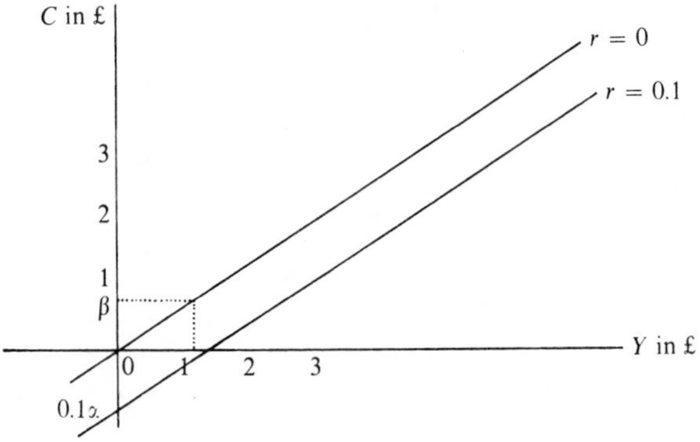

Figure 1.1

model into a linear one. Models which preserve constant proportions (constant elasticities) are common and they can be made linear by taking logarithms. Section 12.2 gives an example of this. Even if such a transformation is not possible one can obtain useful results by making and approximating the assumption that the relationship is linear in some small neighbourhood of a particular point of interest, such as an equilibrium value. A natural assumption to make is that the relationship is a straight line which is tangent to the curve at the point concerned. This is discussed in detail in Chapter 14. It is a point at which the linear algebra and the calculus parts of the book join forces.

1.4 Linear algebra

This is the subject of the first ten chapters of this book. It provides a set of rules—an algebra—for the manipulation of systems of linear relationships. It is sometimes known as vector and matrix algebra. The main reason that relationships occur in systems, rather than singly, is simultaneity.

Roughly speaking, two or more relationships are said to form a simultaneous system if they have variables in common and if it is required that the relationships be satisfied at the same time. We illustrate with a simple example from macroeconomics. The national expenditure has several components, including consumer expenditure, investment and government expenditure. But one man's expenditure is another man's income so total expenditure and income are one and the same thing. At the same time consumer expenditure and investment themselves depend upon total incomes. We now have three simultaneous relationships (which need not necessarily be linear).

We are interested to know what level of national income is consistent with all these relationships (if any), and how this will change when government policy changes. Changes in government expenditure will change national income, which will in turn change consumption and investment, which are themselves components of income, and so it goes on. The techniques of linear algebra help to unravel (or 'solve') an interdependent system such as this. The main idea is that by one means or another the system of interest can be reduced to a set of linear equations. These may be very complicated (examples can be seen by looking forward to Sections 8.3, 8.8 and 18.3), but by suitable definitions they may be written down and manipulated using very few symbols. For example, a linear version of the three simultaneous relationships mentioned above would be

$$\begin{aligned} Y &= C + I + G \\ C &= \alpha r + \beta Y \\ I &= \gamma + \delta r + \epsilon Y \end{aligned} \quad \text{or} \quad \left\{ \begin{aligned} Y - C - I &= G \\ -\beta Y + C &= \alpha r \\ -\epsilon Y + I &= \gamma + \delta r. \end{aligned} \right.$$

We shall see that this whole system can be written in the very compact form

$$\mathbf{A}\boldsymbol{x} = \boldsymbol{b}$$

where the *matrix* **A**, and the *vectors* $\boldsymbol{x}$ and $\boldsymbol{b}$ are given by

$$\mathbf{A} = \begin{bmatrix} 1 & -1 & -1 \\ -\beta & 1 & 0 \\ -\epsilon & 0 & 1 \end{bmatrix}, \quad \boldsymbol{x} = \begin{bmatrix} Y \\ C \\ I \end{bmatrix}, \quad \boldsymbol{b} = \begin{bmatrix} G \\ \alpha r \\ \gamma + \delta r \end{bmatrix},$$

in which case the 'solution' for $\boldsymbol{x}$ in terms of $\boldsymbol{b}$ would (under certain conditions) be

$$\boldsymbol{x} = \mathbf{A}^{-1}\boldsymbol{b},$$

where the process of finding the quantity $\mathbf{A}^{-1}$ is known. This is rather similar to solving the very simple equation

$$3x = 6$$

by writing

$$x = 3^{-1}.6 = \tfrac{1}{3}.6 = 2.$$

The ability to handle large systems in this simple way is a great asset to an economist. The excellent introductory chapter to Hadley (1961) describes many applications.

Here is a program which calculates a solution to this macroeconomic model.

```
100  ALPHA = -0.15E8
110  BETA = 0.75
120  GAMMA = 0.15E7
130  DELTA = -1.0E8
140  EPSIL = 0.1 : REM CANNOT USE 'EPSILON' BECAUSE IT
                   CONTAINS THE RESERVED WORD 'ON'
150  R = 0.1
160  INPUT "GOVERNMENT EXPENDITURE";G : C = 0 : I = 0
170  Y = C + I + G
180  C = C - (C - ALPHA*R - BETA*Y)
190  I = I - (I - GAMMA - DELTA*R - EPSIL*Y)
200  PRINT "INCOME       = ",Y/1E6," £M"
210  PRINT "CONSUMPTION = ",C/1E6," £M"
220  PRINT "INVESTMENT   = ",I/1E6," £M"
230  GOTO 170
```

This program asks you to suggest a level of government expenditure (try starting with 1.0E9, that is, 1 with nine zeros, or one thousand million). It then calculates the solutions to the equations by a simple (but inefficient) iterative process. For simplicity and brevity the version given here has no way of terminating. It will keep on going until you intervene to stop it. It prints the current values of the variables at each iteration and so you can watch the progress of the algorithm towards the solution and you can decide when you think that things are changing sufficiently slowly that you are 'near enough' to a solution. You can check that you have indeed found a solution by making sure that the three equations are satisfied. (You should be very near a solution after about 120 iterations, but, depending on the internal accuracy of your machine you may never reach an exact solution.) By suitable variation of the level of government expenditure you should be able to establish the Keynesian government expenditure multiplier effect on equilibrium income. With the values given in the program it is 20/3 or approximately 6.667.

A full understanding of how the algorithm works is not necessary, but to give a general idea, note that line 180 is not an equation but an instruction to calculate a new value in terms of a set of old ones. The values of C which appear on the left of the assignment statement are to be the current values and all of those which appear on the right are the values calculated in the previous pass through the loop. The expression in parentheses in line 180 is the difference between the previous value of consumption and what it ought to be if income were at the level calculated in the previous statement. If it is too high then the difference is positive and the line adjusts the old value of C downwards to give a new value. Similarly for investment in line 190. Note that an algorithm as crude as this can only be relied upon because of the linearity of the system. In general it could not be guaranteed to work. Note also that the fact that the variables are changing slowly from one iteration to the next is not a guarantee that a solution is nearby. Fortunately, in this particular case we can always make a direct check of whether a particular set of values constitutes a solution.

To illustrate that difficulties can arise even in a case as simple as this, try changing the value given to EPSIL in line 140 to 0·25. You will find that the algorithm will fail. There are good mathematical and economic reasons for this, which we will come to when we discuss the theory of systems of linear equations in Chapter 8.

1.5 Analysis

The term 'analysis' refers to a large group of topics but we shall concentrate on the calculus. This is the most useful single piece of mathematical technique available to economists.

The central problem is, how fast does one quantity change in response to changes in another? For example, what is the rate of change of the balance of payments with respect to changes in the exchange rate; the rate of change of a firm's profit with respect to output; the rate of change of social welfare with respect to a redistributive income tax; the rate of change of demand with respect to price changes; the rate of change of the price level with respect to changes in the wage rate?

If we can find these 'slopes' we have a way of analysing a large class of economic problems. Many of them can be formulated as maximizing or minimizing something, usually subject to some constraints. For example, finding the best way of allocating scarce resources; maximizing profits or minimizing costs subject to the prevailing technology; finding the socially optimum bus fare in a congested town given the behaviour of private car-owners; finding the best rate of investment and hence the best rate of economic growth given current capital stock and technology. All these problems are discussed below.

At a maximum or a minimum the rate of change of the thing one wishes to maximize or minimize must be zero. Otherwise one could do better by either increasing or reducing the value of the choice variable(s). This simple observation forms the basis of the theory of optimization.

1.6 Preliminaries

This introductory chapter ends with a few notes on some of the elementary rules of arithmetic and some notation. The basic rules for manipulating numbers cause considerable difficulty to people who are new to the subject, or who have lost touch with it. The only way to become thoroughly familiar with them is by practising exercises from a suitable elementary text. If in doubt in a particular case it is nearly always possible to resolve the difficulty by trying a few simple cases with suitable numerical values. For instance, is it true that

$$\begin{aligned}(x+y)/x &= x/x + y/x \\ &= 1 + y/x\ ?\end{aligned}$$

What about

$$\begin{aligned}x/(x+y) &= x/x + x/y \\ &= 1 + x/y\ ?\end{aligned}$$

You can quickly answer this by trying, say, $x = 2$ and $y = 3$ and seeing if the two sides of the equations are the same. Note, however, that whilst you can always prove a proposition to be false in this way, you cannot prove it to be true; $2 + 2 = 4$ and $2 \times 2 = 4$, but it is not true in general that $Y + Y = Y \times Y$.

By real number we mean what one normally means by number: 3, −2, 1·5, $\sqrt{2}$. The word 'real' is used to distinguish these numbers from complex numbers which involve the 'imaginary' quantity $\sqrt{-1}$. (Try evaluating this on your calculator or computer. If it gives you an answer then the machine is suspect.) These are explained in Chapter 9 but they are not essential for an understanding of the rest of the book.

Positive and negative whole numbers, such as 1, −1, 67 and −10, are known as *integers*.

The *absolute value*, or *modulus*, of a number (denoted by two vertical lines) is that number but with a positive sign, so that $|-3| = 3$, $|-8{\cdot}5| = 8{\cdot}5$, $|6| = 6$.

The sum and difference of two positive numbers pose no problems, but remember that if a negative number is to be subtracted from anything, then this is equivalent to *adding* the absolute value of the number; for example:

$$2 - (-3) = 2 + 3 = 5.$$

The product of one negative number and one positive number is a negative number, but the product of two negative numbers is *positive*:

$$-2.(+3) = -6, \qquad -2.(-3) = 6.$$

(Note that a dot is often used to denote multiplication rather than ×, and even that is frequently omitted.)

The square root of a positive number is some number which, when multiplied by itself, yields that positive number; for example:

$$\sqrt{4} = 2 \text{ or } -2, \quad \text{since } 2.2 = 4, \text{ and } (-2)(-2) = 4.$$

Since the product of negative numbers is positive, every positive number has *two* square roots, one positive and one negative, and a negative number has no square roots at all (hence $\sqrt{-1}$ is imaginary). In some calculations one ends up with the square root of a number which is not a perfect square and it is often convenient to leave a square root in the solution (known as a *surd*) although it is best to simplify it as much as possible first; for example:

$$\sqrt{27} = \sqrt{(9.3)} = \pm 3\sqrt{3}$$

$$\frac{3}{\sqrt{3}} = \frac{3\sqrt{3}}{\sqrt{3}.\sqrt{3}} = \frac{3\sqrt{3}}{3} = \sqrt{3}.$$

If we wish to make a statement which applies to all numbers, then we often use letters like x, y or a. For example,

$$3(x + 2) = 3x + 6$$

is a true statement whatever value is given to x, so it is convenient to leave x as an unspecified number. Very often x will be referred to as a *variable*.

If we write x^n, then x is said to have the *index* n, or to be 'raised to the power of n', and it means that x is to be multiplied by itself n times. Although indices are commonly positive integers, negative numbers and fractional indices are perfectly allowable in most circumstances. Now, we shall assume it to be the case that

$$x^a.x^b = x^{a+b}$$

for any numbers x, a and b such that x^a and x^b are defined. This is easily verified by simple examples:

$$2^2.2^3 = 4.8 = 32$$

$$2^{2+3} = 2^5 = 32.$$

Consider $x^{\frac{1}{2}}$. Using this rule

$$x^{\frac{1}{2}}.x^{\frac{1}{2}} = x^{(\frac{1}{2}+\frac{1}{2})} = x,$$

so that $x^{\frac{1}{2}}$ must be the same thing as $\sqrt{x}$:

$$x^{\frac{1}{2}} = \sqrt{x}.$$

Similarly

$$x^{\frac{1}{3}} = \sqrt[3]{x} \text{ (the cube root of } x)$$

and

$$x^{1/n} = \sqrt[n]{x}.$$

It should now be clear that such a quantity may not be defined. (−2 has no (real) square root so that $(-2)^{\frac{1}{2}}$ is not defined.)

Similarly,

$$x^{-a}.x^{a} = x^{a-a} = x^{0}$$

but by convention

$$x^{0} = 1, \quad \text{whatever } x,$$

so that

$$x^{-a}.x^{a} = 1.$$

Hence,

$$x^{-a} = \frac{1}{x^{a}}, \quad x \neq 0$$

so that we can easily interpret negative indices. In particular

$$1/x = x^{-1}.$$

Two further rules are that

$$(x^{a})^{b} = x^{ab} \quad \text{and} \quad (xy)^{a} = x^{a}y^{a}.$$

For example,

$$(2^2)^3 = (4)^3 = 64 = 2^6 = 2^{2\,.\,3} \quad \text{and} \quad (2\,.\,3)^2 = 2^2\,.\,3^2 = 4\,.\,9 = 36.$$

We can now interpret something like $x^{-\frac{5}{3}}$ as $1/(\sqrt[3]{x})^5$.

Remember that an *equation* is a statement that whatever is on the left-hand side is the *same thing* as whatever is on the right. Therefore any operation carried out on one side must also be carried out on the other For example, if we have

$$3 - 2x = 7$$

then, subtracting 3 from both sides of the equation,

$$-2x = 7 - 3,$$

and dividing both sides by −2,

$$x = \frac{7-3}{-2} = -2$$

and we have *solved* for the variable x.

Brackets in expressions are important because they remove ambiguities. For instance:

$$3(x + 2) \neq 3x + 2.$$

They are a very common source of error. Too few brackets may lead to statements with meaning different from what was intended, whilst too many do not matter, so use them freely if in doubt.

Inequalities are very much like equations, except that = is replaced by $<, \leqslant, >$ or $\geqslant$, meaning respectively less than, less than or equal to, greater than, greater than or equal to. One might have

$$2x + 2 \leqslant 4y + 6$$

or

$$2x \leqslant 4y + 4$$

or

$$x \leqslant 2y + 2,$$

so that if y is given the value 3, then x must be less than or equal to 8. There is one important point: if an inequality is multiplied (or divided) by a negative number, then the sense of the inequality must be reversed. For instance:

$$2 < 3$$

but

$$-2 > -3.$$

The symbol $\approx$ is also used, meaning 'is approximately equal to'.

If we have a long list of variables, it is often convenient to use a single letter with one or more *subscripts* to identify them, rather than attempt to give a different letter to each. Thus x_1 might be the first variable, x_2 the second, and so on, rather than x and y. If we wish to talk in general terms and to avoid giving a specific value to a subscript, we give it a letter such as i, j or k. Hence

$$x_i, \quad i = 1, 3, 6$$

would refer to x_1, x_3 and x_6.

Since subscripted variables very often have to be added together, a very useful special notation is used for this, known as the *sigma* notation. Many readers will already be familiar with it because of its extensive use in statistical theory.

$$\sum_{k=a}^{b} x_k$$

just means that the numbers, $x_a, x_{a+1}, \ldots, x_k, \ldots, x_b$, identified by the subscript k, which is to start at a and increase in steps of one to b, are to be added together. Thus, for example

$$\sum_{j=3}^{6} \alpha_j = \alpha_3 + \alpha_4 + \alpha_5 + \alpha_6$$

or, if $x_1 = 1, x_2 = -2, x_3 = 3$ and $x_4 = -\frac{1}{2}$ then

$$\sum_{i=1}^{4} x_i = 1 + (-2) + 3 + (-\tfrac{1}{2}) = 1\tfrac{1}{2}.$$

We have already seen an example of the use of subscripted variables when discussing additivity in Section 1.3. In computer programming the alternative name 'array' is used. Thus in the second program of Section 1.3 $C(1)$, $C(2)$ and $C(3)$ are elements of an array. The computing equivalent of the sigma notation can be achieved by the use of the FOR . . . NEXT loop:

```
100  X(1) = 1
110  X(2) = -2
120  X(3) = 3
130  X(4) = -0.5
140  Z = 0
150  FOR I = 1 TO 4 : REM START I AT 1
160  Z = Z + X(I)
170  NEXT I : REM INCREASE I BY 1 AND GO BACK TO 'FOR'
                 UNLESS I >= 4
180  PRINT Z
```

This program is the equivalent of the example just given. Should we wish to add $X(1)$ to $X(3)$ we could replace line 150 by

```
150  FOR I = 1 TO 4 STEP 2
```

or alternatively we could replace lines 150 and 160 by

```
150  FOR I = 1 TO 2
160  Z = Z + X(2*I - 1)
```

To see how this works try executing each step by hand.

The meaning and usage of subscripted variables should become clearer as the first few chapters of this book are read. Problem 3.8.4 gives some practice in manipulating the sigma notation.

Finally, some pieces of shorthand which are useful:

iff (Instead of 'if') means 'if and only if'. Thus, the statement, 'A is true *iff* B is true' means that if the statement A is true then the statement B must also be true *and* conversely, if B is true then A must also be true. That is, A is necessary and sufficient for B, and conversely.

$\Rightarrow$ As in '$A \Rightarrow B$', means that A *implies* B, or if A is true then B must be true. That is, 'A only if B' and 'B if A'.

$\Leftrightarrow$ Means A *iff* B.

$\forall$ Means 'for all' or 'for every'. For example, in Definition 3.2, '$\forall i$' means that $x_i = y_i$ for every value of i between 1 and n. This is sometimes written: '$i = 1, 2, \ldots, n$'.

$\exists$ Means 'there exists'.

s.t., :, or | Means 'such that'. Thus, if λ and δ are numbers, the statement that '$\forall \lambda$, $\exists \delta$ s.t. $\delta > \lambda$' means that for any arbitrarily chosen number, λ, it is always possible to find a larger one, δ.

2 Vectors and matrices

2.1 Vectors

We start with some definitions.

D2.1 A *scalar* is a real (or complex) number.

The significance of 'real (or complex)' may not be clear at this stage. The phrase is included so as to make the definition as general as possible, but the difference between real and complex numbers is not explained until Sections 9.2 and 14.3. For the moment ignore the words 'or complex'.

D2.2 A *vector* is an ordered, one-dimensional array of scalars–a list of scalars; for example, the number 3 is a scalar, but (3, 2) is a vector, because it is a list containing more than one real number. The *order* matters; (3, 2) is a different vector from (2, 3). Another example of a vector is $(-1, \frac{1}{2}, 5)$. These elements could also be written as a column:

$$\begin{bmatrix} -1 \\ \frac{1}{2} \\ 5 \end{bmatrix}.$$

By convention, a distinction is made between *row vectors* and *column vectors*, the distinction being simply that they are written down differently. In general, we denote vectors thus:

$$\boldsymbol{x} = \begin{bmatrix} x_1 \\ x_2 \\ \vdots \\ x_n \end{bmatrix} \quad \text{or} \quad \boldsymbol{x} = (x_1, x_2, \ldots, x_n)$$

depending on whether we want $\boldsymbol{x}$ to be a column vector or a row vector, where n is some integer.

Each x with a subscript is called an *element* (or *component*) of the vector. So the above example is a column or row vector with n elements. We use some letter like n to specify the number of elements in order to maintain generality. At some later stage in a piece of analysis we can, if we wish, give a specific value to n. This must be some positive integer. Examples have already been given where $n = 2$ and $n = 3$. Notice that in the special case where $n = 1$, a vector reduces to a scalar. If we wish to specify a *general* element of a vector, we use a letter as a subscript, so that x_i is the ith element of the vector $\boldsymbol{x}$. Again, i may be given any integer value, with $1 \leqslant i \leqslant n$. For example, a_5 is the fifth element of a vector $\boldsymbol{a}$; if $\boldsymbol{z} = (-1, \frac{1}{2}, 5)$ then $z_2 = \frac{1}{2}$.

It is often said that a vector with n elements is a vector 'of dimension n'. Notice that the word 'dimension' is being applied to a vector here, and not to an array as in the definition of a vector, D2.2. In the latter case it is the array that is 'one-dimensional' indicating that an element of the array may be represented using *one* subscript. As we shall see, elements of two-dimensional arrays require two subscripts, in which case we would have a *matrix*.

Suppose that we wanted to write down the quantities of all the goods purchased by an individual in a certain period of time. A single number, or scalar, could only be used to record the quantity of one good. Hence we would make a list, or one-dimensional array, or vector of the purchases, with as many entries as there were goods to buy, one entry for each good. If there were ten goods then we would have a vector with ten elements, or to put it another way, a vector of dimension ten. More generally, n goods would yield a vector of dimension n. Note that each position in the list would be associated with a particular good and would be measured in its own particular units: pints of milk, boxes of eggs, pounds of meat, tons of coal and so on, so that it would be meaningless to add these physical quantities up or otherwise attempt to represent them by a scalar. Suppose now, that we wanted to record simultaneously the purchases of these same goods by a second individual. Clearly we would form a second list, and the two together would form a two-dimensional array, or a matrix. If we made lists for further individuals we would still have a two-dimensional array, because any entry could be identified by two subscripts, one representing the particular good and the other representing the particular individual. If we wanted to record all these purchases at several different points in time then we would have to use an additional subscript to identify a particular element, fixing the time or place, and so we would have to use a three-dimensional array. Thus in this case, one dimension of the array would be accounted for by the list of goods, one dimension by the list of individuals, and one dimension by the list of points in time (or of places). There is no restriction on the lengths of any of these lists.

Vast amounts of data can be contained in arrays. For instance our array with 100 goods, 100 individuals at 100 different points in time would contain 1,000,000 elements. One of the difficulties in the computer programming associated with empirical work in economics is to arrange things in such a way that the sizes of the arrays of data do not exceed the storage capacity of the computer's memories.

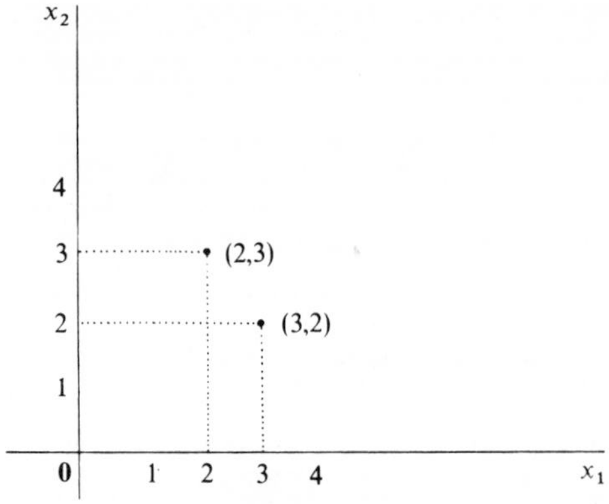

Figure 2.1

It is useful to be able to represent vectors diagrammatically by plotting them on a graph. On two-dimensional paper we can represent vectors with two elements by measuring the value of the first element of the vector along a horizontal *axis*, and the value of the second element on a vertical *axis*. The vector is then represented by the point with the corresponding *coordinates* (see Figure 2.1).

This way of representing a vector, using axes at right angles, is sometimes said to be a representation in (two-dimensional) *Euclidean space*. For three-element vectors we need three-dimensional space, and there is in general no geometrical way of representing vectors with more elements. It is important to realize that, although the diagram is a useful aid to the understanding of the concepts, the properties and techniques for manipulating vectors are completely independent of any geometry. This is one reason why mathematics is so useful in economics–a person who can only manipulate diagrams is limited more or less to analysing a world with two goods, two countries, two people, two firms, and so on, but the mathematical concepts generalize naturally.

Note that there is no way of distinguishing between row and column vectors with the same elements on this diagram, but it does show the difference between $(3, 2)$ and $(2, 3)$. The vector can be thought of either as the line segment joining the point to the origin, or simply as the point itself (that is, a specified location in the space). We shall usually take the latter view, although the former does emphasize the fact that a vector is a quantity having both a *magnitude* (corresponding to its length) and a *direction*, as opposed to a simple scalar which just has a magnitude.

2.2 Matrices

A vector has only one dimension; each element has only one subscript. This means that the elements can be arranged in a single row or a single column. In this respect a vector differs from a matrix.

D2.3 A *matrix* is a *two*-dimensional, *rectangular* array of scalars.

For example,

$$\begin{bmatrix} 2 & \frac{1}{2} \\ 3 & 0 \\ 1 & -5 \end{bmatrix}$$

has 3 rows and 2 columns. The word 'rectangular' is important. The following is *not* a matrix:

$$\begin{bmatrix} 1 & 0 \\ 2 & \end{bmatrix}.$$

'Rectangular' means that each row and column is complete; that is, every row (and column) has the same number of elements. The following is an example of a *square* matrix

$$\begin{bmatrix} -2 & 3 & 6 \\ 7 & 1 & 8 \\ 9 & -5 & \frac{1}{2} \end{bmatrix}$$

because it contains the same number of rows as columns.

Row vectors and column vectors are special cases of matrices. A row vector can be thought of as a matrix with only one row, and a column vector as a matrix with only one column.

Capital letters are generally used to denote matrices which are not vectors; for vectors, the corresponding small letters are used. **Bold face** type is used to distinguish vectors and matrices from scalars.

By convention, the second subscript changes as one moves along a row and the first changes as one moves down a column. This means that the first subscript identifies the row to which an element belongs and the second subscript identifies the column, so that q_{ij} would be the element in the ith row and jth column of a matrix $\mathbf{Q}$.

Also by convention, we usually use the subscript i to represent rows and j to represent columns. This, however, is not always the case since i and j may have been 'used up' for some other purpose, so one might want to write z_{kl} for instance. In general we denote matrices thus:

$$\mathbf{A} = \begin{bmatrix} a_{11} & a_{12} & \dots & a_{1n} \\ a_{21} & a_{22} & \dots & a_{2n} \\ \vdots & \vdots & & \vdots \\ a_{m1} & a_{m2} & \dots & a_{mn} \end{bmatrix}.$$

Sometimes this statement is abbreviated to

$$\mathbf{A} = (a_{ij})$$

which is read, '$\mathbf{A}$ is a matrix whose elements are denoted by a_{ij}'. In texts both square and round brackets are used for matrices and vectors, but there is no difference. Two straight lines should not be used, however, since these are used to denote determinants, which are discussed in Chapter 6.

The above example has m rows and n columns and so we say that it is an $m \times n$ matrix. There is no restriction on the relationship between m and n. If $m = n$, we say that the matrix is 'square'. Thus, a 10×10 matrix is square with 10 rows and 10 columns. An $n \times 1$ matrix is a column vector with n elements and a $1 \times n$ matrix is a row with n elements. The $m \times n$ matrix $\mathbf{A}$ can also be thought of as a row of n column vectors, or as a column of m row vectors. For example, if the row vector $\boldsymbol{a}_2$ is defined as $(a_{21}, a_{22}, \ldots, a_{2n})$, and if in general,

$$\boldsymbol{a}_i = (a_{i1}, a_{i2}, \ldots, a_{im}), \quad i = 1, 2, \ldots, m.$$

then the matrix $\mathbf{A}$ can be represented as a column of those row vectors:

$$\mathbf{A} = \begin{bmatrix} \boldsymbol{a}_1 \\ \boldsymbol{a}_2 \\ \vdots \\ \boldsymbol{a}_m \end{bmatrix}.$$

The word 'array' is also used for subscripted variables in computer programming. We have already seen an example of the use of vectors in programs in the previous chapter where $C(I)$ and $X(I)$ were introduced. When BASIC first encounters an array most versions assume that it has ten elements unless a previous declaration to the contrary has been made in a DIM statement:

```
100  DIM X(4), Y(20,20), Z(4,5,6)
```

It is a peculiarity of BASIC that the first element is always indexed by 0 rather than by 1. Thus X is a one-dimensional array with the five elements $X(0)$, $X(1)$, $X(2)$, $X(3)$ and $X(4)$. Y is a 21×21 two-dimensional array and Z is a three-dimensional array. Once declared, either explicitly or by default, all the elements are assumed to be zero until otherwise specified. (This is not the case with all languages.)

Try the following.

```
160  FOR I = 0 TO 5
170  FOR J = 0 TO 5
180  PRINT I, J ;
190  NEXT J
200  PRINT
210  NEXT I
```

This will print out the ij indices in the form of an array. Note the use of two nested FOR ... NEXT loops. You may find it useful to trace the operation of the program through with a pencil and paper in order to understand how programs work. The semicolon at the end of line 180 causes the next ij pair to be printed on the same line as the previous one (otherwise a new line of print would be created each time a PRINT statement is encountered). The PRINT in line 200 is to create a new row of the matrix each time a row is completed.

The following is an extension which will print a small multiplication table.

```
100  DIM X(5,5,)
110  FOR I = 0 TO 5
120  FOR J = 0 TO 5
130  X(I,J) = I*J
140  NEXT J
150  NEXT I
160  FOR I = 0 TO 5
170  FOR J = 0 TO 5
180  PRINT X(I,J); : REM NOT THE SAME AS BEFORE
190  NEXT J
200  PRINT
210  NEXT I
```

2.3 Problems

1. Solve the systems:

(*a*) $$x_1 + x_2 = 3$$
$$4x_1 - 2x_2 = 0$$

(*b*) $$-3x_1 + 3x_2 = 45$$
$$2x_1 + x_2 = 3$$

that is, find values of x_1 and x_2 which satisfy both relationships simultaneously.

2. The relationship between two variables x_1 and x_2 given by

$$x_2 = a + bx_1$$

where a and b are constants, is said to be 'the equation of a straight line'. a is the 'intercept' and b is the 'slope'. Plot this relationship on a graph in the following cases:

(*a*) $a = 0$; $b = 1$;

(*b*) $a = 0$, $b = 2$;

(*c*) $a = -1$, $b = 2$;

(*d*) $a = 1$, $b = -2$.

Show that the relationship satisfies the definition of linearity if and only if $a = 0$, but that if $a \neq 0$ then the relationship can be very easily converted into a linear one.

3. To produce one unit of coal a nationalized coal industry uses $\frac{1}{6}$ unit of coal and $\frac{1}{3}$ unit of electricity. To produce one unit of electricity the generating industry uses $\frac{1}{2}$ unit of coal and $\frac{1}{12}$ unit of electricity. If the government decides that a total of ten units of coal and ten units of electricity are required for domestic consumption in a certain year, how many units should

it direct the two industries to produce? What would happen to these required outputs if the consumption of electricity went up by 1 unit?

4. Suppose that p is the price of some commodity, S is the quantity that producers are willing to supply and D is the quantity that consumers would like to buy, and that

$$S = a + bp \quad (a > 0, \quad b > 0)$$

$$D = c + dp \quad (c > 0, \quad d < 0).$$

Interpret these relationships and find an expression for the price which would make the supply equal the demand. What extra conditions are necessary to ensure that this price is positive?

Suppose now that a tax of $100t$ per cent is imposed so that suppliers only receive a price of $(1-t)p$ for each unit they sell. The constant b now becomes $(1-t)b$. What happens to the equilibrium price? Will the whole of the tax be 'passed on' to the consumers?

3 Operations on vectors

Having defined what we mean by vectors and matrices we now begin to define various operations which can be carried out on them. On the whole, these are very similar to the familiar operations of addition, subtraction and multiplication for ordinary numbers. However, there are very important differences which must be understood; for instance there is nothing corresponding to the operation of division for vectors, and the vector operation of transposition has no meaning for ordinary numbers.

For the purposes of this chapter, let

$$\boldsymbol{x} = \begin{bmatrix} x_1 \\ x_2 \\ \vdots \\ x_n \end{bmatrix} \quad \text{and} \quad \boldsymbol{y} = \begin{bmatrix} y_1 \\ y_2 \\ \vdots \\ y_n \end{bmatrix},$$

being column vectors with the same number of elements.

3.1 Transposition

The simplest operation is to transform a column into its corresponding row (or row into column). This is called the operation of transposition.

D3.1 The *transpose* of $\boldsymbol{x}$, denoted by $\boldsymbol{x}'$, is the corresponding row (or column). For example, if $\boldsymbol{x} = \begin{bmatrix} 2 \\ 3 \end{bmatrix}$ then $\boldsymbol{x}' = (2, 3)$, and if $\boldsymbol{x} = (-1, 2)$ then $\boldsymbol{x}' = \begin{bmatrix} -1 \\ 2 \end{bmatrix}$. Hence, note that $(\boldsymbol{x}')' = \boldsymbol{x}$.

3.2 Equality

D3.2 Two vectors are *equal* if and only if the corresponding elements are the same–that is, $\boldsymbol{x} = \boldsymbol{y}$ if and only if $x_i = y_i \ \forall i$.

Definition D3.2 has two prerequisites:

1 The two vectors being compared must be either both columns or both rows.
2 They must both have the same number of elements.

Equality is an example of a relationship which is always meaningful for two real numbers (two numbers are either equal or they are not), but which will not even be defined when dealing with vectors if these two requirements are not met. To check the equality of two vectors, the elements are taken pair-wise to see if they are the same. Two vectors are equal if they are one and the same thing.

3.3 Addition

D3.3 If the *sum* of two vectors $\boldsymbol{x}$ and $\boldsymbol{y}$ is given by

$$\boldsymbol{z} = \boldsymbol{x} + \boldsymbol{y},$$

then

$$z_i = x_i + y_i, \quad i = 1, 2, \ldots, n.$$

The same requirements apply as for equality. For instance

$$\begin{bmatrix} 3 \\ 2 \\ 4 \end{bmatrix} + \begin{bmatrix} -1 \\ 5 \\ -3 \end{bmatrix} = \begin{bmatrix} 3 + (-1) \\ 2 + 5 \\ 4 + (-3) \end{bmatrix} = \begin{bmatrix} 2 \\ 7 \\ 1 \end{bmatrix}.$$

If

$$\boldsymbol{x} = \begin{bmatrix} x_1 \\ x_2 \end{bmatrix} \quad \text{and} \quad \boldsymbol{y} = \begin{bmatrix} y_1 \\ y_2 \end{bmatrix},$$

then

$$\boldsymbol{z} = \boldsymbol{x} + \boldsymbol{y} = \begin{bmatrix} (x_1 + y_1) \\ (x_2 + y_2) \end{bmatrix}.$$

Addition can be represented geometrically as in Figure 3.1. The point $\boldsymbol{z} = \boldsymbol{x} + \boldsymbol{y}$ is found by joining the vectors $\boldsymbol{x}$ and $\boldsymbol{y}$ to the origin and completing the parallelogram.

To illustrate an economic application, suppose that $\boldsymbol{x}$ represents the vector of quantities of goods which a consumer buys in some period, where the element x_1 is, say, the number of apples, x_2 is the number of pears, and so on.

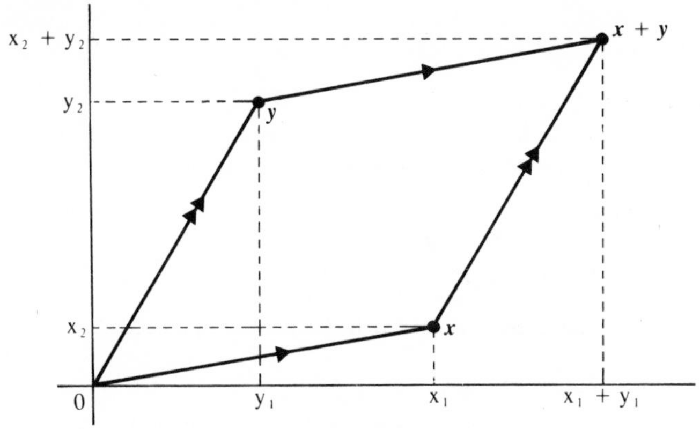

Figure 3.1

And suppose that $\boldsymbol{y}$ represents quantities of the same goods which some other consumer buys in the same period. Then the sum $\boldsymbol{z}$ is the vector of their total purchases. It is easy to see how this particular example could be extended to give the vector of total purchases of all goods in an economy, by having one vector for each consumer and then summing them.

3.4 Product with a scalar

D3.4 The *product* of a vector $\boldsymbol{x}$ and scalar λ is given by

$$\lambda \boldsymbol{x} = \begin{bmatrix} \lambda x_1 \\ \lambda x_2 \\ \vdots \\ \lambda x_n \end{bmatrix}.$$

For example, if $\boldsymbol{x} = \begin{bmatrix} 3 \\ 2 \\ 4 \end{bmatrix}$ then $5\boldsymbol{x} = \begin{bmatrix} 15 \\ 10 \\ 20 \end{bmatrix}$.

This can be shown geometrically, in the case where $\lambda = 2$ and $n = 2$, as in Figure 3.2.

The product $2\boldsymbol{x}$ lies on the same straight line through the origin as the original vector did; since it increases each element by the same proportion, it moves along a ray. The same is true for any value of λ. If λ is negative, the resultant will be in the opposite quadrant. This is why λ is called a scalar; it 'scales' the vector up or down while keeping the same direction (or reversing it if $\lambda < 0$).

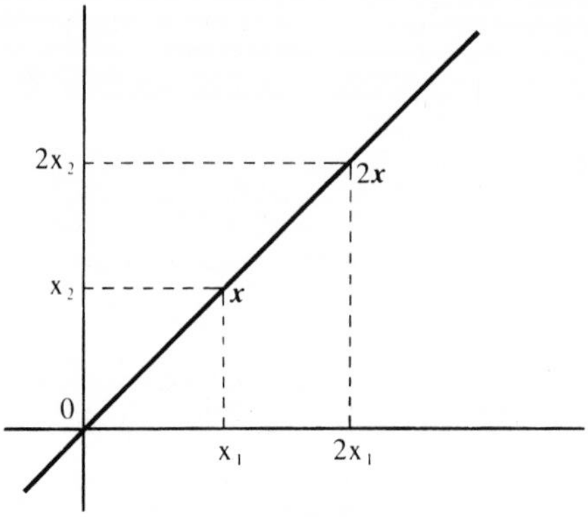

Figure 3.2

Formally, the *difference* between two vectors, $\boldsymbol{x}-\boldsymbol{y}$, is obtained by combining the operations of addition and multiplication by a scalar: $\boldsymbol{x}-\boldsymbol{y}=\boldsymbol{x}+(-1)\boldsymbol{y}$. In practice, one simply subtracts the elements of $\boldsymbol{y}$ from those of $\boldsymbol{x}$, pairwise. The geometry of this is left as an exercise.

3.5 Scalar product

The product of two vectors that we shall now define is called the *scalar product*, which should be distinguished from the product of a vector and a scalar. It is also sometimes called the dot product or the Euclidean inner product. The word 'product' has to be qualified as there are alternative ways of defining the multiplication of vectors; for example, the 'cross product', used by theoretical physicists.

D3.5 The *scalar product* of a row vector $\boldsymbol{x}'$ and a column vector $\boldsymbol{y}$ is given by

$$\boldsymbol{x}'\cdot\boldsymbol{y}=(x_1,x_2,\ldots,x_n)\begin{bmatrix} y_1 \\ y_2 \\ \vdots \\ y_n \end{bmatrix}=x_1y_1+x_2y_2+x_3y_3+\ldots+x_ny_n$$

$$=\sum_{i=1}^{n} x_iy_i.$$

There must be the same number of elements in $\boldsymbol{x}$ and $\boldsymbol{y}$. The scalar product is only defined when one has a row vector first and column vector second. $\boldsymbol{x}$ and $\boldsymbol{y}$ were both column vectors, so $\boldsymbol{x}$ had to be transposed to give $\boldsymbol{x}'\cdot\boldsymbol{y}$. In practice the dot and/or prime are sometimes omitted. It is then assumed that whatever transpositions are necessary will be carried out in order to give a row first and a column second. In this book transpositions will always be written explicitly.

For example, let

$$x = \begin{bmatrix} 3 \\ 2 \\ 4 \end{bmatrix} \quad \text{and} \quad y = \begin{bmatrix} -1 \\ 5 \\ -3 \end{bmatrix}$$

then

$$\begin{aligned} x' \cdot y &= (3, 2, 4)\begin{bmatrix} -1 \\ 5 \\ -3 \end{bmatrix} \\ &= 3.(-1) + 2.5 + 4.(-3) \\ &= -3 + 10 - 12 = -5. \end{aligned}$$

The implication of having a *row* first and a *column* second is that the result is a single number, or scalar. A column into a row would give a matrix as we shall see. Hence,

$$x' \cdot y \neq y \cdot x' \quad \text{although} \quad x' \cdot y = y' \cdot x,$$

so the importance of ensuring that the order and transpositions are correct should be clear. Here we have an example of a property of ordinary numbers, that $ab = ba$, which vectors do not have.

As an example of an economic application, return to the previous discussion (Section 3.3), where x was a choice vector for a consumer. If we now let

$$p = \begin{bmatrix} p_1 \\ p_2 \\ \vdots \\ p_n \end{bmatrix}$$

be a vector of prices, each corresponding to its respective good, then the scalar product $p' \cdot x$ will be his total expenditure. In a theory of consumer choice one might reasonably require that he chooses x subject to the condition (known as the budget constraint) that

$$p' \cdot x \leqslant m$$

where his income is m. It is very convenient to be able to write expenditures so concisely. If x now becomes the total purchases vector for the whole economy, then the scalar product is the value of national expenditure, or the national income.

As another example consider a firm which is producing one output from a number of different inputs. The first element in the vector x represents the volume of output and the remaining elements the various inputs, and we adopt the convention of assigning a positive value to the output and negative values to the inputs.

For example,

$$x = \begin{bmatrix} +6 \\ -3 \\ -1 \\ \vdots \end{bmatrix}$$

We then have a corresponding price vector $\boldsymbol{p}$ where p_1 is the price at which the output is sold and $p_2, p_3, \ldots, p_n$ are the prices paid for the inputs. The scalar product $\boldsymbol{p}' \cdot \boldsymbol{x}$ will then give the *profit* of the firm for any vector $\boldsymbol{x}$. If the technology of the firm restricts its choice of $\boldsymbol{x}$, so that it must choose a vector within the set of possible production vectors, then the firm's profit-maximizing problem is to maximize $\boldsymbol{p}' \cdot \boldsymbol{x}$, where $\boldsymbol{p}$ is assumed fixed, subject to the constraint that it chooses a technologically feasible production vector. This is a typical example of a problem of *constrained optimization*, which we shall be considering in Chapter 17.

Again, suppose that $\boldsymbol{x}$ is a total net output vector for a planned economy, and the p_i are the 'weights', or relative importances, that the planning commission attaches to the various goods. Then the commission, when it searches for the 'socially optimal' and feasible amounts of each good it should direct manufacturing units to produce, is faced with a problem that is mathematically similar to that of the profit-maximizing firm.

Note that division of one vector by another is not defined in any sense, although something analogous to division is defined for *square* matrices, in Chapter 7.

Here is a program that asks you to specify the elements of three vectors, $\boldsymbol{x}, \boldsymbol{y}$ and $\boldsymbol{p}$. It then calculates $\boldsymbol{z} = (\boldsymbol{x} + \boldsymbol{y})$ and the scalar product $\boldsymbol{p} \cdot \boldsymbol{z}$.

```
100  INPUT "WHAT IS THE DIMENSION OF THE VECTOR";N
110  DIM X(N), Y(N), Z(N), P(N)
120  FOR I = 1 TO N
130  PRINT "X(";I")"; : INPUT X(I)
140  NEXT I
150  FOR I = 1 TO N
160  PRINT "Y(";I")"; : INPUT Y(I)
170  NEXT I
180  FOR I = 1 TO N
190  PRINT "P(";I")"; : INPUT P(I)
200  NEXT I
210  PRINT
220  FOR I = 1 TO N
230  Z(I) = X(I) + Y(I)
240  NEXT I
250  PRINT "X   Y   Z   P"
260  FOR I = 1 TO N
```

```
270 PRINT X(I),Y(I),Z(I),P(I)
280 NEXT I
290 PRINT
300 S=0
310 FOR I=1 TO N : REM ADD TOGETHER ...
320 S=S+P(I)*Z(I) : REM ... THE PRODUCTS OF CORRESPONDING
                         ELEMENTS OF P AND Z
330 NEXT I
340 PRINT "THE SCALAR PRODUCT OF P AND X + Y IS";S
```

3.6 Euclidean norm

It is useful to have a definition of the distance of a vector from the origin: its 'length'. There are many possible definitions of length, one of which is a 'Pythagorean' definition, which follows from the theorem that the length of the hypotenuse of a right-angle triangle is the square root of the sum of the squares of the other two sides.

D3.6 The length or *Euclidean norm* of a vector $\boldsymbol{x}$, denoted by $\|\boldsymbol{x}\|$, is given by

$$\|\boldsymbol{x}\| = \sqrt{(\boldsymbol{x}' \cdot \boldsymbol{x})}$$

$$= \sqrt{\left(\sum_{i=1}^{n} x_i^2\right)}$$

the positive square root being taken by convention. See Figure 3.3.

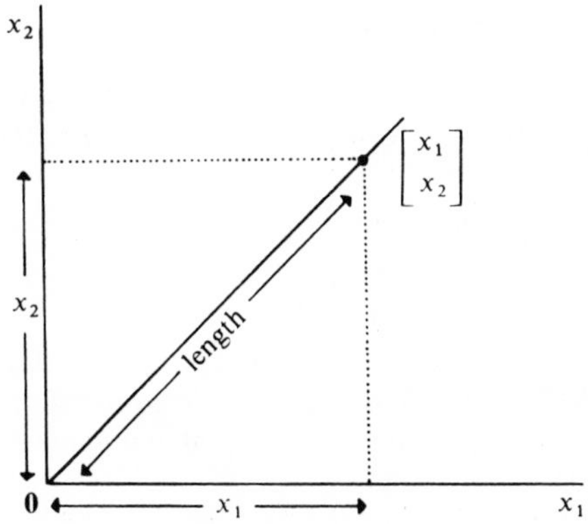

Figure 3.3

Note that

$$x' \cdot x = (x_1, \ldots, x_n) \begin{bmatrix} x_1 \\ \vdots \\ x_n \end{bmatrix}$$

$$= x_1 x_1 + x_2 x_2 + \ldots + x_n x_n$$

which is the sum of the squares of the elements.

For example, if

$$x = \begin{bmatrix} 3 \\ 4 \end{bmatrix},$$

then

$$x' \cdot x = 3^2 + 4^2 = 25$$

and so

$$\|x\| = \sqrt{25} = 5.$$

As an example from statistical theory, note that if the x_i were observations of a random variable, obtained by random sampling, then, apart from a factor of $1/\sqrt{n}$ (where n is the sample size), the norm of x would be the square root of the second moment of the sample, about the origin.

The *distance* between two vectors can be defined as the norm of the difference between them, $\|x - y\|$. The geometry is left as an exercise.

If you add the following to the previous program it will calculate the norm of the sum of the vectors x and y that you have specified.

```
400  S = 0
410  FOR I = 1 TO N
420  S = S + Z(I)*Z(I)
430  NEXT I
440  S = SQR(ABS(S)) : REM ABS IS USED TO GIVE MODULUS OF S
                           TO AVOID SQUARE ROOT OF A NEGATIVE
                           NUMBER
450  PRINT " THE NORM OF X + Y IS"; S
```

Of course this will give the norm of a single vector x if you specify y as the zero vector, and the distance between x and y if y is entered with a reversed sign.

3.7 Orthogonality

D3.7 If the inner product of two vectors is zero, then the vectors are *orthogonal*. That is, if $x' \cdot y = 0$, then x and y are orthogonal.

This is geometrically equivalent to being at right-angles. For example, the vectors $\begin{bmatrix} 1 \\ 0 \end{bmatrix}$ and $\begin{bmatrix} 0 \\ 1 \end{bmatrix}$ lie on the axes (see Figure 3.4) and are clearly at right angles.

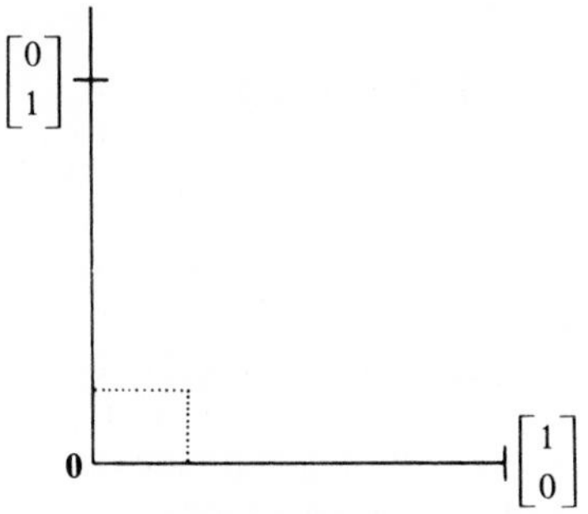

Figure 3.4

To confirm this, note that $(1, 0)\begin{bmatrix}0\\1\end{bmatrix} = 1.0 + 0.1 = 0.$

Also, if

$$x = \begin{bmatrix}2\\1\end{bmatrix} \quad \text{and} \quad y = \begin{bmatrix}1\\-2\end{bmatrix},$$

then

$$\begin{aligned} x' \cdot y &= (2, 1)\begin{bmatrix}1\\-2\end{bmatrix} \\ &= 2 + (-2) = 0. \end{aligned}$$

As an exercise, you can confirm that these two vectors are at right angles by sketching them.

D3.8 If we have a collection of vectors which are

1 Mutually (or pairwise) orthogonal, and
2 Each of unit length,

then it is called an *orthonormal* set.

A set of orthogonal vectors can be converted to unit length by multiplying each by a suitable scalar to produce an orthonormal set of vectors. (See Problems 3.8.3 and 3.8.7.)

There is an infinite number of such sets, but a particularly important set, which corresponds to the ordinary axes, is given by

$$e_1 = \begin{bmatrix}1\\0\\0\\\vdots\\0\\0\end{bmatrix}, \ldots, e_i = \begin{bmatrix}0\\0\\\vdots\\1\\0\\0\end{bmatrix} \leftarrow i\text{th element}, \ldots, e_n = \begin{bmatrix}0\\0\\\vdots\\0\\0\\1\end{bmatrix}.$$

It is easily shown that

$$e_i' \cdot e_j = 0 \quad \text{if} \quad i \neq j$$

and

$$e_i' \cdot e_j = 1 \quad \text{if} \quad i = j,$$

confirming that they have the required properties.

Notice that in this definition we have a slight departure from the procedure so far established; a *vector* e_i carries a subscript. We could try to give each vector a different letter, but this is tedious and one runs out of letters rather quickly. This notation is obviously convenient; the i simultaneously identifies which vector in the set it is, and what position the 1 should occupy.

3.8 Problems

1. If $x_1 = \begin{bmatrix} 1 \\ 2 \\ 3 \end{bmatrix}$, $x_2 = \begin{bmatrix} 1 \\ 0 \\ 4 \end{bmatrix}$, $x_3 = \begin{bmatrix} -5 \\ -6 \\ -17 \end{bmatrix}$, calculate $3x_1 + 2x_2 + x_3$.

2. If $x = \begin{bmatrix} 1 \\ 2 \end{bmatrix}$ and $y = \begin{bmatrix} 4 \\ -2 \end{bmatrix}$, find the scalar product $x' \cdot y$.

Sketch and show that x and y are orthogonal. Give an example of two three-element vectors which are orthogonal.

3. Find the Euclidean length of the vector $\begin{bmatrix} 2 \\ 3 \\ -1 \end{bmatrix}$. Convert this to a vector which has the same direction but has length of unity.

4. Show that

(*a*) $\sum_i (x_i + y_i) = \sum_i x_i + \sum_i y_i$

(*b*) $\sum_i \lambda x_i = \lambda \sum_i x_i$, λ a scalar

(*c*) $\sum_i \sum_j a_{ij} x_j = \sum_j \sum_i a_{ij} x_j$

$$= \sum_j x_j \sum_i a_{ij}.$$

5. Show that $\|\lambda x\| = |\lambda| \, \|x\|$.

6. Investigate the geometry of the measure of distance between $\boldsymbol{x}$ and $\boldsymbol{y}$, $\|\boldsymbol{x}-\boldsymbol{y}\|$. Show that

(*a*) $\|\boldsymbol{x}-\boldsymbol{y}\| > 0$ unless $\boldsymbol{x}=\boldsymbol{y}$

(*b*) $\|\boldsymbol{x}-\boldsymbol{y}\| = \|\boldsymbol{y}-\boldsymbol{x}\|$.

It is also true that if $\boldsymbol{z}$ is a third vector,

$$\|\boldsymbol{x}-\boldsymbol{z}\| + \|\boldsymbol{z}-\boldsymbol{y}\| \geqslant \|\boldsymbol{x}-\boldsymbol{y}\|.$$

Interpret this. Can you prove it?

7. Derive a technique for normalizing a vector (that is, making its norm = 1) which applies to vectors of any finite dimension.

8. Let $\boldsymbol{p} = \begin{bmatrix} 1 \\ 4 \\ 0 \\ 7 \end{bmatrix}$, $\boldsymbol{x} = \begin{bmatrix} 2 \\ 6 \\ -1 \\ -3 \end{bmatrix}$, $\boldsymbol{y} = \begin{bmatrix} 4 \\ -2 \\ -1 \\ 1 \end{bmatrix}$. Find $\boldsymbol{p}'\cdot\boldsymbol{x}$ and $\boldsymbol{p}'\cdot\boldsymbol{y}$ and then verify that $\boldsymbol{p}'\cdot\boldsymbol{x} + \boldsymbol{p}'\cdot\boldsymbol{y} = \boldsymbol{p}'\cdot(\boldsymbol{x}+\boldsymbol{y})$.

4 Operations on matrices

4.1 Addition

To add two matrices we add the corresponding elements in each matrix, in the same way as the corresponding elements of each vector are added in vector addition:

D4.1 If $\mathbf{A}$ is the matrix $\begin{bmatrix} a_{11} \dots a_{1n} \\ \vdots \quad \vdots \\ a_{m1} \dots a_{mn} \end{bmatrix}$, and $\mathbf{B} = \begin{bmatrix} b_{11} \dots b_{1n} \\ \vdots \quad \vdots \\ b_{m1} \dots b_{mn} \end{bmatrix}$, has the same number of rows and columns, then the matrix $\mathbf{C} = \mathbf{A} + \mathbf{B}$ is defined by

$$c_{ij} = a_{ij} + b_{ij}, \forall i, \forall j.$$

The matrices must be of the same size (just as vectors have to be); otherwise the addition operation is not defined. For example, if

$$\mathbf{A} = \begin{bmatrix} 1 & 2 \\ 0 & 1 \end{bmatrix} \quad \text{and} \quad \mathbf{B} = \begin{bmatrix} 2 & 3 \\ 1 & 4 \end{bmatrix}$$

then

$$\mathbf{A} + \mathbf{B} = \begin{bmatrix} 1+2 & 2+3 \\ 0+1 & 1+4 \end{bmatrix} = \begin{bmatrix} 3 & 5 \\ 1 & 5 \end{bmatrix}.$$

It is clear that $\mathbf{A}+\mathbf{B}=\mathbf{B}+\mathbf{A}$ and that $\mathbf{A}+(\mathbf{B}+\mathbf{C})=(\mathbf{A}+\mathbf{B})+\mathbf{C}$; two useful results in matrix algebra.

4.2 Multiplication by scalars

To multiply a matrix by a scalar, each element in the matrix is multiplied by the scalar:

D4.2 If $\mathbf{C} = \lambda\mathbf{A}$ where λ is any scalar, then $c_{ij} = \lambda a_{ij}$, $\forall i, j$.

Taking the matrix **A** above and $\lambda = 2$,

$$2\mathbf{A} = \begin{bmatrix} 2 & 4 \\ 0 & 2 \end{bmatrix}.$$

A matrix of any size can be multiplied by a scalar; it does not matter how many rows and columns it has.

4.3 Matrix products

There are several alternative ways of multiplying matrices together. The most common and most useful method is given here. Informally, to obtain the product, **AB**, of two matrices, we take the *first* row of **A** and the *first* column of **B** and obtain the scalar product of those two vectors. The result is the element in the *first* row and *first* column of the product matrix.

To obtain the element in the *second* row and the *first* column we take the *second* row in **A** and form the scalar product with the *first* column of **B**, and so on.

Hence the *row* in **A** and the *column* in **B** are used to identify the position of the resultant element in the new matrix. As with vectors, if this operation is to be defined, restrictions are needed on the sizes of **A** and **B**. In this case, **A** must have the same number of columns as **B** has rows.

D4.3 Let **A** be considered as a column of n-element row vectors,

$$\mathbf{A} = \begin{bmatrix} \boldsymbol{a}_1 \\ \boldsymbol{a}_2 \\ \vdots \\ \boldsymbol{a}_m \end{bmatrix}, \text{ an } m \times n \text{ matrix.}$$

Let **B** be considered as a row of n-element column vectors,

$$\mathbf{B} = [\boldsymbol{b}_1, \boldsymbol{b}_2, \ldots, \boldsymbol{b}_p], \text{ an } n \times p \text{ matrix.}$$

Now, if the matrix $\mathbf{C} = \mathbf{AB}$, then c_{ij} is defined as the inner product of $\boldsymbol{a}_i$ with $\boldsymbol{b}_j$; that is

$$c_{ij} = \boldsymbol{a}_i \cdot \boldsymbol{b}_j, \qquad i = 1, \ldots, m$$
$$j = 1, \ldots, p$$

$$= \sum_{k=1}^{n} a_{ik} b_{kj}, \forall i, \forall j.$$

When **A** has the same number of columns as **B** has rows, **A** and **B** are said to be ‘conformable for multiplication’.

It is not usually true that $\mathbf{AB} = \mathbf{BA}$. If $\mathbf{AB}$ is defined, $\mathbf{BA}$ need not be. In the definition, $\mathbf{BA}$ would be defined only if $m = p$. This would allow the operation, but $\mathbf{AB}$ would still be a different product from $\mathbf{BA}$, because in the first case, $\mathbf{A}$'s rows are multiplied by $\mathbf{B}$'s columns, whereas in the second case, $\mathbf{B}$'s rows are multiplied by $\mathbf{A}$'s columns.

For example,

$$\begin{bmatrix} 1 & 2 \\ 0 & 1 \end{bmatrix}\begin{bmatrix} 2 & 3 \\ 1 & 4 \end{bmatrix} = \begin{bmatrix} 1.2+2.1 & 1.3+2.4 \\ 0.2+1.1 & 0.3+1.4 \end{bmatrix} = \begin{bmatrix} 4 & 11 \\ 1 & 4 \end{bmatrix};$$

$$\begin{bmatrix} 2 & 3 \\ 1 & 4 \end{bmatrix}\begin{bmatrix} 1 & 2 \\ 0 & 1 \end{bmatrix} = \begin{bmatrix} 2 & 7 \\ 1 & 6 \end{bmatrix};$$

so that $\mathbf{BA}$ and $\mathbf{AB}$ are completely different. If $\mathbf{A}$ and $\mathbf{B}$ happen to be matrices such that $\mathbf{AB} = \mathbf{BA}$, then $\mathbf{A}$ and $\mathbf{B}$ are said to *commute*.

The product of an $m \times n$ matrix with a $k \times p$ matrix is an $m \times p$ matrix *iff* $n = k$: $(m \times n)(n \times p) = m \times p$. If $n \neq k$, then the product is not defined. In particular, $(m \times n)(n \times 1) = m \times 1$ and $(1 \times m)(m \times n) = 1 \times n$, so that a column vector *pre*multiplied by a matrix is also a column vector, and a row *post*multiplied by a matrix is also a row.

Note that the operation of multiplying a vector by a matrix has two rather special properties: if $\mathbf{A}$ is any $m \times n$ matrix and $\boldsymbol{x}$ and $\boldsymbol{y}$ are two $n \times 1$ columns, then

$$\mathbf{A}(\boldsymbol{x} + \boldsymbol{y}) = \mathbf{A}\boldsymbol{x} + \mathbf{A}\boldsymbol{y}$$

and

$$\mathbf{A}(\lambda \boldsymbol{x}) = \lambda \mathbf{A}\boldsymbol{x}, \quad \text{for any scalar } \lambda.$$

These are the two requirements for an operation to be linear, and so a matrix is an example of what is known as a *linear operator*. We shall come across several other examples in the course of this book.

With the definition of matrix multiplication established we can now see how a system of equations can be written in matrix form. Take the system used in Problem 2.3.1(*a*):

$$x_1 + x_2 = 3$$
$$4x_1 - 2x_2 = 0.$$

This is equivalent to

$$\begin{bmatrix} 1 & 1 \\ 4 & -2 \end{bmatrix}\begin{bmatrix} x_1 \\ x_2 \end{bmatrix} = \begin{bmatrix} 3 \\ 0 \end{bmatrix}.$$

Note how the coefficients of the matrix correspond to those of the original system. If we now let

$$\mathbf{A} = \begin{bmatrix} 1 & 1 \\ 4 & -2 \end{bmatrix}, \quad \boldsymbol{x} = \begin{bmatrix} x_1 \\ x_2 \end{bmatrix} \quad \text{and} \quad \boldsymbol{b} = \begin{bmatrix} 3 \\ 0 \end{bmatrix}$$

we see that the system can be very compactly written as

$$\mathbf{A}x = b.$$

We shall see how to solve such a matrix equation in Chapters 7 and 8.

We can further illustrate by considering the Leontief, *input-output* model (for more detail see Dorfman, Samuelson and Solow, 1958). We suppose that we have an economy with n industries, each producing one good, and let

$$\mathbf{A} = (a_{ij}), \quad a_{ij} \geqslant 0, \quad i, j = 1, 2, \ldots, n,$$

where a_{ij} (known as the *technology coefficient*) is the number of units of input i required to produce *one* unit of good j. Suppose that we require net outputs of the goods in the amounts $f_1, f_2, \ldots, f_n$ for consumers' use (called *final demands*). The problem is, given the technology coefficients and the final demands, what should the gross output of each industry, $x_1, x_2, \ldots, x_n$, be? (Cf. Problem 2.3.3 above.)

For each industry it must be that the total amount produced is equal to what is needed for final consumption, plus what is needed as inputs to other industries (*intermediate demands*):

$$f_i + a_{i1}x_1 + a_{i2}x_2 + \ldots + a_{in}x_n = x_i \quad \text{for} \quad i = 1, 2, \ldots, n.$$

Note that, for a sensible solution, the a_{ij} must be such that a vector x can be found with $x_i \geqslant 0, i = 1, 2, \ldots, n$.

In matrix form, the set of n equations, of which the above is an example, can be written as

$$f + \mathbf{A}x = x$$

where

$$f = \begin{bmatrix} f_1 \\ f_2 \\ \vdots \\ f_n \end{bmatrix}, \quad x = \begin{bmatrix} x_1 \\ x_2 \\ \vdots \\ x_n \end{bmatrix}, \quad \mathbf{A} = (a_{ij}).$$

This example is further developed in Sections 4.5(*a*); 7.1 and 9.4(*b*).

As another example, consider the elementary theory of Markov chains. Suppose that we form a column vector x^0, such that x_i^0 is the number of objects in the ith 'state'. It might be the number of people in the ith social class, or income group, or age group. Suppose we define a square matrix $\mathbf{P}$ such that p_{ij} is the probability that in any time period an object will transfer from state j into state i (from the second subscript state into the first subscript state). The product $\mathbf{P}x^0$ will be an n-dimensional column vector, x^1 such that

$$x^1 = \mathbf{P}x^0.$$

From the definition of the product

$$x_1^1 = \sum_{j=1}^{n} p_{1j}x_j^0,$$

which is the expected number of objects in the first state at the end of a period. Hence, $\boldsymbol{x}^1$ gives the expected distribution of objects after one period, given the initial distribution $\boldsymbol{x}^0$. Similarly,

$$\boldsymbol{x}^2 = \mathbf{P}\boldsymbol{x}^1 = \mathbf{PP}\boldsymbol{x}^0 = \mathbf{P}^2\boldsymbol{x}^0$$

and

$$\boldsymbol{x}^n = \mathbf{P}^n\boldsymbol{x}^0.$$

Hence, we can calculate the expected distribution of objects (class structure, income distribution, age structure, etc.) at any time by multiplying $\mathbf{P}$ by itself an appropriate number of times and multiplying the result by the initial distribution $\boldsymbol{x}^0$. It is then interesting to ask whether this distribution will always be changing, or whether there will be a tendency to some stable distribution, from an arbitrary initial distribution. We return to this in Section 9.4(*a*).

The following program produces the product of two matrices.

```
100  PRINT "MATRIX A"
110  INPUT "NO OF ROWS"; M
120  INPUT "NO OF COLUMNS"; N
130  DIM A(M,N)
135  :
140  PRINT "MATRIX B"
150  INPUT "NO OF ROWS"; Q
160  IF Q<>N THEN PRINT "MATRICES NOT CONFORMABLE"
170  IF Q<>N THEN STOP
180  INPUT "NO OF COLUMNS"; P
190  DIM B(N,P)
195  :
200  FOR I = 1 TO M
210  FOR J = 1 TO N
220  PRINT "A("I","J")" : INPUT A(I,J)
230  NEXT J, I
240  PRINT
250  PRINT "MATRIX A"
255  :
260  FOR I = 1 TO M
270  FOR J = 1 TO N
280  PRINT A(I,J);
290  NEXT J
300  PRINT
310  NEXT I
320  PRINT
325  :
400  FOR I = 1 TO N
410  FOR J = 1 TO P
420  PRINT "B("I","J")" : INPUT B(I,J)
430  NEXT J, I
```

```
440  PRINT
445  :
450  PRINT "MATRIX B"
460  FOR I = 1 TO N
470  FOR J = 1 TO P
480  PRINT B(I,J);
490  NEXT J
500  PRINT
510  NEXT I
520  PRINT
530  DIM C(M,P)
535  :
600  FOR I = 1 TO M
610  FOR J = 1 TO P
620  C(I,J) = 0                    : REM THIS . .
630  FOR K = 1 TO N                : REM AND THIS . . .
640  C(I,J) = C(I,J) + A(I,K)*B(K,J) : REM AND THIS . . .
650  NEXT K                        : REM AND THIS CALCULATE
                                     THE PRODUCT MATRIX, C
660  NEXT J, I
670  PRINT
675  :
700  PRINT "MATRIX C = AB"
710  FOR I = 1 TO M
720  FOR J = 1 TO P
730  PRINT C(I,J);
740  NEXT J
750  PRINT
760  NEXT I
```

You can check that the program is working correctly by using the worked examples on the previous pages. A more interesting example to try is provided by the matrix **A** and its inverse, $\mathbf{A}^{-1}$ printed on pp. 63–4. This will probably show that more programming work is required to obtain a neat and readable output. If you want to improve its format you will have to get to know the techniques for achieving this which apply to your particular machine (they vary somewhat). If you look carefully at the results this example gives and then try the matrix multiplication by hand you will also have an illustration of some of the numerical problems that can be caused by the inability of a computer to represent some numbers exactly.

You may find it worthwhile storing this program for use at a later stage.

If you wish to follow the development of a Markov chain then add the following lines.

```
800  FOR I = 1 TO M
810  FOR J = 1 TO P
820  B(I,J) = C(I,J)
830  NEXT J, I
840  GOTO 600
```

When this is run **A** must be square with entries which are all positive fractions (probabilities) and columns which add up to unity. **B** must be an $m \times 1$ column vector. The program will print the numbers in each state at each stage of the chain.

4.4 Transposition

The transpose of a matrix is obtained by writing the jth row as the jth column and the ith column and the ith row:

D4.4 If $\mathbf{A} = (a_{ij})$, then $\mathbf{A}' = (a_{ji})$.

For example, if

$$\mathbf{A} = \begin{bmatrix} 1 & 2 \\ 0 & 3 \end{bmatrix}$$

then

$$\mathbf{A}' = \begin{bmatrix} 1 & 0 \\ 2 & 3 \end{bmatrix}.$$

If the matrix is square, as in this example, then the transpose of the matrix can be thought of as the matrix with the same main diagonal, with all the other elements 'reflected' in that diagonal.

4.5 Special matrices

There are a few special matrices which are very useful.

(a) In the real number system, there is a number '1' which, when it is multiplied by any other number x does not change x. That is, $1x = x$, $\forall x$.

The corresponding matrix is known as the *identity matrix*. Each element on the main diagonal of the identity matrix is 1, and all other elements are zero. It is denoted by **I**. Thus, $\mathbf{I}\boldsymbol{x} = \boldsymbol{x}$, and $\boldsymbol{x}'\mathbf{I} = \boldsymbol{x}'$:

$$\begin{bmatrix} 1 & 0 & 0 & 0 \\ 0 & 1 & 0 & 0 \\ 0 & 0 & 1 & 0 \\ 0 & 0 & 0 & 1 \end{bmatrix} \begin{bmatrix} x_1 \\ x_2 \\ x_3 \\ x_4 \end{bmatrix} = \begin{bmatrix} x_1 \\ x_2 \\ x_3 \\ x_4 \end{bmatrix},$$

as can be confirmed by multiplication.

To return to the input-output equation,

$$\begin{aligned} \boldsymbol{f} + \mathbf{A}\boldsymbol{x} &= \boldsymbol{x} \\ &= \mathbf{I}\boldsymbol{x}. \end{aligned}$$

We can write this as

$$f = \mathbf{I}x - \mathbf{A}x$$

or

$$f = (\mathbf{I} - \mathbf{A})x.$$

Further analysis will be found in Sections 7.1 and 9.4.

(*b*) The *null* or *zero* matrix is the matrix which corresponds to zero in the real number system and is a matrix of zeros. It is a matrix **O** such that

$$\mathbf{O}x = \mathbf{0}$$

(where **0** on the right-hand side is a zero *vector*).

(*c*) A *diagonal* matrix is a square matrix with zeros everywhere except on the main diagonal

$$\begin{bmatrix} \lambda_1 & 0 & 0 & 0 \\ 0 & \lambda_2 & 0 & 0 \\ 0 & 0 & \lambda_3 & 0 \\ 0 & 0 & 0 & \lambda_4 \end{bmatrix}$$

where the λs are any scalars.

(*d*) A *symmetric* matrix is a square matrix **A** such that

$$a_{ij} = a_{ji}, \ \forall i, j;$$

that is,

$$\mathbf{A}' = \mathbf{A}.$$

A symmetric matrix is a 'reflection' of itself in the main diagonal.

(*e*) A *skew-symmetric* matrix has the property that $\mathbf{A} = -\mathbf{A}'$. It is similar to a symmetric matrix, except that the corresponding elements have opposite signs; for example,

$$\begin{bmatrix} 0 & 5 & -6 \\ -5 & 0 & 4 \\ 6 & -4 & 0 \end{bmatrix}.$$

4.6 Partitioning

Any matrix can be separated arbitrarily into a number of sub-matrices. For example, we could *partition* **A** as follows:

$$\mathbf{A} = \left[\begin{array}{c|c} \mathbf{B} & \mathbf{C} \\ \hline \mathbf{D} & \mathbf{E} \end{array}\right],$$

and if

$$\mathbf{A} = \begin{bmatrix} 1 & 2 & -3 & 1 \\ 4 & 0 & 6 & 1 \\ 0 & 2 & 2 & 1 \end{bmatrix}$$

we could take

$$\mathbf{B} = \begin{bmatrix} 1 & 2 & -3 \\ 4 & 0 & 6 \end{bmatrix}, \quad \mathbf{C} = \begin{bmatrix} 1 \\ 1 \end{bmatrix}$$

$$\mathbf{D} = [0 \quad 2 \quad 2], \quad \mathbf{E} = [1].$$

Conformable matrices which are suitably partitioned have the property that their product can be expressed in terms of the products of the submatrices as follows:

if

$$\mathbf{A} = \left[\begin{array}{c|c} \mathbf{B} & \mathbf{C} \\ \hline \mathbf{D} & \mathbf{E} \end{array}\right] \quad \text{and} \quad \mathbf{V} = \left[\begin{array}{c|c} \mathbf{W} & \mathbf{X} \\ \hline \mathbf{Y} & \mathbf{Z} \end{array}\right]$$

then

$$\mathbf{AV} = \left[\begin{array}{c|c} \mathbf{BW} + \mathbf{CY} & \mathbf{BX} + \mathbf{CZ} \\ \hline \mathbf{DW} + \mathbf{EY} & \mathbf{DX} + \mathbf{EZ} \end{array}\right].$$

This operation is useful for several reasons. For one thing, it may be very much easier to calculate the submatrix products than to calculate the whole product at once; if **D** is a null matrix, for example. Partitioning can also be a great help in interpretation, in such models as the input-output model or the Markov chain. Suppose that, after a suitable rearrangement of the rows and columns of the input-output matrix, it can be partitioned in the way given for **A** above, with **D** a matrix of zeros. Then we see that the first few industries do not use the outputs of the last few industries as their inputs, and we say that the system is *decomposable* (or segmentable). This has implications for the properties of the solutions to the system. Partitioning is also important in econometrics, for example, in interpreting structural forms and in handling identification problems.

4.7 Problems

1. If $\mathbf{A} = \begin{bmatrix} 2 & 4 \\ -1 & 6 \end{bmatrix}$ and $\mathbf{B} = \begin{bmatrix} 0 & 1 \\ 2 & 2 \end{bmatrix}$, show that $\mathbf{AB} \neq \mathbf{BA}$.

2. If $\mathbf{A} = \begin{bmatrix} 0 & -3 & 6 & -10 \\ 3 & 0 & 9 & \frac{1}{2} \\ -6 & -9 & 0 & 1 \\ 10 & -\frac{1}{2} & -1 & 0 \end{bmatrix}$, calculate $\mathbf{A} + \mathbf{A}'$.

3 Let $\mathbf{A} = \begin{bmatrix} 1 & 1 & 1 \\ 2 & -1 & 2 \\ -1 & -1 & 0 \end{bmatrix}$ and $\mathbf{B} = \begin{bmatrix} -\frac{2}{3} & \frac{1}{3} & -1 \\ \frac{2}{3} & -\frac{1}{3} & 0 \\ 1 & 0 & 1 \end{bmatrix}$.

Find the products **AB** and **BA**. Show that the premultiplication of any three-element column vector y by the product **BA** leaves the vector y unchanged; that is, show that $\mathbf{BA}y = y$. Hence, solve the system of equations:

$$\begin{aligned} x_1 + x_2 + x_3 &= 6 \\ 2x_1 - x_2 + 2x_3 &= 6 \\ -x_1 - x_2 \quad &= -5. \end{aligned}$$

4 If $x = \begin{bmatrix} 1 \\ 1 \\ 1 \end{bmatrix}$ and **A** is a 3×5 matrix, what is the relationship between the columns of **A** and the row vector $x'\mathbf{A}$?

5. Given the matrix $\mathbf{A} = \begin{bmatrix} 2 & 1 \\ 5 & 3 \end{bmatrix}$, find the matrix **B** such that $\mathbf{AB} = \begin{bmatrix} 1 & 0 \\ 0 & 1 \end{bmatrix}$.

6. If x is a column vector with n elements, and y is a column vector with m elements, what is the (matrix) product xy'?

7. A large firm controls five factories. The input and output levels of each factory are given by one column of the matrix (inputs negative, outputs positive)

$$\begin{array}{l} \text{factory} \\ \text{good 1} \\ \text{good 2} \\ \text{good 3} \end{array} \begin{array}{c} \begin{array}{ccccc} a & b & c & d & e \end{array} \\ \begin{bmatrix} 1 & -2 & 0 & 1 & 1 \\ 0 & 3 & -\frac{1}{2} & 1 & -2 \\ -\frac{1}{2} & 1 & 2 & -2 & -1 \end{bmatrix}. \end{array}$$

If the prices of the three goods are given by $\begin{bmatrix} 3 \\ 4 \\ 6 \end{bmatrix}$, find the total profit of the firm. Write down the matrix formula you use for this calculation.

5 Properties of sets of vectors

Having defined all the fundamental operations on vectors that we need, we now investigate the properties possessed by *sets* of vectors.

5.1 Linear combinations

D5.1 Given a set of m n-component vectors $\boldsymbol{a}_1, \boldsymbol{a}_2, \ldots, \boldsymbol{a}_m$, then any vector $\boldsymbol{b}$ given by

$$\boldsymbol{b} = \sum_{i=1}^{m} \lambda_i \boldsymbol{a}_i$$

for some scalars λ_i, $i = 1, \ldots, m$, is a linear combination of the set.

For example,

$$3.\begin{bmatrix}2\\1\end{bmatrix} + 6.\begin{bmatrix}-1\\4\end{bmatrix} = \begin{bmatrix}0\\27\end{bmatrix}$$

and $\begin{bmatrix}0\\27\end{bmatrix}$ is a linear combination of $\begin{bmatrix}2\\1\end{bmatrix}$ and $\begin{bmatrix}-1\\4\end{bmatrix}$. The scalars can be any numbers, including zero.

Geometrically, for two vectors, a linear combination is found by completing the parallelogram, after having found $\lambda_1\boldsymbol{a}_1$ and $\lambda_2\boldsymbol{a}_2$ (see Figure 5.1).

If one fixes any two vectors which do not lie in the same line (i.e. are not *collinear*), then it is possible to 'generate' any point in the plane by taking suitable linear combinations of those two vectors. In general, if one has an n-dimensional space, and a set of n 'non-coplanar', or *linearly independent* vectors, then one can express any vector in the space in terms of a linear

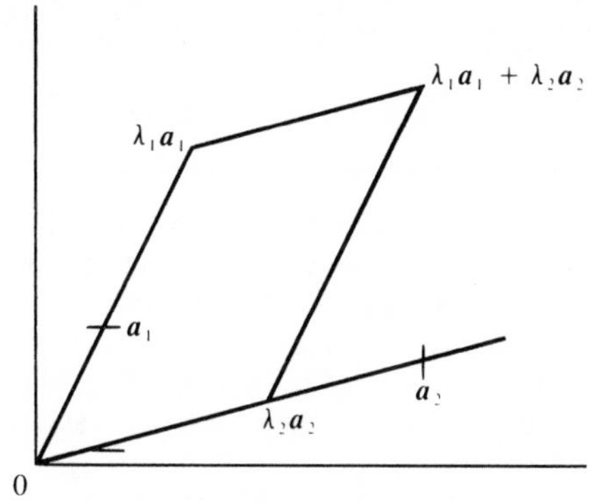

Figure 5.1

combination of that set of n vectors. The concept of linear dependence is fundamental, and we shall use it many times.

5.2 Linear dependence

D5.2 A set of vectors $\{\boldsymbol{a}_1, \ldots, \boldsymbol{a}_m\}$ is said to be *linearly independent* if the statement that $\sum_{i=1}^{m} \lambda_i \boldsymbol{a}_i = \mathbf{0}$ implies that $\lambda_i = 0, \forall i$.

If a set is not linearly independent it is linearly dependent; in other words, if $\exists$ scalars λ_i s.t.

$$\sum_{i=1}^{m} \lambda_i \boldsymbol{a}_i = \mathbf{0}$$

and $\lambda_k \neq 0$ for at least one k, then the set is linearly dependent, because the definition of linear independence is not satisfied, since the zero vector can be obtained as a linear combination of the $\boldsymbol{a}_i$, with at least one non-zero coefficient.

Hence, to check whether the two vectors, $\boldsymbol{a}_1$ and $\boldsymbol{a}_2$, are linearly independent, one tries to find values of λ_1 and λ_2 such that $\lambda_1 \boldsymbol{a}_1 + \lambda_2 \boldsymbol{a}_2 = \mathbf{0}$, excluding the trivial case, $\lambda_1 = 0$ and $\lambda_2 = 0$. If such values can be found, then they are *not* linearly independent, they are linearly dependent.

To illustrate, $\begin{bmatrix} 2 \\ 1 \end{bmatrix}$ and $\begin{bmatrix} -1 \\ 4 \end{bmatrix}$ are linearly independent since no values of λ_1 and λ_2 can be found to give $\lambda_1 \begin{bmatrix} 2 \\ 1 \end{bmatrix} + \lambda_2 \begin{bmatrix} -1 \\ 4 \end{bmatrix} = \begin{bmatrix} 0 \\ 0 \end{bmatrix}$ except $\lambda_1 = 0$, $\lambda_2 = 0$.

The vectors $\begin{bmatrix}2\\1\end{bmatrix}$ and $\begin{bmatrix}-4\\-2\end{bmatrix}$ are linearly dependent since

$$2\begin{bmatrix}2\\1\end{bmatrix}+1\begin{bmatrix}-4\\-2\end{bmatrix}=\begin{bmatrix}0\\0\end{bmatrix} \text{ that is, } \lambda_1=2, \lambda_2=1.$$

Geometrically, if two vectors, each with two elements, are linearly dependent, they lie on the same straight line. On the other hand, if they are linearly independent, they do not and the only way of obtaining a result at the origin would be to take the values $\lambda_1=0, \lambda_2=0$.

In Figure 5.2 $\boldsymbol{a}_1$ and $\boldsymbol{a}_2$ are linearly dependent since $\frac{1}{2}\boldsymbol{a}_1+\boldsymbol{a}_2=\boldsymbol{0}$, but $\boldsymbol{a}_1$ and $\boldsymbol{a}_3$ are linearly independent, since the only way of making $\lambda_1\boldsymbol{a}_1+\lambda_3\boldsymbol{a}_3=\boldsymbol{0}$ is by taking $\lambda_1=\lambda_3=0$.

Note that linear (in)dependence is a property of a *set* of vectors, not of the vectors themselves. For example, a set of linearly independent vectors can be converted to a set of linearly dependent vectors by including the zero vector, because any value of $\lambda \neq 0$, multiplied by the zero vector, will still give the zero vector. We know from above that $\begin{bmatrix}2\\1\end{bmatrix}$ and $\begin{bmatrix}-1\\4\end{bmatrix}$ are linearly independent, but if we add $\begin{bmatrix}0\\0\end{bmatrix}$ to the set it becomes dependent, because

$$0.\begin{bmatrix}2\\1\end{bmatrix}+0.\begin{bmatrix}-1\\4\end{bmatrix}+1.\begin{bmatrix}0\\0\end{bmatrix}=\begin{bmatrix}0\\0\end{bmatrix}$$

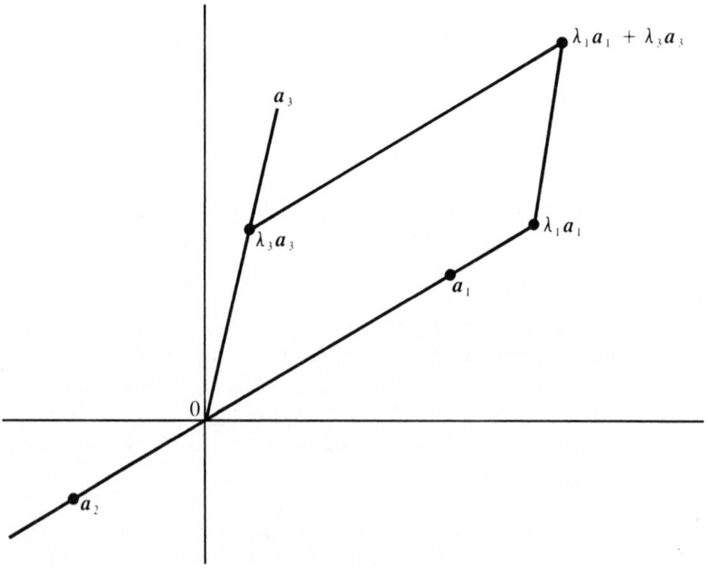

Figure 5.2

and we have found a set of λs, not all zero ($\lambda_3 = 1$), yielding a linear combination of $\mathbf{0}$.

It is not possible to have a set of three vectors, each with two elements, that is linearly independent, as Problem 5.4.1 (*d*) illustrates, and, in general, any set of $n+1$ (or more) vectors with n elements must be linearly dependent. More of this later.

As an application, let a vector $\boldsymbol{a}_1$ represent a feasible production technique for a firm and another vector $\boldsymbol{a}_2$ represent another distinct technique, then the linear combination $\lambda_1\boldsymbol{a}_1 + \lambda_2\boldsymbol{a}_2$ gives yet another feasible technique which may be more profitable, depending on the costs of the various inputs and other considerations. More applications of this type will be found in Problems 5.4.5 and 5.4.6.

The last numerical examples suggest that there may be a relationship between the concepts of linear combination and linear dependence. This is established by the following theorem.

Theorem 5.1 The set of vectors $\{\boldsymbol{a}_1, \ldots, \boldsymbol{a}_m\}$ is linearly dependent *iff* one vector is a linear combination of the others.

Proof. (Technique. Prove that if the second statement is true, it implies the first, and vice versa.)
If: assume one vector is a linear combination of the others. Then $\exists\, k$ s.t.

$$\boldsymbol{a}_k = \sum_{i \neq k} \lambda_i \boldsymbol{a}_i \quad \text{for some } \lambda_i,\ i = 1, 2, \ldots, k-1, k+1, \ldots, n.$$

Hence,

$$\sum_{i \neq k} \lambda_i \boldsymbol{a}_i - \boldsymbol{a}_k = \mathbf{0}$$

which proves that it is a linearly dependent set, since a set of λs has been found such that taking the linear combination using those λs yields zero, and they themselves are not all zeros because they include $\lambda_k = -1$ (the coefficient of $\boldsymbol{a}_k$).
Only if: assume linear dependence. That is

$$\sum_{i=1}^{m} \lambda_i \boldsymbol{a}_i = \mathbf{0} \quad \text{and} \quad \lambda_k \neq 0 \text{ for some } k.$$

Then omitting $\lambda_k \boldsymbol{a}_k$ from the summation,

$$\lambda_k \boldsymbol{a}_k + \sum_{i \neq k} \lambda_i \boldsymbol{a}_i = \mathbf{0}$$

or

$$-\lambda_k \boldsymbol{a}_k = \sum_{i \neq k} \lambda_i \boldsymbol{a}_i.$$

Dividing by $-\lambda_k \neq 0$,

$$a_k = \frac{1}{-\lambda_k} \sum_{i \neq k} \lambda_i a_i$$

$$= \sum_{i \neq k} -\left(\frac{\lambda_i}{\lambda_k}\right) a_i$$

$$= \sum_{i \neq k} \mu_i a_i, \quad \text{where } \mu_i = -\left(\frac{\lambda_i}{\lambda_k}\right)$$

so that one of the vectors, $\boldsymbol{a}_k$, has been written as a linear combination of all the others, using the coefficients μ_i ■

The theorem establishes the equivalence of the two concepts and thus provides an alternative way of defining linear dependence. It again proves as a corollary that any set containing the zero vector is linearly dependent.

Consider the set,

$$\begin{bmatrix}1\\1\end{bmatrix}, \begin{bmatrix}1\\2\end{bmatrix}, \begin{bmatrix}2\\0\end{bmatrix}.$$

By the theorem, for linear dependence there must be values of λ_1 and λ_2 such that

$$\begin{bmatrix}1\\1\end{bmatrix} = \lambda_1 \begin{bmatrix}1\\2\end{bmatrix} + \lambda_2 \begin{bmatrix}2\\0\end{bmatrix};$$

these values are $\lambda_1 = \frac{1}{2}, \lambda_2 = \frac{1}{4}$.

In practice it can be very difficult to spot linear dependence of a given set of vectors directly. Theorem 5.1 justifies an approach which is a useful alternative: to look for linear combinations of the vectors which yield others in the set. Problem 5.4.1 illustrates. However, it is not until we have studied determinants in Chapter 6 that we shall have a method which will always detect linear dependence.

5.3 Bases

The material in this section can cause confusion, but the ideas are fairly simple. It can be summarized as follows: if one has two linearly independent vectors, each with two elements, then one can write any other two-element vector as a *unique* linear combination of those two vectors. For 'two-dimensional Euclidean space', the vectors $\begin{bmatrix}1\\0\end{bmatrix}$ and $\begin{bmatrix}0\\1\end{bmatrix}$ are used as standard vectors; any vector $\boldsymbol{x}$ can be written as

$$\boldsymbol{x} = x_1 \boldsymbol{e}_1 + x_2 \boldsymbol{e}_2.$$

For example,

$$\begin{bmatrix}3\\6\end{bmatrix} = 3.\begin{bmatrix}1\\0\end{bmatrix} + 6.\begin{bmatrix}0\\1\end{bmatrix}$$

so that if $\begin{bmatrix}1\\0\end{bmatrix}$ and $\begin{bmatrix}0\\1\end{bmatrix}$ are used as the so-called *basis* vectors, then the values of λ used to obtain any other vector as a linear combination of them, are just the elements of that vector. However,

$$\begin{bmatrix}3\\6\end{bmatrix} = 2.\begin{bmatrix}-1\\4\end{bmatrix} + 1.\begin{bmatrix}5\\-2\end{bmatrix}$$

illustrating that $\begin{bmatrix}-1\\4\end{bmatrix}$ and $\begin{bmatrix}5\\-2\end{bmatrix}$ will also do as basis vectors, so that the basis chosen is not unique. The *standard Euclidean basis*, which is composed of the vectors e_i as defined in Section 3.7, is a particularly convenient one to use.

Formally:

D5.3 A set $\{a_1, \ldots, a_m\}$ is said to *generate* (or *span*) E^n if every vector with n elements can be written as a linear combination of the set. The notation E^n is short-hand for *n-dimensional Euclidean space.*

The vectors $\begin{bmatrix}-1\\4\end{bmatrix}$ and $\begin{bmatrix}5\\-2\end{bmatrix}$ span E^2, because any other vector with two elements can be written as a linear combination of these two vectors.

The vectors $\begin{bmatrix}1\\1\\1\end{bmatrix}$ and $\begin{bmatrix}2\\0\\0\end{bmatrix}$ do *not* span E^3 because the vector $\begin{bmatrix}3\\3\\2\end{bmatrix}$, for example, cannot be written as a linear combination of the two vectors. Nor does the addition of the vector $\begin{bmatrix}2\\2\\2\end{bmatrix}$ to the set make it span E^3 because $\begin{bmatrix}2\\2\\2\end{bmatrix}$ is twice $\begin{bmatrix}1\\1\\1\end{bmatrix}$ which means that they are linearly dependent.

As already indicated, the vectors e_i, $i = 1, 2, \ldots, n$, span E^n, but they are also linearly independent, and thus they satisfy the other requirement for a set of basis vectors:

D5.4 A *basis* for E^n is a *linearly independent* set of vectors which spans E^n.

It can be shown that there must be exactly n vectors in a basis for E^n.

Theorem 5.2 The representation of any vector with respect to a *given* basis is unique.

In other words, given an arbitrary vector, there is one, and only one, way of writing that vector as a linear combination of the basis.

Proof. Suppose on the contrary that ∃2 representations of $\boldsymbol{x}$ with respect to the given basis $\{\boldsymbol{b}_1, \ldots, \boldsymbol{b}_n\}$, then

$$\boldsymbol{x} = \sum_{i=1}^{n} \lambda_i \boldsymbol{b}_i$$

and

$$\boldsymbol{x} = \sum_{i=1}^{n} \mu_i \boldsymbol{b}_i,$$

where

$$\lambda_k \neq \mu_k \quad \text{for some } k.$$

This implies that

$$\sum_{i=1}^{n} \lambda_i \boldsymbol{b}_i = \sum_{i=1}^{n} \mu_i \boldsymbol{b}_i.$$

Therefore,

$$\sum_{i=1}^{n} \lambda_i \boldsymbol{b}_i - \sum_{i=1}^{n} \mu_i \boldsymbol{b}_i = \boldsymbol{0}$$

or

$$\sum_{i=1}^{n} (\lambda_i - \mu_i)\, \boldsymbol{b}_i = \boldsymbol{0}, \quad (\lambda_k - \mu_k) \neq \boldsymbol{0} \quad \text{some } k.$$

But this means that $\{\boldsymbol{b}_1, \ldots, \boldsymbol{b}_n\}$ is linearly dependent, which contradicts the assumption that $\{\boldsymbol{b}_i\}$ is a basis, so that the original assumption that there are two distinct representations must have been false. ■

If a vector has n elements it is a point in E^n, *n-dimensional Euclidean space*, and this is why we sometimes say that the vector itself has dimension n. The concept of a basis is vital in the theory of the solution of systems of equations, the subject of Chapter 8. There we will also use the concept of a *subspace of* E^n. If we have a set of vectors in E^n which contains less than n linearly independent vectors, then they cannot span E^n, because not every vector in E^n can be written as a linear combination of them. However, a restricted class of vectors in E^n *can* be written as linear combinations of the set, and (cf. D5.3) we say that the set spans a subspace of E^n. For instance, in Figure 5.2, $\boldsymbol{a}_1$ and $\boldsymbol{a}_3$ span E^2 (and therefore form a basis for E^2), but $\boldsymbol{a}_1$ and $\boldsymbol{a}_2$ only span the subspace consisting of the line through the origin on which they both lie. Any other point on this line can be expressed in terms of $\boldsymbol{a}_1$ and $\boldsymbol{a}_2$, but a point elsewhere cannot. One can easily convince oneself that a subspace has two properties: (*a*) if $\boldsymbol{x}$ is a vector in the subspace then $\lambda\boldsymbol{x}$ is also in the subspace, and (*b*) if $\boldsymbol{y}$ is also in the subspace then so is $\boldsymbol{x}+\boldsymbol{y}$. In many dimensions it can be thought of as a line, plane or hyperplane passing through the origin, its dimensionality being given by the number of linearly independent vectors which span it.

5.4 Problems

1. Are the following sets of vectors linearly dependent or independent?

$$(a)\begin{bmatrix}1\\-1\end{bmatrix},\begin{bmatrix}0\\1\end{bmatrix}\qquad (b)\ (\tfrac{1}{2},-2),(-4,16)\qquad (c)\begin{bmatrix}-2\\3\end{bmatrix},\begin{bmatrix}1\\1\end{bmatrix}$$

$$(d)\begin{bmatrix}-2\\3\end{bmatrix},\begin{bmatrix}1\\1\end{bmatrix},\begin{bmatrix}3\\-2\end{bmatrix}\qquad (e)\begin{bmatrix}2\\3\\4\\5\end{bmatrix},\begin{bmatrix}1\\2\\1\\3\end{bmatrix},\begin{bmatrix}0\\1\\-2\\2\end{bmatrix},\begin{bmatrix}3\\5\\5\\8\end{bmatrix}$$

2. Consider examples (*c*) and (*d*) above. Is it possible to have three two-element vectors which are linearly independent? What about four three-element vectors?

3. Let $\begin{bmatrix}2\\5\end{bmatrix},\begin{bmatrix}1\\3\end{bmatrix}$ be a basis for E^2. Write the vector $\begin{bmatrix}2\\4\end{bmatrix}$ as a linear combination of these basis vectors. Repeat for the basis $\begin{bmatrix}1\\0\end{bmatrix}$ and $\begin{bmatrix}0\\1\end{bmatrix}$.

4. Consider Problem 4.7.3. Are the rows linearly dependent? The columns? Show that the columns of your answer to Problem 4.7.5 are linearly independent.

5. A petrol company can convert one unit of crude oil into three grades of petrol. If it does not use lead additives it obtains amounts given by the vector $\begin{bmatrix}2\\2\\4\end{bmatrix}$. Using the legally permitted maximum of one unit of additives it obtains $\begin{bmatrix}5\\0\\3\end{bmatrix}$. Assuming that intermediate amounts of additives yield pro-

portionately intermediate vectors of outputs, can the company produce the quantities

$$(a)\begin{bmatrix} 7/2 \\ 1 \\ 7/2 \end{bmatrix} \quad (b)\begin{bmatrix} 4 \\ 1/3 \\ 10/3 \end{bmatrix}?$$

If so, how much lead should it use?

6. A certain firm operates two plants, each producing the same three products but in different proportions. If it allocates a fraction λ of its available labour to one plant and a fraction $1-\lambda$ to the other, then the quantities of the product produced by each plant are given by $\lambda\begin{bmatrix} 8 \\ 4 \\ 4 \end{bmatrix}$ and $(1-\lambda)\begin{bmatrix} 2 \\ 6 \\ 10 \end{bmatrix}$ respectively, where the first element of each vector is the quantity of the first product produced per unit time if all the labour were used on that plant, etc. Comment on the possibility of producing the total output vectors

$$(a)\begin{bmatrix} 5 \\ 5 \\ 7 \end{bmatrix} \text{and } (b)\begin{bmatrix} 7 \\ 5 \\ 5 \end{bmatrix}.$$

How will the revenue-maximizing choice of λ be affected by the selling prices p_1, p_2 and p_3 of the goods?

6 Determinants

6.1 Introduction

Some of the characteristics of a vector $\boldsymbol{x}$ can be represented by a scalar, for example, the norm (length) $\|\boldsymbol{x}\|$. Similarly, some of the characteristics of a *square* matrix $\mathbf{A}$ can be represented by a scalar, called the determinant, denoted by $|\mathbf{A}|$. The definition is arbitrary but useful. Before giving it in its general form we shall introduce the concept in a series of stages of increasing generality.

It should be pointed out that there is some debate amongst economists about how much one needs to know about determinants. It is certainly true that evaluating determinants is rather tedious and an inefficient way of solving large numerical problems when using a computer, and that theoretical results can be obtained without them. However, they are extremely useful in expounding various pieces of theory, and they are extensively used in the existing literature. They are used in several different contexts in this book. For a lucid exposition of an alternative approach the reader is referred to Mills (1969).

We start with a 2×2 matrix.

D6.1 The *determinant* of a 2×2, square matrix is given by

$$|\mathbf{A}| = \begin{vmatrix} a_{11} & a_{12} \\ a_{21} & a_{22} \end{vmatrix}$$

$$= a_{11}a_{22} - a_{12}a_{21}.$$

For example, if

$$\mathbf{A} = \begin{bmatrix} 2 & 1 \\ 1 & 1 \end{bmatrix}$$

$$|\mathbf{A}| = 2.1 - 1.1 = 1$$

which is the difference between the product of the elements on the main diagonal, and the product of the elements on the other diagonal.

Similarly, if

$$\mathbf{A}=\begin{bmatrix}2 & 4\\ 2 & 4\end{bmatrix}$$

then

$$|\mathbf{A}|=2.4-4.2=0.$$

Note that in this case the columns are linearly dependent and it will transpire that a determinant is zero if and only if the columns are linearly dependent. This property is useful in testing for linear dependence and independence of sets of vectors.

For a 3×3 matrix, the technique is analogous. For example:

$$\begin{vmatrix}1 & 2 & 3\\ 1 & -2 & -1\\ 1 & 0 & 1\end{vmatrix}$$

$$\begin{aligned}&=1.(-2).1+2.(-1).1+3.1.0-3.(-2).1-2.1.1-1.(-1).0\\ &=-2-2+6-2\\ &=0.\end{aligned}$$

This is obtained by:

1. Multiplying elements on the main diagonal (top left to bottom right), and
2. Moving along the first row to the second column and multiplying parallel to the main diagonal with the element in the third row, first column as the third element, and
3. Multiplying the elements in the diagonal which start with the first row, third column, and
4. Adding the results.
5. Repeating the process, using the opposite diagonals (top right to bottom left) and subtracting this total from the first.

Formally:

D6.2 The *determinant* of a 3×3 matrix is given by

$$\begin{aligned}|\mathbf{A}|=\begin{vmatrix}a_{11} & a_{12} & a_{13}\\ a_{21} & a_{22} & a_{23}\\ a_{31} & a_{32} & a_{33}\end{vmatrix}\\ &=a_{11}a_{22}a_{33}+a_{12}a_{23}a_{31}+a_{13}a_{21}a_{32}\\ &\quad-(a_{13}a_{22}a_{31}+a_{12}a_{21}a_{33}+a_{11}a_{23}a_{32}).\end{aligned}$$

The determinant of a 3×3 matrix can, however, be defined in terms of a set of determinants of 2×2 matrices and, in general, the determinant of an $n \times n$ matrix can be defined in terms of determinants of $(n-1) \times (n-1)$ matrices. Each of these can in turn be defined in terms of a set of determinants of $(n-2) \times (n-2)$ matrices, until the problem is reduced to one of evaluating a series of determinants of 2×2 matrices which can be evaluated by D6.1.

The expression in D6.2 can be obtained by taking the sum of three 2×2 determinants:

$$|\mathbf{A}| = -a_{12}\begin{vmatrix} a_{21} & a_{23} \\ a_{31} & a_{33} \end{vmatrix} + a_{22}\begin{vmatrix} a_{11} & a_{13} \\ a_{31} & a_{33} \end{vmatrix} - a_{32}\begin{vmatrix} a_{11} & a_{13} \\ a_{21} & a_{23} \end{vmatrix},$$

where in each case the determinant is that of the submatrix obtained by deleting the row and column occupied by the element which appears as its coefficient. This is known as the 'expansion down the second column' for obvious reasons.

In determining whether to add or subtract each term, one can consult the 'chessboard' pattern:

$$\begin{matrix} + & - & + \\ - & + & - \\ + & - & + \end{matrix}$$

so that in our case, since we were moving down the second column, the sequence was subtracted, add, subtract.

Expanding further,

$$\begin{aligned} |\mathbf{A}| &= -a_{12}(a_{21}a_{33}-a_{23}a_{31}) + a_{22}(a_{11}a_{33}-a_{13}a_{31}) \\ &\quad - a_{32}(a_{11}a_{23}-a_{13}a_{21}) \\ &= -a_{12}a_{21}a_{33}+a_{12}a_{23}a_{31}+a_{22}a_{11}a_{33}-a_{22}a_{13}a_{31} \\ &\quad - a_{32}a_{11}a_{23}+a_{32}a_{13}a_{21}. \end{aligned}$$

These terms are exactly those which are given in the direct expansion of the 3×3 matrix in D6.2 and it is easily verified that the result would be the same whichever row or column we chose for the expansion. In practical work one tries to minimize calculations by choosing to expand along a row, or down a column, which contains many zeros. (See Problem 6.3.1.)

6.2 Formal definitions

D6.3 The *cofactor* A_{ij} of a_{ij} is $(-1)^{i+j}$ times the determinant of the submatrix obtained by deleting row i and column j from $\mathbf{A}$ (called the *minor* of a_{ij}).

The $(-1)^{i+j}$ corresponds to the 'chessboard' rule; for example, for a_{58}, $(-1)^{i+j} = (-1)^{5+8} = (-1)^{13} = -1$; or for a_{57}, $(-1)^{i+j} = (-1)^{5+7} = (-1)^{12} = +1$.

D.6.4 For any square matrix **A**,

$$|\mathbf{A}| = \sum_j a_{ij}.A_{ij}.$$

This is the expansion along the *i*th row, for any value of *i*.

Equivalently,

$$|\mathbf{A}| = \sum_i a_{ij}.A_{ij}.$$

This is the expansion down the *j*th column, for any value of *j*.

For example, the following is an expansion down the first column:

$$\begin{vmatrix} 0 & 2 & 4 \\ 1 & 3 & 7 \\ 0 & -1 & -2 \end{vmatrix}$$

$$= (-1)^{1+1}.0.(1) + (-1)^{2+1}.1.\begin{vmatrix} 2 & 4 \\ -1 & -2 \end{vmatrix} + (-1)^{3+1}.0.(2)$$

$$= +0 - 1.(-4+4) + 0$$

$$= 0.$$

These columns are linearly dependent, since the first column plus twice the second column is the third column.

The following program employs this principle to calculate the determinant of a (3 x 3) matrix.

```
100  PRINT
110  N = 3
120  DIM A(N,N)
130  DIM Z(N-1,N-1)
140  FOR I = 1 TO N
150  FOR J = 1 TO N
160  PRINT "A("I,J")";: INPUT A(I,J)
170  NEXT J, I
180  :
200  PRINT
210  FOR I = 1 TO N
220  FOR J = 1 TO N
230  PRINT A(I,J);
240  NEXT J
250  PRINT
260  NEXT I
270  :
400  DET = 0
410  FOR J = 1 TO N : REM MOVE ALONG THE ROWS OF A
```

```
420   : FOR I = 2 TO N : REM MOVE DOWN COLUMNS OF THE
                             SUBMATRIX, Z
430   :     FOR K = 1 TO N :                   REM DEFINE
                                                SUBMATRIX...
440   :     IF K < J THEN Z(I-1,K) = A(I,K) :   REM Z FROM A BY...
450         IF K > J THEN Z(I-1,K-1) = A(I,K) : REM OMITTING ROW 1
                                                AND COL J FROM A
460   : NEXT K, I
470   GOSUB 10000 : REM CALCULATE VALUE OF MINOR FOR Z
480   DET = DET + (−1)↑(1 + J) * A(1,J) * MINR : REM SUM PRODUCTS
                                                   OF ELEMENTS IN
                                                   FIRST ROW OF A
                                                   WITH THEIR
                                                   COFACTORS
490   NEXT J
500   PRINT
510   PRINT "DETERMINANT IS" DET
520   STOP
530   :
9999   REM SUBROUTINE E TO CALCULATE DETERMINANT OF A
       (2 x 2) DIRECTLY
10000  MINR = Z(1,1) * Z(2,2) − Z(1,2) * Z(2,1)
10010  RETURN
```

Since this program requires the evaluation of a 2 x 2 determinant on several occasions the required code is written in the form of a subroutine at line 10000 which is called at line 470 each time it is needed. It would be a useful exercise in programming and in the theory of determinants to generalize this program so that it would deal with matrices of a general dimension. Note, however, that it is not a very efficient way of calculating determinants of large matrices and if you need a routine for practical work you should take one from one of the standard sources for such routines. (In fact some versions of BASIC have matrix routines ready built into them.) If you try the program with a matrix having large elements which you know to have a zero determinant you may, depending on the accuracy of your machine, see how the limited numerical accuracy can give problems.

Determinants have a lot of properties which we shall need to know, but before stating them we give a geometrical interpretation of the determinant which may assist an understanding of some of them. As always, these properties follow from the formal definition, and do not rely in any way on geometry. Consider two vectors, $\boldsymbol{a} = \begin{bmatrix} a_1 \\ a_2 \end{bmatrix}$ and $\boldsymbol{b} = \begin{bmatrix} b_1 \\ b_2 \end{bmatrix}$ in E^2 as shown in Figure 6.1.

We shall show that the shaded area enclosed by $\boldsymbol{a}$, $\boldsymbol{b}$ and the origin is in fact one half of the determinant of the matrix formed by using $\boldsymbol{a}$ and $\boldsymbol{b}$ as columns. This area can be found by adding the areas of the rectangles of

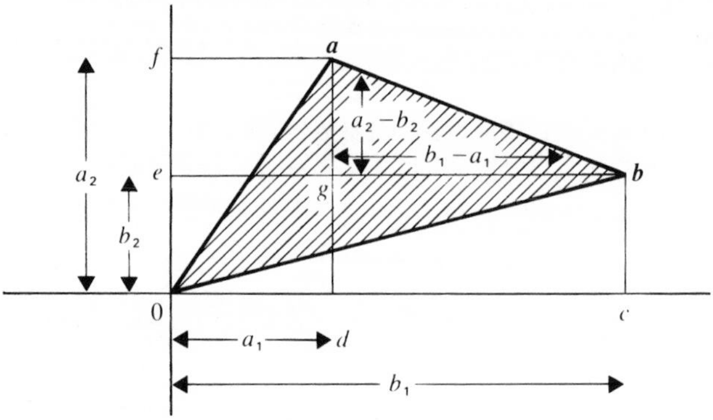

Figure 6.1

0*fad* and 0*ebc*, subtracting the area 0*egd* which has been 'counted twice', adding the area of the triangle *abg*, to give the area of the whole figure, 0*fabc*, and then subtracting the area of the two triangles, 0*fa* and 0*bc* (remembering that the area of a triangle is half the base multiplied by the perpendicular height). Thus

$$\begin{aligned}\text{area} &= a_2a_1+b_2b_1-b_2a_1+\tfrac{1}{2}(b_1-a_1)(a_2-b_2)\\ &\quad -\tfrac{1}{2}a_1a_2-\tfrac{1}{2}b_1b_2\\ &= \tfrac{1}{2}b_1a_2-\tfrac{1}{2}b_2a_1\\ &= \tfrac{1}{2}\begin{vmatrix} b_1 & a_1\\ b_2 & a_2\end{vmatrix}.\end{aligned}$$

This property generalizes, so that the determinant of three vectors in E^3 is proportional to the *volume* enclosed between them and the origin, and for higher dimensional vectors the determinant is proportional to a *hypervolume.*

We come now to a series of results concerning matrices. You can confirm each of them using the above computer program for evaluating determinants.

Theorem 6.1 A matrix with a row (or column) of zeros has a zero determinant.

Proof. Immediate: Simply choose that row or column upon which to expand the matrix. ∎

In terms of the geometry, if one of three vectors in E^3 is $\mathbf{0}$, then the other two must lie on some plane passing through $\mathbf{0}$, so the enclosed three-dimensional volume is zero.

Theorem 6.2 If any single row (or column) of a matrix is multiplied by a scalar λ, then the determinant is also multiplied by λ.

Proof. Let **A** be the original matrix and **A*** be identical with **A**, except that one row (or column) is multiplied by λ. Then choosing that row (column) for expansion,

$$|\mathbf{A}^*| = \sum_j (\lambda a_{ij}).(A_{ij})$$

$$= \lambda \sum_j a_{ij} A_{ij} = \lambda |\mathbf{A}|. \blacksquare$$

As an exercise, you can now show as a corollary that if a square matrix of dimension n is multiplied by λ, then its determinant is multiplied by λ^n.

Theorem 6.3 The interchange of two adjacent rows or columns changes the sign of $|\mathbf{A}|$.

Proof.

$$|\mathbf{A}| = \sum_j a_{ij} A_{ij}$$

but

$$A_{ij} = (-1)^{i+j}.M_{ij},$$

where M_{ij} is the minor (see D6.3).

Now interchange row i with $i+1$ and expand along $i+1$ to give

$$\sum_j a_{ij}.(-1)^{i+1+j}.M_{ij}$$

since the elements in the minors are unchanged. But

$$(-1)^{i+1+j} = (-1).(-1)^{i+j},$$

and so we have

$$(-1) \sum_j a_{ij}(-1)^{i+j}.M_{ij} = -|\mathbf{A}|. \blacksquare$$

This applies for an interchange between any two rows (or columns), because whichever rows (or columns) one selected, their interchange can only be achieved by an *odd* number of *adjacent* interchanges.

Theorem 6.4 A matrix with two rows or columns the same has a determinant of zero.

Proof. Expand along one of the two identical rows to obtain $|\mathbf{A}|$. Now interchange one identical row for the other, and expand along the row in the original position. But this expansion involves the same elements and so must yield the same result, although by Theorem 6.3 the sign has changed; hence $|\mathbf{A}| = -|\mathbf{A}|$, which is a property exclusive to zero. $\blacksquare$

Theorem 6.5 Any expansion using the 'wrong' cofactors yields zero.

This means that if one expands along some row (or column), but uses the cofactors of some other row (or column), then the result will be zero. For example,

$$\sum_j a_{ij} A_{kj} = 0 \quad \text{if} \quad k \neq i.$$

Proof. The elements in row k never appear in the summation $\sum_j a_{ij} A_{kj}$ if $k \neq i$, because A_{kj} involves submatrices with row k and column j deleted.

So if we replace row k with row i, this will not affect the value of the summation. But it will now be the expansion of the determinant of a matrix with two rows the same. Hence, from theorem 6.4,

$$\sum_j a_{ij} A_{kj} = 0. \quad \blacksquare$$

To confirm this change **A(1,J)** in line 480 of the above program to **A(2,J)** or **A(3,J)**.

Theorem 6.6 The addition of a scalar multiple of any row (column) to another row (column) leaves a determinant unchanged.

Proof. Without loss of generality, suppose we add $\lambda \times$ row k to row 1, to give $\mathbf{A}^*$. Then the determinant of $\mathbf{A}^*$ can be obtained by expanding along the first row:

$$|\mathbf{A}^*| = \sum_j a^*_{1j} A^*_{1j}.$$

But

$$a^*_{1j} = a_{1j} + \lambda a_{kj} \quad \text{and} \quad A^*_{1j} = A_{1j}$$

so

$$|\mathbf{A}^*| = \sum_j a_{1j} A_{1j} + \lambda \sum_j a_{kj} A_{1j}.$$

But the second term is zero, because it is an expansion along row k, using cofactors of row 1. Hence

$$|\mathbf{A}^*| = |\mathbf{A}|. \quad \blacksquare$$

Corollary: If the rows (columns) are linearly dependent, then $|\mathbf{A}| = 0$.

Proof. By Theorem 5.1 one row, say the first, must be a linear combination of the others. By Theorem 6.6, subtracting this combination from the first row cannot change the determinant. But then we have a determinant of a matrix containing a row of zeros, which is zero by Theorem 6.1. $\blacksquare$

Since its is also true that if $|\mathbf{A}| \neq 0$ then the rows (columns) are linearly independent, we have a useful method for testing vectors for linear dependence. This method will always work and is the one promised at the end of Section 5.2. Linear dependence can often be detected by inspection, and since the calculations involved in evaluating determinants can be laborious, it is worthwhile looking carefully at a problem before going ahead with determinant evaluations. For example, consider the problem of determining whether the two three-element vectors $\begin{bmatrix} 2 \\ 1 \\ 3 \end{bmatrix}, \begin{bmatrix} 4 \\ 2 \\ 0 \end{bmatrix}$ are linearly dependent. A difficulty in using determinants to investigate this is that they do not form a square matrix as they stand.

One solution is to take the top two rows and check whether the determinant of the resulting 2×2 submatrix is zero. If it is not, then the two vectors are linearly independent. But the converse is not necessarily true; the determinants of *all* possible 2×2 submatrices of the two vectors must be zero for them to be linearly dependent. In this case $\begin{vmatrix} 2 & 4 \\ 1 & 2 \end{vmatrix} = 0$, but $\begin{vmatrix} 1 & 2 \\ 3 & 0 \end{vmatrix} = -6$ and so the vectors are linearly independent. We are touching on the concept of *rank* here, which will be discussed more fully in Chapter 8.

6.3 Problems

1. Calculate the determinant of the matrix $\begin{bmatrix} 2 & 1 & 3 \\ 0 & 0 & -5 \\ -2 & 1 & 3 \end{bmatrix}$

(*a*) directly;
(*b*) by expansion along the third row;
(*c*) by expansion along the second row.

How does the value of the element in the first row and third column affect the result?

2. Show that if two matrices $\mathbf{A}$ and $\mathbf{B}$ differ only in the ith row (or jth column), then

$$|\mathbf{A}| + |\mathbf{B}| = |\mathbf{C}|$$

where $\mathbf{C}$ is a matrix which differs from $\mathbf{A}$ and $\mathbf{B}$ only in its ith row (or jth column), which is the sum of the corresponding rows (or columns) or $\mathbf{A}$ and $\mathbf{B}$.

3. Evaluate,

(*a*) $\begin{vmatrix} 2 & 4 \\ 1 & 3 \end{vmatrix}$ (*b*) $\begin{vmatrix} 3 & 1 & 1 \\ 2 & 1 & 2 \\ 1 & 3 & 2 \end{vmatrix}$ (*c*) $\begin{vmatrix} 3 & 1 & 4 & 0 & 3 \\ 0 & 0 & 3 & 0 & 1 \\ 1 & 2 & 3 & 0 & 5 \\ 3 & 2 & 4 & 2 & 0 \\ 5 & 0 & 3 & 0 & 4 \end{vmatrix}$ (*d*) $\begin{vmatrix} 2 & 4 & 8 \\ 1 & 3 & 5 \\ 3 & 8 & 14 \end{vmatrix}$.

4. Determine the number of linearly independent vectors in the following sets:

(*a*) $\begin{bmatrix} -2 \\ 5 \end{bmatrix}, \begin{bmatrix} 4 \\ -10 \end{bmatrix}$ (*b*) $\begin{bmatrix} 3 \\ 2 \\ 0 \end{bmatrix}, \begin{bmatrix} 0 \\ 1 \\ 3 \end{bmatrix}, \begin{bmatrix} 1 \\ 0 \\ 2 \end{bmatrix}$

(*c*) $\begin{bmatrix} 1 \\ 2 \end{bmatrix}, \begin{bmatrix} 2 \\ 1 \end{bmatrix}, \begin{bmatrix} -1 \\ 3 \end{bmatrix}$ (*d*) $\begin{bmatrix} 2 \\ -3 \\ 1 \end{bmatrix}, \begin{bmatrix} -1 \\ 1 \\ 2 \end{bmatrix}, \begin{bmatrix} 1 \\ 1 \\ -12 \end{bmatrix}$

(*e*) $\begin{bmatrix} 1 \\ 2 \\ 3 \end{bmatrix}, \begin{bmatrix} 2 \\ 4 \\ 6 \end{bmatrix}, \begin{bmatrix} -1 \\ -2 \\ -3 \end{bmatrix}$, (*f*) $\begin{bmatrix} 0 \\ 0 \\ 0 \end{bmatrix}$.

5. Find values of λ such that

$$\begin{vmatrix} (-3-\lambda) & 0 & 0 \\ 0 & (4-\lambda) & \sqrt{3} \\ 0 & \sqrt{3} & (6-\lambda) \end{vmatrix} = 0.$$

6.* Prove, as concisely as possible, that

(*a*) $$\begin{vmatrix} 1 & b+c & b^2+c^2 \\ 1 & c+a & c^2+a^2 \\ 1 & a+b & a^2+b^2 \end{vmatrix} = \begin{vmatrix} 1 & a & a^2 \\ 1 & b & b^2 \\ 1 & c & c^2 \end{vmatrix}.$$

(*b*) $$\begin{vmatrix} 1 & 1 & 1 \\ a & b & c \\ a^3 & b^3 & c^3 \end{vmatrix} = (b-c)(c-a)(a-b)(a+b+c).$$

7 The matrix inverse

We are now in a position to deal with sets of linear, simultaneous equations which have the general matrix form $\mathbf{A}x = b$. For example, in the Leontief interindustry model, the equation $(\mathbf{I} - \mathbf{A})x = f$ was derived; the problem was to find the value of x, if any, which would satisfy this equation. The matrix of the system is $(\mathbf{I} - \mathbf{A})$.

7.2 Definition

Let us suppose a matrix $\mathbf{B}$ exists, such that $\mathbf{BA} = \mathbf{I}$. Then if we have the standard form,

$$\mathbf{A}x = b,$$

premultiplying by $\mathbf{B}$,

$$\mathbf{BA}x = \mathbf{B}b$$

and since

$$\mathbf{BA}x = \mathbf{I}x = x,$$

we have

$$x = \mathbf{B}b.$$

Hence, if we know how to calculate $\mathbf{B}$, we can multiply by b to yield the appropriate value of the vector x. This matrix is called the *inverse* of $\mathbf{A}$, and is denoted $\mathbf{A}^{-1}$.

D7.1 A matrix $\mathbf{A}^{-1}$ s.t. $\mathbf{A}^{-1}\mathbf{A} = \mathbf{I}$ is the *inverse* of $\mathbf{A}$, if it exists.

For example, if $(\mathbf{I} - \mathbf{A})x = f$, then $x = (\mathbf{I} - \mathbf{A})^{-1}f$, if $(\mathbf{I} - \mathbf{A})^{-1}$ exists.

The conditions under which an inverse will exist, and therefore the conditions under which a system of equations will be soluble, are discussed below. Note that this way of solving whole systems is analogous to the way a single (scalar) equation

$$ax = b$$

would be solved, by writing

$$x = a^{-1}b = \frac{b}{a}$$

as was mentioned in Section 1.3.

7.2. Adjoints

One more definition is required before the calculation of inverses can be described.

D7.2 The *adjoint* of $\mathbf{A}$, denoted by $\mathbf{A}^+$, is the transposed matrix of cofactors of $\mathbf{A}$.

The element a_{11}^+ of $\mathbf{A}^+$ is the cofactor of a_{11} of matrix $\mathbf{A}$. But the cofactor of a_{21} of $\mathbf{A}$ becomes element a_{12}^+ of $\mathbf{A}^+$, because of the *transpose*. In general the *ij*th element of the adjoint is the cofactor of the *ji*th element of the original matrix. An example of a calculation of an adjoint will be found below.

We now prove a theorem which points the way to a technique for calculating inverses.

Theorem 7.1 $\mathbf{AA}^+ = |\mathbf{A}|\,\mathbf{I}$ where $\mathbf{A}$ and $\mathbf{I}$ are $n \times n$ matrices.

Proof. On the right-hand side we have, remembering that $|\mathbf{A}|$ is scalar:

$$\begin{bmatrix} |\mathbf{A}| & 0 & 0 & 0 & \dots & 0 \\ 0 & |\mathbf{A}| & 0 & 0 & \dots & 0 \\ 0 & 0 & |\mathbf{A}| & 0 & \dots & 0 \\ 0 & 0 & 0 & |\mathbf{A}| & \dots & 0 \\ \vdots & & & & & \vdots \\ 0 & 0 & 0 & 0 & \dots & |\mathbf{A}| \end{bmatrix}.$$

On the left-hand side let $\mathbf{AA}^+ = \mathbf{B}$ and consider the *ii*th element of $\mathbf{B}$:

$$b_{ii} = \sum_{k=1}^{n} a_{ik}a_{ki}^+, \quad i = 1, 2, \dots, n$$

that is, running along the ith row of $\mathbf{A}$, with k the changing (column) subscript and picking out the kith element of the adjoint $\mathbf{A}^+$ (running down the ith column), which will be a_{ki}^+. But, by definition, a_{ki}^+ is the cofactor of the *ik*th element in the original matrix, that is

$$a^+_{ki} = A_{ik}.$$

So

$$b_{ii} = \sum_k a_{ik} A_{ik}$$

which is the expansion of the determinant of **A** along the *i*th row. Hence

$$b_{ii} = |\mathbf{A}|.$$

Now consider b_{ij}, $i \neq j$:

$$b_{ij} = \sum_k a_{ik} a^+_{kj}$$

$$= \sum_k a_{ik} A_{jk} \quad (i \neq j)$$

$$= 0$$

because it is the expansion along the *i*th row using the cofactors corresponding to the *j*th row, where $j \neq i$. (An expansion using wrong cofactors.) Thus, **B** has the determinant of **A** down the main diagonal and zeros everywhere else, so the left- and right-hand sides are the same. ∎

Let us illustrate the theorem by using

$$\mathbf{A} = \begin{bmatrix} 1 & 2 & 4 \\ 1 & 3 & 7 \\ 1 & -1 & -2 \end{bmatrix}.$$

Then

$$|\mathbf{A}| = -6 + 14 - 4 - 12 + 4 + 7 = 3.$$

Calculating the cofactors,

$$\mathbf{A}^+ = \begin{bmatrix} 1 & 0 & 2 \\ 9 & -6 & -3 \\ -4 & 3 & 1 \end{bmatrix}$$

and

$$\mathbf{AA}^+ = \begin{bmatrix} 3 & 0 & 0 \\ 0 & 3 & 0 \\ 0 & 0 & 3 \end{bmatrix}$$

as the theorem predicts.

Corollary of Theorem 7.1 If $|\mathbf{A}| \neq 0$, then $\mathbf{A}^{-1} = (1/|\mathbf{A}|)\,\mathbf{A}^{+}$.

Proof.

$$\mathbf{AA}^{+} = |\mathbf{A}|\,\mathbf{I}.$$

Premultiplying by $\mathbf{A}^{-1}$,

$$\mathbf{A}^{-1}\mathbf{AA}^{+} = \mathbf{A}^{-1}|\mathbf{A}|\,\mathbf{I}.$$

By definition,

$$\mathbf{A}^{-1}\mathbf{A} = \mathbf{I} \quad \text{and} \quad \mathbf{IA}^{+} = \mathbf{A}^{+}$$

so

$$\mathbf{A}^{+} = |\mathbf{A}|\,\mathbf{A}^{-1}.$$

And, since $|\mathbf{A}| \neq 0$, we can divide by it to give

$$\mathbf{A}^{-1} = \frac{1}{|\mathbf{A}|}\,\mathbf{A}^{+}. \quad \blacksquare$$

This is our fundamental result as far as inverting matrices is concerned, because it tells us when the inverse is defined (when $|\mathbf{A}| \neq 0$), and also gives us a method of actually finding it.

Using the previous example to illustrate,

$$\mathbf{A}^{-1} = \begin{bmatrix} \frac{1}{3} & 0 & \frac{2}{3} \\ 3 & -2 & -1 \\ -\frac{4}{3} & 1 & \frac{1}{3} \end{bmatrix}$$

and it is easy to confirm that $\mathbf{AA}^{-1} = \mathbf{I}$.

You can extend the program for evaluating 3 x 3 determinants from the previous chapter to give the matrix inverse as follows. Change line 120 to

```
120   DIM A(N,N), B(N,N)
```

The matrix B will be the inverse. Then add the following lines

```
520   IF ABS(DET) < 1.0E-6 THEN PRINT "MATRIX NOT
      INVERTIBLE"
530   IF ABS(DET) < 1.0E-6 THEN STOP
540   :
600   FOR L = 1 TO N
610   :     FOR J = 1 TO N
620   :          FOR I = 1 TO N
630   :               FOR K = 1 TO N
640   :               IF K < J AND I < L THEN
                            Z(I,K) = A(I,K)
650   :               IF K < J AND I > L THEN
                            Z(I-1,K) = A(I,K)
```

```
660  :              IF K>J AND I<L THEN
                           Z(I,K-1) = A(I,K)
670  :              IF K>J AND I>L THEN
                           Z(I-1,K-1) = A(I,K)
680  :     NEXT K,I
690  :     GOSUB 10000
700  :     B(J,L) = (-1)↑(L+J)*MINR/DET : REM NOTE
                                          B(J,L) NOT B(L,J) SO AS
                                          TO GIVE THE
                                          TRANSPOSE
710  NEXT J,L
720  PRINT "MATRIX INVERSE"
730  FOR I = 1 TO N
740  FOR J = 1 TO N
750  PRINT B(I,J);
760  NEXT J
770  PRINT
780  NEXT I
790  END
```

Lines 600 to 670 contrive to construct all the 2 x 2 submatrices by deleting row L and column K from the matrix A. Then the minor is calculated in line 670 and the inverse is constructed in line 680 by calculating the cofactors (i.e. signing the minors), transposing and dividing by the determinant. Note that the routine is particularly inefficient because the minors of the first row are calculated twice, once for the determinant and once for the adjoint. This could be avoided but it would make the program less readable. In lines 520 and 530 a test is made against an arbitrary 'tolerance', to see that the matrix is not singular. In principle one would like to test if the determinant is exactly zero. But as you may have noticed numerical inaccuracies may yield a nonzero determinant even when it is truly zero. In computing it is usually unwise to expect two numbers to be exactly equal (unless they are integers as in the case of the index variables in a FOR . . . NEXT loop).

We now know that:

Theorem 7.2 A square matrix has an inverse *iff* the determinant is nonzero.

D7.3 A matrix with a nonzero determinant, and hence an inverse, is said to be *nonsingular* or regular).

We can now apply these last calculations to the solution of the system,

$$x_1 + 2x_2 + 4x_3 = 1$$

$$x_1 + 3x_2 + 7x_3 = 1$$

$$x_1 - x_2 - 2x_3 = 1.$$

Writing in matrix notation:

$$\begin{bmatrix} 1 & 2 & 4 \\ 1 & 3 & 7 \\ 1 & -1 & -2 \end{bmatrix} \begin{bmatrix} x_1 \\ x_2 \\ x_3 \end{bmatrix} = \begin{bmatrix} 1 \\ 1 \\ 1 \end{bmatrix},$$

i.e. $\mathbf{A}\boldsymbol{x} = \boldsymbol{b}$.

Using the inverse from above,

$$\begin{bmatrix} x_1 \\ x_2 \\ x_3 \end{bmatrix} = \begin{bmatrix} \frac{1}{3} & 0 & \frac{2}{3} \\ 3 & -2 & -1 \\ -\frac{4}{3} & 1 & \frac{1}{3} \end{bmatrix} \begin{bmatrix} 1 \\ 1 \\ 1 \end{bmatrix} = \begin{bmatrix} 1 \\ 0 \\ 0 \end{bmatrix}$$

i.e. $\boldsymbol{x} = \mathbf{A}^{-1}\boldsymbol{b}$, so the solution is $x_1 = 1, x_2 = 0, x_3 = 0$, which is obviously the correct solution by inspection of the original problem.

Very often the rules of matrix algebra, including the inverse, are used to make deductions about systems which are quite general and are just specified by letters, as opposed to the previous example where actual values for the elements of **A** and $\boldsymbol{b}$ were known. For instance, in econometrics, a *structural form* for a stochastic model (that is, a set of linear behavioural equations and identities) is often written

$$\mathbf{B}\boldsymbol{y} + \Gamma \boldsymbol{z} = \boldsymbol{u}$$

where $\boldsymbol{y}$ is a vector of values for variables determined by the system, $\boldsymbol{z}$ a vector of values of variables which are determined outside the system, and $\boldsymbol{u}$ a vector of random disturbances.

Then

$$\mathbf{B}^{-1}\mathbf{B}\boldsymbol{y} = -\mathbf{B}^{-1}\Gamma \boldsymbol{z} + \mathbf{B}^{-1}\boldsymbol{u}$$

and so

$$\boldsymbol{y} = \Pi \boldsymbol{z} + \boldsymbol{v},$$

where

$$\Pi = -\mathbf{B}^{-1}\Gamma$$

and

$$\boldsymbol{v} = \mathbf{B}^{-1}\boldsymbol{u}.$$

This is known as the *reduced form* and, since it tells us exactly how the variables determined by the system depend on the others, it is the set of equations which is usually used for statistical estimation. (An example is worked out in Section 8.7.) The *identification* problem is the problem of discovering whether it is possible to obtain knowledge of the elements of the matrices **B** and Γ (the structural parameters) from the estimates obtained for the reduced form matrix Π, together with any *a priori* information we may have about **B** and Γ.

You are asked to investigate some of the properties of inverses in the following problems.

7.3 Problems

1. Show that if $\mathbf{A}$ and $\mathbf{B}$ are square, nonsingular matrices, then

$$(\mathbf{AB})^{-1} = \mathbf{B}^{-1}\mathbf{A}^{-1}.$$

2. Show that

(*a*) $(\mathbf{A}^{-1})^{-1} = \mathbf{A}$

(*b*) $(\mathbf{A}^{-1})' = (\mathbf{A}')^{-1}$

where $\mathbf{A}$ is nonsingular.

(*c*) $(\mathbf{AB})' = \mathbf{B}'\mathbf{A}'$ for any conformable matrices.

3. Invert the following matrices:

(*a*) $\begin{bmatrix} 2 & -2 & 3 \\ 1 & 0 & -3 \\ 3 & 4 & 0 \end{bmatrix}$ (*b*) $\begin{bmatrix} 1 & 1 & 1 \\ 2 & -1 & 2 \\ -1 & -1 & 0 \end{bmatrix}$ (*c*) $\begin{bmatrix} 1 & 1 & 1 \\ 2 & -1 & 2 \\ 3 & 0 & 3 \end{bmatrix}$

(*d*) $\begin{bmatrix} 3 & 0 & 1 & 0 \\ 2 & 1 & 0 & 4 \\ 0 & 3 & 2 & 0 \\ 0 & 0 & 0 & 1 \end{bmatrix}$.

In each case verify your results by checking that $\mathbf{AA}^{-1} = \mathbf{I}$.

4. (*a*) A certain economy has exactly one technique for producing each of n goods and the technique for the jth good is represented by the jth column of a matrix $\mathbf{A}$ where a_{ij} is the number of units of good i consumed in the production of one unit of good j. Given any vector of nonnegative final demands $\boldsymbol{f}$ for the goods, the required vector of total outputs $\boldsymbol{x}$ is given by

$$\boldsymbol{x} = [\mathbf{I} - \mathbf{A}]^{-1}\boldsymbol{f}.$$

By considering the case of two goods only, derive a condition on the matrix $\mathbf{A}$ which ensures that $\boldsymbol{x}$ will be feasible (that is, nonnegative) for any vector $\boldsymbol{f}$. Interpret and generalize.

$$(b) \quad \text{if } \mathbf{A} = \begin{bmatrix} \frac{1}{2} & 0 & 0 \\ \frac{1}{4} & \frac{1}{2} & \frac{1}{4} \\ \frac{3}{4} & \frac{1}{4} & \frac{1}{2} \end{bmatrix}$$

show by calculation that every element of $[\mathbf{I} - \mathbf{A}]^{-1}$ is nonnegative and verify that $\mathbf{A}$ satisfies the conditions found in (*a*).

5. (*a*) If $\mathbf{A}^+$ is the adjoint of a symmetric matrix $\mathbf{A}$, prove that $\mathbf{A}^+$ is symmetric, and deduce that the inverse of a nonsingular symmetric matrix is symmetric.

(*b*) If a matrix $\mathbf{A}$ is partitioned such that $\mathbf{A} = \begin{bmatrix} \mathbf{A}_{11} & \mathbf{A}_{12} \\ \mathbf{A}_{21} & \mathbf{A}_{22} \end{bmatrix}$

where $\mathbf{A}_{11}$ and $\mathbf{A}_{22}$ are square but not necessarily of the same order and both nonsingular and if $\mathbf{A}^{-1} = \mathbf{B} = \begin{bmatrix} \mathbf{B}_{11} & \mathbf{B}_{12} \\ \mathbf{B}_{21} & \mathbf{B}_{22} \end{bmatrix}$ is partitioned in the same way, show that, if $\mathbf{A}_{21} = \mathbf{0}$,

$$\mathbf{B}_{11} = \mathbf{A}_{11}^{-1}, \qquad \mathbf{B}_{12} = -\mathbf{A}_{11}^{-1}\mathbf{A}_{12}\mathbf{A}_{22}^{-1}, \qquad \mathbf{B}_{21} = \mathbf{0} \qquad \text{and} \qquad \mathbf{B}_{22} = \mathbf{A}_{22}^{-1}.$$

8 Solving systems of equations

There is in general no reason to suppose that any system of equations has a solution, or that, if a solution is found, it is unique. We must therefore ask what conditions are required to guarantee the existence of a solution for a system. This requires the concept of the 'rank' of a matrix.

The reader might find it helpful to read the elementary introduction to this topic by Carl Christ, which is reproduced in Johnson (1971), pp. 105-7.

8.1 Rank

D8.1 The *row rank* of $\mathbf{A}$ is the number of linearly independent rows in $\mathbf{A}$, and the *column rank* is the number of linearly independent columns.

For example, we know from Chapter 7 that

$$\begin{vmatrix} 1 & 2 & 4 \\ 1 & 3 & 7 \\ 1 & -1 & -2 \end{vmatrix} = 3.$$

This determinant is nonzero and the rows of this matrix are therefore linearly independent. The columns are also linearly independent, and so the row rank = column rank = 3.

It can be shown that:

Theorem 8.1 The row rank of any matrix is equal to the column rank. We therefore simply refer to the rank of $\mathbf{A}$, denoted rank $(\mathbf{A})$.

If $\mathbf{A}$ is $n \times n$ and has rank n, the inverse of $\mathbf{A}$ exists, and we see that we now have a set of equivalent criteria for the existence of the inverse of a square, $n \times n$ matrix, $\mathbf{A}$:

$$\begin{aligned} \mathbf{A}^{-1} \text{ exists } iff \ |\mathbf{A}| \neq 0 \\ &\Leftrightarrow \text{rank}(\mathbf{A}) = n \\ &\Leftrightarrow \mathbf{A} \text{ is nonsingular} \\ &\Leftrightarrow \text{columns and rows of } \mathbf{A} \text{ are bases for } E^n. \end{aligned}$$

The last statement follows from the definition of a basis, given in Section 5.3. If $\mathbf{A}$ is square, each column is a vector with n elements, and if $\mathbf{A}$ is nonsingular there are exactly n linearly independent columns. Therefore, they satisfy the requirements of a basis. This becomes important in the next few sections.

Obviously, if $\mathbf{A}$ is $n \times m$, and not square, then the rank of $\mathbf{A}$ cannot exceed the smaller of the two dimensions of $\mathbf{A}$. In other words

$$\text{rank}(\mathbf{A}) \leqslant \min(n, m)$$

where 'min(n, m)' is whichever is the smaller of n and m.

We now have a way of determining the rank of a matrix:

Theorem 8.2 A matrix has rank k *iff* $\exists$ at least one $k \times k$ nonsingular submatrix, and every $(k+1) \times (k+1)$ submatrix is singular.

Hence, to check the rank of, say, an 8×5 matrix, one checks *all* possible 5×5 submatrices. If they are all singular, one then tries all possible 4×4 submatrices, and so on, until a nonsingular submatrix is found.

D8.2 The matrix $\mathbf{A}$ has *full rank* if rank $(\mathbf{A})$ is actually equal to $\min(n, m)$.

In the following sections, techniques are outlined for solving systems of equations which can be written in the general form $\mathbf{A}\boldsymbol{x} = \boldsymbol{b}$, where $\mathbf{A}$ is a known matrix, $\boldsymbol{b}$ is a known vector and $\boldsymbol{x}$ is to be determined. There are various types of systems to be considered.

8.2 Nonsingular matrix

If $\mathbf{A}$ is square and of full rank, then $\mathbf{A}^{-1}$ exists and there is a *unique* solution given by $\boldsymbol{x} = \mathbf{A}^{-1}\boldsymbol{b}$. There are no special problems in this case.

8.3 Singular matrix

If $\mathbf{A}$ is square but rank$(\mathbf{A}) < n$ (so $|\mathbf{A}| = 0$), then there are two possibilities. When looking for a solution to $\mathbf{A}\boldsymbol{x} = \boldsymbol{b}$, one is asking whether there is a linear combination of the columns of $\mathbf{A}$ which yields $\boldsymbol{b}$. If the vectors $\boldsymbol{a}_1$, $\boldsymbol{a}_2, \ldots, \boldsymbol{a}_n$ are the columns of $\mathbf{A}$, then

$$\mathbf{A}\boldsymbol{x} = \boldsymbol{a}_1 x_1 + \boldsymbol{a}_2 x_2 + \ldots \boldsymbol{a}_n x_n$$

where $x_1, x_2, \ldots, x_n$ are the elements of $\boldsymbol{x}$. If these vectors form a basis for E^n (that is, they are linearly independent), it is possible, by definition, to write any arbitrary vector $\boldsymbol{b}$ as a unique linear combination of them, and this was the situation in Section 8.2. However, if rank($\mathbf{A}$) is less than n, the columns are linearly dependent and they do not span the whole of E^n. It is possible that $\boldsymbol{b}$ lies outside the *subspace* spanned by them, in which case there will not be a solution to the system. If $\boldsymbol{b}$ does lie in the subspace spanned by the columns of $\mathbf{A}$ then $\boldsymbol{b}$ can be written as a linear combination of the columns. The system can be solved and there are in fact an *infinite* number of ways of writing $\boldsymbol{b}$ as a linear combination of them, and hence an infinite number of solutions. For example, suppose $\mathbf{A}$ is 2×2 with columns $\boldsymbol{a}_1$ and $\boldsymbol{a}_2$. If $\boldsymbol{a}_1$ and $\boldsymbol{a}_2$ are linearly dependent, rank($\mathbf{A}$) = 1, and they lie on a straight line through the origin in E^2. If the vector $\boldsymbol{b}$ lines on the same line, then there will be an infinite number of solutions for $\boldsymbol{x}$. On the other hand, $\boldsymbol{b}$ may lie off the line in which case there is obviously no way of solving the problem.

We check whether $\boldsymbol{b}$ lies within or outside the space spanned by the columns of $\mathbf{A}$ by forming a new matrix,

$$[\mathbf{A}, \boldsymbol{b}]$$

that is, $\mathbf{A}$ with the inclusion of an extra column, $\boldsymbol{b}$. Let rank($\mathbf{A}$) = k. If rank([$\mathbf{A}$, $\boldsymbol{b}$]) > k, then by adding $\boldsymbol{b}$ we have added one more linearly independent column to the matrix. Therefore the vector $\boldsymbol{b}$ does not lie within the space spanned by the columns of $\mathbf{A}$, and the system is *inconsistent* (there is *no* solution).

Stated formally:

1 If rank([$\mathbf{A}$, $\boldsymbol{b}$]) > rank($\mathbf{A}$), then the system is inconsistent.
2 If rank ([$\mathbf{A}$, $\boldsymbol{b}$]) = rank($\mathbf{A}$), then the system is consistent and there is an infinite number of solutions.

Some examples follow.

Consider

$$x_1 + x_2 = 1$$
$$2x_1 + 2x_2 = 3.$$

In matrix notation,

$$\begin{bmatrix} 1 & 1 \\ 2 & 2 \end{bmatrix} \begin{bmatrix} x_1 \\ x_2 \end{bmatrix} = \begin{bmatrix} 1 \\ 3 \end{bmatrix}.$$

$|\mathbf{A}| = 0$ and so rank($\mathbf{A}$) $\neq 2$. But there are 1×1 submatrices with nonzero determinants and so rank($\mathbf{A}$) = 1.

Now,

$$[\mathbf{A}, \boldsymbol{b}] = \begin{bmatrix} 1 & 1 & 1 \\ 2 & 2 & 3 \end{bmatrix}.$$

Certainly, rank([$\mathbf{A}$, $\boldsymbol{b}$]) $\leqslant 2$. Taking the first and third columns to form a 2×2 submatrix, we find it has a determinant of 1. Hence, rank([$\mathbf{A}$, $\boldsymbol{b}$]) = 2, and the system is inconsistent and has no solution. This is obvious by inspection of the system. It is not possible to find two numbers which add to 1 and also add to $\frac{3}{2}$.

Now consider

$$\begin{bmatrix} 1 & 2 & 7 \\ 3 & 3 & 6 \\ 2 & 2 & 4 \end{bmatrix} \begin{bmatrix} x_1 \\ x_2 \\ x_3 \end{bmatrix} = \begin{bmatrix} 4 \\ 3 \\ 2 \end{bmatrix}.$$

$|\mathbf{A}| = 0$, therefore $\text{rank}(\mathbf{A}) < 3$, But $\begin{vmatrix} 1 & 2 \\ 3 & 3 \end{vmatrix} = -3$, so $\text{rank}(\mathbf{A}) = 2$, and it is also the case that $\text{rank}([\mathbf{A}, \boldsymbol{b}]) = 2$. This means that one equation (that is, one row of $[\mathbf{A}, \boldsymbol{b}]$) is a linear combination of the others. It therefore does not add any information and we can delete it to eliminate the dependence, giving

$$\begin{bmatrix} 1 & 2 & 7 \\ 3 & 3 & 6 \end{bmatrix} \begin{bmatrix} x_1 \\ x_2 \\ x_3 \end{bmatrix} = \begin{bmatrix} 4 \\ 3 \end{bmatrix}.$$

Unfortunately, the matrix is no longer square. It can be converted to a square matrix by taking some terms over to the right-hand side. We know that we can do this in such a way as to leave a nonsingular 2×2 matrix on the left, since we have already established that $\text{rank}(\mathbf{A}) = 2$.

Moving the terms involving x_3 to the right we obtain

$$\begin{bmatrix} 1 & 2 \\ 3 & 3 \end{bmatrix} \begin{bmatrix} x_1 \\ x_2 \end{bmatrix} = \begin{bmatrix} 4 - 7x_3 \\ 3 - 6x_3 \end{bmatrix}.$$

This gives solutions for x_1 and x_2 in terms of x_3, which we find by calculating the inverse. Let

$$\mathbf{B} = \begin{bmatrix} 1 & 2 \\ 3 & 3 \end{bmatrix} \quad \text{so} \quad \mathbf{B}^+ = \begin{bmatrix} 3 & -2 \\ -3 & 2 \end{bmatrix}, \quad |\mathbf{B}| = -3.$$

$$\mathbf{B}^{-1} = \frac{1}{|\mathbf{B}|}\mathbf{B}^+ = -\tfrac{1}{3}\begin{bmatrix} 3 & -2 \\ -3 & 1 \end{bmatrix} = \begin{bmatrix} -1 & \frac{2}{3} \\ 1 & -\frac{1}{3} \end{bmatrix}$$

so

$$\begin{bmatrix} x_1 \\ x_2 \end{bmatrix} = \begin{bmatrix} -1 & \frac{2}{3} \\ 1 & -\frac{1}{3} \end{bmatrix} \begin{bmatrix} 4 - 7x_3 \\ 3 - 6x_3 \end{bmatrix} = \begin{bmatrix} -2 + 3x_3 \\ 3 - 5x_3 \end{bmatrix},$$

or

$$x_1 = -2 + 3x_3 \qquad x_2 = 3 - 5x_3.$$

Hence, once an arbitrary value is chosen for x_3, then x_1 and x_2 are determined. For instance, if $x_3 = 1$, $x_1 = 1$ and $x_2 = -2$. Substituting these values in the original equations confirms that this is a solution:

$$1.1 + 2.-2 + 7.1 = 4$$

$$3.1 + 3.-2 + 6.1 = 3$$

$$2.1 + 2.-2 + 4.1 = 2.$$

One can also confirm that the values $x_1 = -2 + 3x_3$ and $x_2 = 3 - 5x_3$ satisfy the system for *any* arbitrary value of x_3, and hence we see that there is an *infinite* number of possible solutions, one for each value of x_3. We could equally well have solved in terms of x_1 or x_2. This procedure can be formally justified as follows.

Let $\text{rank}(\mathbf{A}) = k = \text{rank}([\mathbf{A}, \boldsymbol{b}])$, and let (r_i, b_i), $i = 1, 2, \ldots, n$, be the rows of $[\mathbf{A}, \boldsymbol{b}]$. Suppose the *first* k rows of $[\mathbf{A}, \boldsymbol{b}]$ are linearly independent; that is,

$$(r_j, b_j) = \sum_{i=1}^{k} \lambda_{ij}(r_i, b_i), \quad j = k + 1, \ldots, n \text{ for some } \lambda_{ij}.$$

Equivalently,

$$r_j = \sum_{i=1}^{k} \lambda_{ij} r_i, \quad b_j = \sum_{i=1}^{k} \lambda_{ij} b_i.$$

But if $\boldsymbol{x}$ is a solution to the first k equations, so that

$$r_i\boldsymbol{x} = b_i \quad i = 1, \ldots, k$$

then

$$r_j\boldsymbol{x} = \sum_{i=1}^{k} \lambda_{ij} r_i \boldsymbol{x} = \sum_{i=1}^{k} \lambda_{ij} b_i = b_j, \quad j = k + 1, \ldots, n$$

so that $\boldsymbol{x}$ also satisfies the remaining $(n - k)$ equations. Therefore these can be deleted, and we can be sure that any vector satisfying the first k equations will also satisfy the remaining $(n - k)$ equations.

Partitioning

$$\begin{bmatrix} \mathbf{A}_{11} & \mathbf{A}_{12} \\ \mathbf{A}_{21} & \mathbf{A}_{22} \end{bmatrix} \begin{bmatrix} \boldsymbol{x}_1 \\ \boldsymbol{x}_2 \end{bmatrix} = \begin{bmatrix} \boldsymbol{b}_1 \\ \boldsymbol{b}_2 \end{bmatrix}$$

so that $\mathbf{A}_{11}$ is our $k \times k$ nonsingular submatrix, we can now rewrite

$$\mathbf{A}_{11}\boldsymbol{x}_1 + \mathbf{A}_{12}\boldsymbol{x}_2 = \boldsymbol{b}_1,$$

deleting the last rows, or

$$\mathbf{A}_{11}\boldsymbol{x}_1 = \boldsymbol{b}_1 - \mathbf{A}_{12}\boldsymbol{x}_2.$$

So

$$\boldsymbol{x}_1 = \mathbf{A}_{11}^{-1}[\boldsymbol{b}_1 - \mathbf{A}_{12}\boldsymbol{x}_2].$$

This is a solution for the k variables in $\boldsymbol{x}_1$ in terms of the remaining $(n-k)$ variables.

In general, a nonsingular $k \times k$ submatrix may not appear conveniently in the top left-hand corner, but the principles involved are just the same. Note that in some contexts the values of the remaining $(n-k)$ variables are always fixed at zero, in which case it is said that the resulting solution is a *basic* solution.

There is a third possibility which we have yet to consider.

8.4 Nonsquare matrix

Here again, $\text{rank}([\mathbf{A}, \boldsymbol{b}]) \geqslant \text{rank}(\mathbf{A})$. If the system is consistent, that is, if $\text{rank}([\mathbf{A}, \boldsymbol{b}]) = \text{rank}(\mathbf{A})$, then one can proceed to a solution by partitioning, and the same procedure is used as in the case of 8.3: one finds the largest nonsingular submatrix, ignores additional equations and takes any remaining variables to the right-hand side. Again, inconsistency means that there is no solution.

8.5 Homogeneous systems

In the special case where $\boldsymbol{b} = \mathbf{0}$, we have a *homogeneous* system. It is often of interest to know the conditions under which there are values of $\boldsymbol{x}$ other than $\mathbf{0}$ that solve such a system ($\boldsymbol{x} = \mathbf{0}$ is known as the *trivial* solution).

If $\mathbf{A}$ is nonsingular, then there is only the trivial solution, since we can invert and $\mathbf{A}^{-1}\mathbf{0} = \mathbf{0}$, and this is unique. But if $\mathbf{A}$ is $n \times n$ and has rank $<n$, then this implies an infinite number of solutions found in accordance with the technique 8.3 above. There is no question of inconsistency here, since, by the definition of linear dependence, zero can be written as a nontrivial linear combination of the (linearly dependent) columns of $\mathbf{A}$. The solution of homogeneous systems is necessary in the discussion of eigenvalues and vectors in the next chapter.

To summarize, in the nonhomogeneous case, if the matrix is square and nonsingular, there is a unique solution. Otherwise there may either be no solution at all, or an infinity of solutions. In the homogeneous case there will be nontrivial solutions if the matrix is singular.

No computer program for solving systems of equations is given in this chapter. In the case of 3×3 nonsingular systems this may be achieved easily by putting together the routines for matrix inversion and for matrix multiplication given in the earlier chapters. A program which dealt with systems of any size and with all of the possible situations outlined in sections 8.2 to 8.5 would be too long and complex for this book. Standard programs for this task are readily available and they use techniques which are both faster and yield more accurate results than those given here.

8.6 Cramer's rule

This is a device which can be useful in certain situations. It enables one to write down the solution for any one of the xs without calculating the whole of the inverse matrix. It is, however, exactly equivalent to calculating those elements of the inverse which would actually be used.

Let us assume that we have a matrix $\mathbf{A}$ that is square, either because it was originally square or through partitioning and rearrangement. Then the solution will take the form:

$$\begin{bmatrix} x_1 \\ \vdots \\ x_n \end{bmatrix} = \begin{bmatrix} a^{11} & \dots a^{1n} \\ \vdots & \\ a^{n1} & \dots a^{nn} \end{bmatrix} \begin{bmatrix} b_1 \\ \vdots \\ b_n \end{bmatrix}$$

or

$$x = \mathbf{A}^{-1} b$$

where $\mathbf{A}^{-1} = (a^{ij})$. Then, if we only want the value of x_1, say, the only elements of $\mathbf{A}^{-1}$ that are needed are those in the first row, and the other rows of $\mathbf{A}^{-1}$ are irrelevant. Additionally, some of the bs may be zero so that not even all of the first row is needed.

Cramer's rule assists us to exploit this, and to calculate only those cofactors of $\mathbf{A}$ which are necessary. To find the value of x_k, we find $1/|\mathbf{A}|$ and multiply that by another determinant; namely the determinant of the matrix $\mathbf{A}$ with the vector $\boldsymbol{b}$ replacing the kth column:

$$\begin{vmatrix} a_{11} & a_{12} & \dots & a_{1k-1} & b_1 & a_{1k+1} & a_{1n} \\ a_{21} & \dots & \dots & a_{2k-1} & b_2 & a_{2k+1} & a_{2n} \\ \vdots & & & \vdots & \vdots & \vdots & \vdots \\ a_{n1} & \dots & \dots & \dots & b_n & \dots & a_{nn} \end{vmatrix}.$$

To see why this works, consider the value of x_k. From first principles, this is given by

$$x_k = \frac{1}{|\mathbf{A}|} \sum_j b_j a_{kj}^{+} \quad \text{where} \quad \mathbf{A}^{+} = (a_{ij}^{+})$$

$$= \frac{1}{|\mathbf{A}|} \sum_j b_j A_{jk}.$$

If we use Cramer's rule, expanding the new determinant down the kth column the same result is obtained because the cofactor of b_j is the cofactor of a_{jk}, that is A_{jk}.

Cramer's rule is merely a computational technique. It comes to no more than a way of organizing one's calculations on paper, but it is very convenient if one needs only a few of the xs.

You can easily demonstrate the validity of Cramer's rule in the case of a 3×3 system with the program for evaluating determinants from Chapter 6. Evaluate the **A** matrix and then the **A** matrix with the vector $\boldsymbol{b}$ replacing the kth column. The ratio should then be the solution for the kth unknown.

8.7 Cramer's rule applied to an economic problem

Let us take the following linear macroeconomic model, using a fairly standard notation:

$$Y = C + I + G$$

$$C = \alpha + \beta Y \qquad \alpha > 0, 0 < \beta < 1$$

$$I = \gamma + \delta r \qquad \gamma > 0, \delta < 0$$

$$M = \tau Y + \lambda r \qquad \tau > 0, \lambda < 0.$$

We must decide which variables to regard as *exogenous* (predetermined, independent, policy) and which as *endogenous* (jointly dependent, dependent). We have four independent equations, so in general we can solve for the *equilibrium values* of four endogenous variables, which are consistent with the four equations and the independently fixed values of the other variables. We shall (somewhat arbitrarily) assume that:

The endogenous variables are Y, C, I, r
The exogenous variables are G and M.

We first arrange the system so that the endogenous variables appear on the left-hand side and the exogenous variables appear on the right-hand side and then write in matrix notation,

$$\begin{bmatrix} 1 & -1 & -1 & 0 \\ -\beta & 1 & 0 & 0 \\ 0 & 0 & 1 & -\delta \\ \tau & 0 & 0 & \lambda \end{bmatrix} \begin{bmatrix} Y \\ C \\ I \\ r \end{bmatrix} = \begin{bmatrix} G \\ \alpha \\ \gamma \\ M \end{bmatrix}.$$

Suppose we want to determine r. We first find $|\mathbf{A}|$ by expanding down the second column,

$$|\mathbf{A}| = -(-1)(-\lambda\beta) + (\lambda + \delta\tau)$$
$$= \lambda(1 - \beta) + \delta\tau.$$

We assume that this is nonzero. Replacing the fourth column with the column $\boldsymbol{b}$, we have

$$r = \frac{1}{|\mathbf{A}|} \begin{vmatrix} 1 & -1 & -1 & G \\ -\beta & 1 & 0 & \alpha \\ 0 & 0 & 1 & \gamma \\ \tau & 0 & 0 & M \end{vmatrix}$$

$$= \frac{-\beta M - \alpha\tau + M - \gamma\tau - G\tau}{\lambda(1-\beta) + \delta\tau}$$

$$= \frac{M(1-\beta) - \tau(\alpha + \gamma + G)}{\lambda(1-\beta) + \delta\tau}.$$

(This is the *reduced form* of the structure. See Section 7.2 above.) For instance, if G changes by ΔG, then the change in r, Δr, is given by

$$\Delta r = \frac{-\tau \Delta G}{\lambda(1-\beta) + \delta\tau} \quad \text{since } \Delta M = \Delta\alpha = \Delta\gamma = 0.$$

Note that $|\mathbf{A}| < 0$ on the assumptions given above. As is usually the case, its absolute value is the reciprocal of the Keynesian multiplier (see also Section 14.2(*b*)). Since $\tau > 0$, Δr and ΔG are positively related. At this stage the reader should stop and interpret this result and, if he wishes, confirm it diagrammatically. As an exercise one could also solve for national income Y and discuss the conditions on the slopes of the functions under which one would expect fiscal policy (changing G) to be more or less effective than monetary policy (changing M) in changing equilibrium income. A great deal of economic analysis can be extracted from a simple model of this kind. On the other hand, one must be aware of its limitations; for instance, we have shown how one equilibrium compares with another, but we have tacitly assumed that there are forces to take the system from one to another (that is, that the system is *stable*). Hence, the name of the technique–*comparative statics*. This is the subject of Chapter 18. We shall be discussing some simple *dynamics* as an application of the theory of eigenvalues in the next chapter.

8.8 Problems

1. In Problem 2.3.4, we had a system of three linear equations,

$$S = a + bp \quad (a > 0, b > 0)$$
$$D = c + dp \quad (c > 0, d < 0)$$
$$S = D.$$

Using Cramer's rule, solve for p and discuss the effect on p of an increase in the constant c; that is, an upward shift in the demand curve.

2. Consider Problem 4.7.3. You have already solved the system of equations by use of the given inverse. Check your solution by using Cramer's rule to solve the system.

3. Solve the equations:

$$x_1 + x_2 + x_3 = 6$$
$$2x_1 + ax_2 + 2x_3 = c$$
$$-x_1 - x_2 + bx_3 = d$$

when

$$(a)\quad a=2,\quad b=-1,\quad c=12,\quad d=-6$$

$$(b)\quad a=-1,\quad b=-1,\quad c=6,\quad d=-5$$

$$(c)\quad a=-1,\quad b=0,\quad c=6,\quad d=-5.$$

4. The following is a model of two trading nations:

$$Y_1 = C_1 + I_1 + X_1 - M_1 \qquad Y_2 = C_2 + I_2 + X_2 - M_2$$

$$C_1 = c_1 Y_1 \qquad C_2 = c_2 Y_2$$

$$M_1 = m_1 Y_1 \qquad M_2 = m_2 Y_2$$

where Y_i is income of country i
C_i is consumption of country i
X_i is exports of country i
M_i is imports of country i
I_i is investment of country i, which is exogenously determined
$i = 1, 2$.

If $X_1 = M_2$ and $M_1 = X_2$, calculate the equilibrium values of the two national incomes and find the effect of a change in investment in country 1 on the level of income of country 2. Interpret the results.

5. Solve the following equations

$$\begin{aligned} 2x_1 - x_2 + x_3 &= 6 \\ -3x_1 + x_2 + x_3 &= 4 \\ x_1 + 2x_2 + ax_3 &= b \end{aligned}$$

when

$$(a)\quad a=-2,\quad b=-2$$

$$(b)\quad a=-12,\quad b=-2$$

$$(c)\quad a=-12,\quad b=-62$$

6. Where possible solve the following systems of equations:

(*a*)

$$\begin{aligned} x_1 + x_2 + 2x_3 + 3x_4 &= 0 \\ x_1 \qquad + x_3 + 5x_4 &= 1 \\ x_1 + 2x_2 + 3x_3 \qquad &= 3 \end{aligned}$$

(*b*)

$$\begin{aligned} x_1 + 3x_2 + 4x_3 &= 14 \\ 2x_1 + x_2 + x_3 &= 2 \\ 7x_1 + 11x_2 + 14x_3 &= 46 \end{aligned}$$

(c)

$$\begin{aligned} x_1 + 2x_2 + x_3 &= 4 \\ 2x_1 + x_2 + x_3 &= 7 \\ 5x_1 + 4x_2 + 3x_3 &= 10 \end{aligned}$$

(d)

$$\begin{aligned} x_1 + 3x_2 + 4x_3 &= 14 \\ 2x_1 + x_2 + x_3 &= 2 \\ x_1 + 3x_2 - x_3 &= 5 \\ 5x_1 + 5x_2 + x_3 &= 9 \end{aligned}$$

(e)

$$\begin{aligned} 3x_1 + 5x_2 + 4x_3 \qquad\quad &= 0 \\ x_1 + 2x_2 + 2x_3 - 3x_4 &= 0 \\ x_1 \qquad - 2x_3 + 14x_4 &= 0. \end{aligned}$$

9 Eigenvalues and difference equations

9.1 Introduction

The input-output problem formulated in Section 5.3 was to find a vector $\boldsymbol{x}$ such that

$$f + \mathbf{A}x = x$$

given the vector f and the square matrix $\mathbf{A}$ (see also Problem 2.3.3). This is known as the equation of the *open* input-output model, because some net final outputs, given by f, are produced. A special case occurs when all transfers of goods are made within an economy, with no net final outputs, in which case $f = \mathbf{0}$ and we have the *closed* model. Then we seek a vector $\boldsymbol{x}$ such that

$$\mathbf{A}x = x.$$

In other words, given $\mathbf{A}$ (different from $\mathbf{I}$) we want a vector which, when premultiplied by $\mathbf{A}$, is unchanged. This is a particular example of an *eigenvalue* problem. One might expect that this particular problem is rather unlikely to have a solution unless the technology matrix $\mathbf{A}$ has rather special properties, because it is rather unlikely that we could produce all goods in exactly the right proportions. We shall see what these conditions are below.

In general we ask: is it possible to find a vector $\boldsymbol{x}$, and a scalar λ, such that for a given $n \times n$ matrix $\mathbf{A}$

$$\mathbf{A}x = \lambda x$$

that is, such that premultiplication by $\mathbf{A}$ changes the length of $\boldsymbol{x}$, but not its direction? We shall see that in general the answer is yes; in fact, there will be up to n distinct *eigenvalues* and up to n linearly independent associated *eigenvectors*. For example,

$$\begin{bmatrix} 2 & -1 \\ -1 & 2 \end{bmatrix}\begin{bmatrix} 1 \\ -1 \end{bmatrix} = \begin{bmatrix} 3 \\ -3 \end{bmatrix} = 3\begin{bmatrix} 1 \\ -1 \end{bmatrix}$$

so $\lambda = 3$ and $x = (1, -1)'$ satisfy the equation for this matrix. So do $\lambda = 1$, $x = (1, 1)'$.

It turns out that just as a single scalar, the determinant, gave quite a bit of information about the matrix, the n eigenvalues contain an amazingly large proportion of the information contained in the total of n^2 scalars in the matrix. In fact, in many applications–in stability analysis of dynamic economic models for instance–they tell us *all* we need to know.

D9.1 If $\mathbf{A}$ is a square matrix, and if a scalar λ and a vector $x \neq \mathbf{0}$ satisfy $\mathbf{A}x = \lambda x$, then λ is an *eigenvalue* (or *latent root* or *characteristic value*) of $\mathbf{A}$ and x is a corresponding *eigenvector* (*latent vector*, *characteristic vector*).

The case $x = \mathbf{0}$ is excluded, because in that case any λ would give $\mathbf{A}x = \lambda x$, and the problem is trivial. An eigenvector is not unique, since if x is an eigenvector, $\mu(\mathbf{A}x) = \mu(\lambda x)$ and so $\mathbf{A}(\mu x) = \lambda(\mu x)$, so that μx is also an eigenvector, where μ is any nonzero scalar. We say that an eigenvector is 'only determined up to a scalar multiple'.

One might compare this with finding the identity matrix in Section 4.5(*a*), when given a *vector*, x we had to find a *matrix* $\mathbf{I}$ such that $\mathbf{I}x = x$. In finding the eigenvector, the question has been turned around: given a *matrix* $\mathbf{A}$, does there exist a *vector* x such that $\mathbf{A}x = x$ multiplied by some scalar?

9.2 Calculation of eigenvalues

The equation $\mathbf{A}x = \lambda x$ can be rewritten

$$\mathbf{A}x - \lambda x = \mathbf{0}$$

or

$$\mathbf{A}x - \lambda \mathbf{I}x = \mathbf{0}$$

or

$$[\mathbf{A} - \lambda\mathbf{I}]x = \mathbf{0}$$

We want a solution, $x \neq \mathbf{0}$, for this homogeneous system of equations, the matrix of the system being $[\mathbf{A} - \lambda\mathbf{I}]$.

From Section 8.5, the matrix $[\mathbf{A} - \lambda\mathbf{I}]$ must be singular if there is to be a nontrivial solution. In other words, if there is to be a nontrivial solution, then we must choose values for λ such that

$$|\mathbf{A} - \lambda\mathbf{I}| = 0.$$

But,

$$[\mathbf{A}-\lambda\mathbf{I}] = \begin{bmatrix} a_{11} & a_{12} & \dots & a_{1n} \\ a_{21} & a_{22} & \dots & a_{2n} \\ \vdots & \vdots & & \vdots \\ a_{n1} & a_{n2} & \dots & a_{nn} \end{bmatrix} - \begin{bmatrix} \lambda & 0 & \dots & 0 \\ 0 & \lambda & \dots & 0 \\ \vdots & \vdots & & \vdots \\ 0 & 0 & \dots & \lambda \end{bmatrix}$$

$$= \begin{bmatrix} a_{11}-\lambda & a_{12} & \dots & a_{1n} \\ a_{21} & a_{22}-\lambda & \dots & a_{2n} \\ \vdots & \vdots & & \vdots \\ a_{n1} & a_{n2} & \dots & a_{nn}-\lambda \end{bmatrix}$$

that is, the matrix **A** with λ subtracted from all the elements on the main diagonal.

Expanding the determinant of this matrix produces an expression of the form

$$b_n\lambda^n + b_{n-1}\lambda^{n-1} + b_{n-2}\lambda^{n-2} + \dots + b_1\lambda + b_0$$

which is known as the *characteristic polynomial*, where the bs are scalars involving the elements of **A**. The problem now becomes that of finding the *roots* of the polynomial; that is, values of λ which, when substituted in this expression, yield zero.

In general, an nth-order polynomial has n different solutions and in the sequel we shall assume this to be the case. In fact, there are two complications here. First, two or more roots may 'coincide' to give less than n distinct values, and second, some of the roots may involve the 'imaginary' square roots of negative numbers, to give so-called *complex* roots. We shall assume that the former problem does not arise. (Slight perturbation of some coefficients will get rid of it.) The latter problem is mentioned briefly in the context of an economic example below, and will be returned to in the chapters on analysis (Section 14.3).

For example, let

$$\mathbf{A} = \begin{bmatrix} 3 & 8 & 1 \\ 0 & 4 & 3 \\ 0 & 3 & 4 \end{bmatrix}$$

and so

$$[\mathbf{A}-\lambda\mathbf{I}] = \begin{bmatrix} 3-\lambda & 8 & 1 \\ 0 & 4-\lambda & 3 \\ 0 & 3 & 4-\lambda \end{bmatrix}.$$

Hence we require values for λ such that

$$|\mathbf{A}-\lambda\mathbf{I}| = (3-\lambda)(4-\lambda)(4-\lambda) - 9(3-\lambda) = 0.$$

This is the *characteristic equation*.

One method of solving this is to multiply out this expression to obtain a cubic polynomial in λ (that is, an expression involving λ^3) and use a standard formula to obtain solutions. However, in this case things are rather simpler. Rewriting,

$$(3-\lambda)\{(4-\lambda)(4-\lambda)-9\}=0.$$

One solution then becomes obvious; $\lambda = 3$. But this is not the only possibility, since we can find values of λ which make the term in curly brackets zero; such that

$$(4-\lambda)(4-\lambda)-9=0.$$

This is now a quadratic polynomial to be solved, so that we are looking for two values of λ which make the left-hand side zero. Again, there are several approaches. In this case the answers are obvious by inspection—we have to make the product of the two terms involving λ come to $+9$; so they must each be $+3$ or -3, implying values of λ of 1 and 7. Alternatively we could multiply out the factors to give

$$16-8\lambda+\lambda^2-9=0$$

or

$$\lambda^2-8\lambda+7=0.$$

In this case the left-hand side is easily written in the form,

$$(\lambda-7)(\lambda-1)=0$$

whence we again see that $\lambda = 1$ and $\lambda = 7$ are solutions. Note the general technique here: given

$$\lambda^2+b\lambda+c=0$$

where b and c are constants, one tries to *factorize* into the form

$$(\lambda-h)(\lambda-k)=0$$

where h and k must be such that $hk = c$ and $(h+k) = -b$. Such values of h and k can often be found by guesswork.

If even this fails, one can resort to a well-known standard formula: if

$$a\lambda^2+b\lambda+c=0$$

then the solutions are

$$\lambda_1=\frac{1}{2a}\{-b+\sqrt{(b^2-4ac)}\},\quad \lambda_2=\frac{1}{2a}\{-b-\sqrt{(b^2-4ac)}\}.$$

You should check that this formula works in the above example. Note, once again, that b^2-4ac might be zero, so that λ_1 and λ_2 'coincide', or it might be negative so that λ_1 and λ_2 involve the 'imaginary' square roots of negative numbers.

The latter case is dealt with in the following way. We define i as the square root of -1;

$$\mathrm{i} = \sqrt{-1}, \quad \mathrm{i}^2 = -1.$$

Now, this number does not exist in the ordinary way, but accepting the *definition* at its face value, it is found that a whole algebra can be built up using it which is indispensible in understanding dynamic systems. If

$$b^2 - 4ac < 0$$

we write

$$\lambda_1 = \frac{1}{2a}\{-b + \mathrm{i}\sqrt{(4ac - b^2)}\}, \quad \lambda_2 = \frac{1}{2a}\{-b - \mathrm{i}\sqrt{(4ac - b^2)}\}$$

where the square roots are now well defined. The eigenvalues now have the form

$$\lambda_1 = x + \mathrm{i}y, \quad \lambda_2 = x - \mathrm{i}y.$$

They have two components, a real part and an imaginary part and are known as *complex* numbers. In this case, as is usual, they occur in pairs of *complex conjugates*. More of this in Section 14.3.

The three eigenvalues are 1, 3 and 7. They should all make the matrix $[\mathbf{A} - \lambda\mathbf{I}]$ singular, and it is easy to confirm this by looking at the matrix above and making the substitutions. The eigenvalues of this matrix turn out to be positive and real numbers. The positivity is related to the fact that the original matrix was positive; that is, a matrix with all its elements positive.

Theorem 9.1 Any positive matrix has at least one real, positive eigenvalue (but possibly some negative and complex ones also). This is part of a theorem of great importance in mathematical economics, statistics, and the theory of games.

The following theorem gives a useful sufficient condition which guarantees that no problems with imaginary numbers will arise.

Theorem 9.2 If the matrix is symmetric, all the eigenvalues are real. This is sufficient but it is certainly not necessary as the example we have just given illustrates.

The following program will illustrate the calculation of the eigenvalues of a 2×2 matrix using the above formula for finding the roots of a quadratic equation. Lines 190 to 470 are intended to illustrate the material in Section 9.5 below and they may be omitted for the moment. Also, the case of complex roots is catered for although an explanation of the theory of these must wait until Section 14.3.

```
100  PI = 3.14159
110  INPUT "A(1,1)";A(1,1)
120  INPUT "A(1,2)";A(1,2)
130  INPUT "A(2,1)";A(2,1)
```

```
140 INPUT "A(2,2)";A(2,2)
150 A = 1
160 B = - (A(1,1) + A(2,2))
170 C = (A(1,1) * A(2,2) - A(1,2) * A(2,1))
180 GOTO 510
190 :
200 INPUT "HOW MANY POINTS";N
210 IF N > 999 THEN PRINT "LESS THAN 1000" : GOTO 200
220 DIM X(N)
230 INPUT "INITIAL VALUE OF X(0)";X(0) : MAX = X(0) : MIN = X(0)
240 INPUT "INITIAL VALUE OF X(1)";X(1)
250 :
300 FOR T = 2 TO N : REM CALCULATE X(T)
310 X(T) = (- B/A) * X(T-1) - (C/A) * X(T-2)
320 NEXT T
330 FOR T = 0 TO N : REM FIND MAX AND MIN
340 IF X(T) > MAX THEN MAX = X(T)
350 IF X(T) < MIN THEN MIN = X(T)
360 NEXT T
370 :
400 RANGE = MAX - MIN : REM PLOT THE RESULTS
410 SCALE = 40/RANGE
420 PRINT "MIN = ";MIN;
430 PRINT "MAX = ";MAX
440 FOR T = 0 TO N
450 PRINT T; TAB(SCALE * (X(T) - MIN) + 5); "*"
460 NEXT T
470 :
500 PRINT : REM FIND EIGENVALUES
510 TEST = B * B - 4 * A * C
520 IF TEST < 0 GOTO 590
530 L1 = (- B + SQR(TEST))/(2 * A)
540 L2 = (- B - SQR(TEST))/(2 * A)
550 PRINT
560 PRINT "EIGENVALUES ARE"; L1;"AND";L2
570 STOP
580 PRINT
590 PRINT "EIGENVALUES ARE COMPLEX"
600 REAL = - B/(2 * A)
610 IMAGINARY = SQR(- TEST)/(2 * A)
620 MDULUS = SQR(REAL*REAL + IMAGINARY*IMAGINARY)
630 IF REAL <> 0 THEN ARGUMENT = ATN(IMAGINARY/REAL)
640 IF REAL = 0 THEN ARGUMENT = PI/2
650 PERIOD = 2 * PI/ARGUMENT
660 PRINT "REAL PART IS", REAL
670 PRINT "IMAGINARY PARTS ARE", IMAGINARY
680 PRINT "MODULUS IS", MDULUS
```

```
690 PRINT "ARGUMENT IS", ARGUMENT
700 IF ARGUMENT >= 0 THEN PRINT "PERIOD IS", PERIOD
710 END
```

Of course it is very limiting to only be able to deal with 2×2 matrices. You might wish to extend the program to handle 3×3 matrices. This will involve solving a cubic equation. One way of doing this is to find one root by a trial and error process, a program for which is given by Kemeny and Kurtz (1971, section 8.2). Then, knowing one root the problem may be reduced to one of solving a quadratic for which the above routine can be used. For serious computational work with larger systems one needs to use one of the readily available standard routines, which operate on quite different principles.

9.3 Calculation of eigenvectors

We have that, for some eigenvalue λ_1,

$$[\mathbf{A} - \lambda_1 \mathbf{I}]\, \boldsymbol{x}_1 = \mathbf{0}$$

where $\boldsymbol{x}_1$ is the eigenvector corresponding to λ_1. Consider the case $\lambda_1 = 3$; $[\mathbf{A} - \lambda_1 \mathbf{I}]$ becomes

$$\begin{bmatrix} 0 & 8 & 1 \\ 0 & 1 & 3 \\ 0 & 3 & 1 \end{bmatrix}$$

and so $\boldsymbol{x}_1 = (x_{11}, x_{21}, x_{31})'$ must satisfy the equation

$$\begin{bmatrix} 0 & 8 & 1 \\ 0 & 1 & 3 \\ 0 & 3 & 1 \end{bmatrix} \begin{bmatrix} x_{11} \\ x_{21} \\ x_{31} \end{bmatrix} = \begin{bmatrix} 0 \\ 0 \\ 0 \end{bmatrix}.$$

Since the last two columns are linearly independent we must have $x_{21} = 0$, $x_{31} = 0$, but x_{11} is arbitrary because the first column in the matrix $[\mathbf{A} - 3\mathbf{I}]$ is a column of zeros. So we can let $x_{11} = 1$, to give

$$x_1 = \begin{bmatrix} 1 \\ 0 \\ 0 \end{bmatrix}$$

as an eigenvector corresponding to $\lambda = 3$. Notice again, that it is only determinate up to a scalar multiple so $\boldsymbol{x}_1 = (2, 0, 0)'$ or $\boldsymbol{x}_1 = (-5, 0, 0)'$ would do just as well. This problem could have been solved by finding the rank of $[\mathbf{A} - 3\mathbf{I}]$ and manipulating the matrix by the techniques outlined previously. But in this example, we can solve by inspection.

Now, take $\lambda_2 = 7$. The equation for $\boldsymbol{x}_2$ becomes

$$\begin{bmatrix} -4 & 8 & 1 \\ 0 & -3 & 3 \\ 0 & 3 & -3 \end{bmatrix} \begin{bmatrix} x_{12} \\ x_{22} \\ x_{32} \end{bmatrix} = \begin{bmatrix} 0 \\ 0 \\ 0 \end{bmatrix}.$$

Let us solve this by standard techniques as an exercise. The rank is 2, because the bottom row, multiplied by -1, becomes identical with the second row. So we can delete the last equation and move the elements containing the third element of the vector $\boldsymbol{x}_2$ to the right-hand side, since this leaves a non-singular 2×2 matrix on the left-hand side. Rewriting, we have

$$\begin{bmatrix} -4 & 8 \\ 0 & -3 \end{bmatrix} \begin{bmatrix} x_{12} \\ x_{22} \end{bmatrix} = \begin{bmatrix} -x_{32} \\ -3x_{32} \end{bmatrix}.$$

Inverting the matrix to obtain a solution,

$$\begin{bmatrix} x_{12} \\ x_{22} \end{bmatrix} = \frac{1}{12} \begin{bmatrix} -3 & -8 \\ 0 & -4 \end{bmatrix} \begin{bmatrix} -x_{32} \\ -3x_{32} \end{bmatrix}.$$

Hence

$$x_{12} = \tfrac{27}{12}\, x_{32} = \tfrac{9}{4}\, x_{32}$$

$$x_{22} = \tfrac{12}{12}\, x_{32} = x_{32}.$$

We can choose x_{32} arbitrarily, so we choose to eliminate the fraction to give

$$\boldsymbol{x}_2 = \begin{bmatrix} 9 \\ 4 \\ 4 \end{bmatrix}.$$

Similarly, for $\lambda_3 = 1$ we have

$$\boldsymbol{x}_3 = \begin{bmatrix} 7 \\ -2 \\ 2 \end{bmatrix}.$$

This completes the solution of the eigenvalue and eigenvector problem, let us now check that, say, $\boldsymbol{x}_2 = (9, 4, 4)'$ is in fact an eigenvector corresponding to the eigenvalue $\lambda_2 = 7$, by showing that

$$\mathbf{A}\boldsymbol{x}_2 = \lambda_2 \boldsymbol{x}_2.$$

Now

$$\mathbf{A}\boldsymbol{x}_2 = \begin{bmatrix} 3 & 8 & 1 \\ 0 & 4 & 3 \\ 0 & 3 & 4 \end{bmatrix} \begin{bmatrix} 9 \\ 4 \\ 4 \end{bmatrix}$$

$$= \begin{bmatrix} 63 \\ 28 \\ 28 \end{bmatrix} = \begin{bmatrix} 7.9 \\ 7.4 \\ 7.4 \end{bmatrix} = 7.\begin{bmatrix} 9 \\ 4 \\ 4 \end{bmatrix}$$

$$= \lambda_2 \boldsymbol{x}_2$$

as required.

We now continue to use this example in order to illustrate the rather extraordinary result which makes the theory of eigenvalues and vectors so very useful. We form a new matrix $\mathbf{Q}$, whose columns are the three eigenvectors, $\boldsymbol{x}_1, \boldsymbol{x}_2$ and $\boldsymbol{x}_3$, and then calculate the matrix product, $\mathbf{Q}^{-1}\mathbf{A}\mathbf{Q}$:

$$\mathbf{Q} = \begin{bmatrix} 1 & 9 & 7 \\ 0 & 4 & -2 \\ 0 & 4 & 2 \end{bmatrix}.$$

Hence,

$$\mathbf{Q}^{-1} = \tfrac{1}{8}\begin{bmatrix} 8 & 5 & -23 \\ 0 & 1 & 1 \\ 0 & -2 & 2 \end{bmatrix}.$$

And so

$$\mathbf{Q}^{-1}\mathbf{A}\mathbf{Q} = \tfrac{1}{8}\begin{bmatrix} 8 & 5 & -23 \\ 0 & 1 & 1 \\ 0 & -2 & 2 \end{bmatrix}\begin{bmatrix} 3 & 63 & 7 \\ 0 & 28 & -2 \\ 0 & 28 & 2 \end{bmatrix}$$

$$= \tfrac{1}{8}\begin{bmatrix} 24 & 0 & 0 \\ 0 & 56 & 0 \\ 0 & 0 & 8 \end{bmatrix}$$

$$= \begin{bmatrix} 3 & 0 & 0 \\ 0 & 7 & 0 \\ 0 & 0 & 1 \end{bmatrix},$$

so that $\mathbf{Q}^{-1}\mathbf{A}\mathbf{Q}$ is a diagonal matrix with the eigenvalues on the diagonal in an order which corresponds to the order in which we took the eigenvectors in the columns of $\mathbf{Q}$. More generally, it is true that for any square matrix $\mathbf{A}$ there exists a nonsingular matrix $\mathbf{Q}$ such that $\mathbf{Q}^{-1}\mathbf{A}\mathbf{Q}$ is either diagonal or 'almost' diagonal; the result is known as the *Jordan canonical form*. (If $\mathbf{Q}^{-1}\mathbf{A}\mathbf{Q}$ is 'almost' diagonal then $\mathbf{A}$ has repeated roots and small 'blocks' appear down the diagonal, each block involving only 1s, 0s and one eigenvalue. A matrix with repeated roots may, or may not, have a pure diagonal form.) The following theorem states the result which is exploited in the following sections on applications.

Theorem 9.3 Let **A** be a matrix with distinct eigenvalues and let **Q** be the matrix whose columns are the eigenvectors of **A**. then $\mathbf{Q}^{-1}\mathbf{AQ}$ is a diagonal matrix with the eigenvalues on the diagonal.

In stating this theorem we have presupposed that $\mathbf{Q}^{-1}$ exists, a supposition which is justified by

Theorem 9.4 The eigenvectors corresponding to distinct eigenvalues are linearly independent; if all eigenvalues are distinct the vectors form a basis for E^n.

Note that the columns of **Q** may contain complex numbers if some of the eigenvalues are complex. This will not occur if the matrix is symmetric by Theorem 9.2.

Theorem 9.5 The eigenvectors corresponding to distinct eigenvalues of a *symmetric* matrix are orthogonal.

Proof. Let $\boldsymbol{x}_1$ and $\boldsymbol{x}_2$ be two eigenvectors of **A**, so that

$$\mathbf{A}\boldsymbol{x}_1 = \lambda_1 \boldsymbol{x}_1 \quad \text{and} \quad \mathbf{A}\boldsymbol{x}_2 = \lambda_2 \boldsymbol{x}_2.$$

Premultiplying each equation by $\boldsymbol{x}_2'$ and $\boldsymbol{x}_1'$, respectively,

$$\boldsymbol{x}_2' \mathbf{A}\boldsymbol{x}_1 = \lambda_1 \boldsymbol{x}_2' \boldsymbol{x}_1, \qquad \boldsymbol{x}_1' \mathbf{A}\boldsymbol{x}_2 = \lambda_2 \boldsymbol{x}_1' \boldsymbol{x}_2.$$

Transposing the first equation

$$\boldsymbol{x}_1' \mathbf{A}'\boldsymbol{x}_2 = \lambda_1 \boldsymbol{x}_1' \boldsymbol{x}_2 \quad \text{and} \quad \boldsymbol{x}_1' \mathbf{A}\boldsymbol{x}_2 = \lambda_2 \boldsymbol{x}_1' \boldsymbol{x}_2,$$

or, since **A** is symmetric,

$$\boldsymbol{x}_1' \mathbf{A}\boldsymbol{x}_2 = \lambda_1 \boldsymbol{x}_1' \boldsymbol{x}_2 \quad \text{and} \quad \boldsymbol{x}_1' \mathbf{A}\boldsymbol{x}_2 = \lambda_2 \boldsymbol{x}_1' \boldsymbol{x}_2$$

and so

$$\lambda_1 \boldsymbol{x}_1' \boldsymbol{x}_2 = \lambda_2 \boldsymbol{x}_1' \boldsymbol{x}_2.$$

Hence, if $\lambda_1 \neq \lambda_2$ we have $\boldsymbol{x}_1' \boldsymbol{x}_2 = 0$ as required. ∎

Since they can also be normalized, they can form an orthonormal basis for E^n. You can confirm that in this case

$$\mathbf{Q}'\mathbf{Q} = \mathbf{I}$$

so that

$$\mathbf{Q}^{-1} = \mathbf{Q}'.$$

If the eigenvalues of **A** are not distinct then these results may or may not still apply—in practice they often do. If not, similar, but weaker results are available. The process of finding $\mathbf{Q}^{-1}\mathbf{AQ}$ is called the *diagonalization of* **A**. In the worked example we found the eigenvalues first and then the eigenvectors (the elements of **Q**) from them, and so the process of computing $\mathbf{Q}^{-1}\mathbf{AQ}$ may appear somewhat pointless. However, in many applications, we only need to know of the *existence* of a matrix which diagonalizes **A**, without actually needing to know what it is.

9.4 Applications

(*a*) In Section 4.3, we developed a model which gave a vector x^n after n transitions from an initial vector x^0 by

$$x^n = \mathbf{P}^n x^0$$

where $\mathbf{P}^n$ was a transition matrix. We were interested in knowing whether $\mathbf{P}^n$ tended towards some fixed matrix, $\mathbf{P}$ say, as n became large. To answer this question, let $\mathbf{S}$ diagonalize $\mathbf{P}$ to give $\mathbf{D}$, so that

$$\mathbf{S}^{-1}\mathbf{P}\mathbf{S} = \mathbf{D}$$

and, multiplying by $\mathbf{S}$,

$$\mathbf{P}\mathbf{S} = \mathbf{S}\mathbf{D}$$

and, postmultiplying by $\mathbf{S}^{-1}$,

$$\mathbf{P} = \mathbf{S}\mathbf{D}\mathbf{S}^{-1}.$$

So

$$\begin{aligned} \mathbf{P}^2 &= \mathbf{S}\mathbf{D}\mathbf{S}^{-1}\mathbf{S}\mathbf{D}\mathbf{S}^{-1} = \mathbf{S}\mathbf{D}^2\mathbf{S}^{-1} \\ &\vdots \\ \mathbf{P}^n &= \mathbf{S}\mathbf{D}^n\mathbf{S}^{-1}. \end{aligned}$$

Now, if $\mathbf{D}$ is a diagonal matrix, $\mathbf{D}^2$ is just a diagonal matrix with the squares of the elements of $\mathbf{D}$ in the corresponding positions, so that $\mathbf{D}^n$ just has the nth power of the eigenvalues on the main diagonal. Hence a necessary and sufficient condition for the stability of this process, if the roots are all real, is that $1 \geqslant \lambda_i \geqslant -1$, $i = 1, 2, \ldots, n$, since then higher and higher powers become smaller and smaller. (If some complex roots occur then we say that 'all roots must lie inside the unit circle', a statement that will be explained more fully in Section 14.3, but it means that if $\lambda = x + \mathrm{i}y$ then $\sqrt{(x^2+y^2)}$ must be less than unity.) In fact, if $\mathbf{P}$ is a matrix of probabilities, that is, with all columns summing to 1, it can be shown that the root with largest modulus will actually equal one, so that $\mathbf{P}^n$ will certainly tend to a stable matrix if all other roots have modulus *strictly* less than 1 (lie strictly within the unit circle), since then $\mathbf{D}^n$ will tend to a matrix of zeros with one isolated 1 on the diagonal, and

$$x^n = \mathbf{S}\mathbf{D}^n\mathbf{S}^{-1}x^0$$

will tend to a stable vector.

(*b*) In Section 4.3 we derived the equation for the open Leontief model:

$$x = \mathbf{A}x + f$$

and in Section 7.1 we wrote its solution in the form

$$x = (\mathbf{I} - \mathbf{A})^{-1}f.$$

The solution can be rewritten in a different form, however, as follows. Note that x appears on both sides of the Leontief equation, so substituting for x in the right-hand side with x as defined by the original equation,

$$\begin{aligned} x &= \mathbf{A}(\mathbf{A}x + f) + f \\ &= \mathbf{A}^2x + \mathbf{A}f + f. \end{aligned}$$

Repeating,

$$\begin{aligned} x &= \mathbf{A}^2(\mathbf{A}x + f) + \mathbf{A}f + f \\ &= \mathbf{A}^3x + \mathbf{A}^2f + \mathbf{A}f + f. \end{aligned}$$

Repeating n times,

$$x = [\mathbf{I} + \mathbf{A} + \mathbf{A}^2 + \mathbf{A}^3 + \ldots + \mathbf{A}^n]\, f + \mathbf{A}^{n+1}x.$$

Now, if $\mathbf{A}^{n+1}$ tends to the zero matrix as n becomes infinite, we have that

$$x = [\mathbf{I} + \mathbf{A} + \mathbf{A}^2 + \mathbf{A}^3 + \ldots]\, f$$

and, comparing this with the inverse form of the solution above, we see that

$$[\mathbf{I} - \mathbf{A}]^{-1} = [\mathbf{I} + \mathbf{A} + \mathbf{A}^2 + \mathbf{A}^3 + \ldots],$$

which is known as the *series expansion* of the inverse.

Comparing with the previous example we see that this will be valid *iff* all the eigenvalues of $\mathbf{A}$ are strictly less than 1 and strictly greater than -1 (lie within the unit circle if some are complex). If so, then we know that the Leontief problem has a meaningful solution. That is, x has every element nonnegative since $\mathbf{A}$, $\mathbf{A}^2, \ldots$ are all matrices of positive elements. In this case we say that the economy is 'productive'. In an unproductive economy, it would not be possible to produce positive outputs of some goods. The reader might like to reconsider Problem 2.3.3 in the light of this analysis.

The problem for the *closed* Leontief model simply amounts to determining whether $\mathbf{A}$ has an eigenvalue of unity and, if so, the feasible outputs are given by the corresponding eigenvectors.

9.5* Difference equations

Difference equations are used in many economic models. Time is divided up into units of equal length (for example, weeks or years) and the value of a variable in one period is assumed to be determined by, amongst other things, its value in the previous period, the one before that and so on. This may be because decisions are taken only at discrete intervals, because data is available only at certain times, or for various other reasons. What follows is only a very elementary survey, but many good references exist, an outstanding one being Goldberg (1958).

(*a*) *Linear, homogeneous, first-order difference equations*

These are equations of the type

$$z(t) = \alpha z(t-1)$$

or equivalently

$$z(t+1) = \alpha z(t)$$

where α is a constant. It is 'homogeneous' because no other term appears, 'first order' because only t and $t-1$ appear and linear because no terms like $z(t).z(t-1)$ or $\{z(t)\}^2$ occur. Here, t is an index identifying the period in question, $t-1$ is the previous period, and so on. In many texts, t will appear as a subscript: z_t.

If we know the situation at some point in time we can predict what will happen at the next point. So, given $z(0)$, an *initial position* or starting point, we can determine $z(1)$ because it is simply $\alpha z(0)$. Hence,

$$\begin{aligned} z(1) &= \alpha z(0) \\ z(2) &= \alpha z(1) = \alpha^2 z(0) \\ &\vdots \\ z(t) &= \alpha^t z(0). \end{aligned}$$

This is the solution to the equation. It specifies how z behaves as time goes on. If:

(1) $\alpha > +1$, then z will grow continually since α^t will become larger as $t \to \infty$. This can be graphed as in Figure 9.1 and we see that $z(t)$ grows explosively.
(2) $1 > \alpha > 0$, then $z(t)$ will decline towards zero (see Figure 9.2).
(3) $-1 < \alpha < 0$, then $z(t)$ will exhibit a declining ('damped') *cycle*. This is a stable cycle, with a period (the time for a complete cycle) of two time periods (see Figure 9.3).

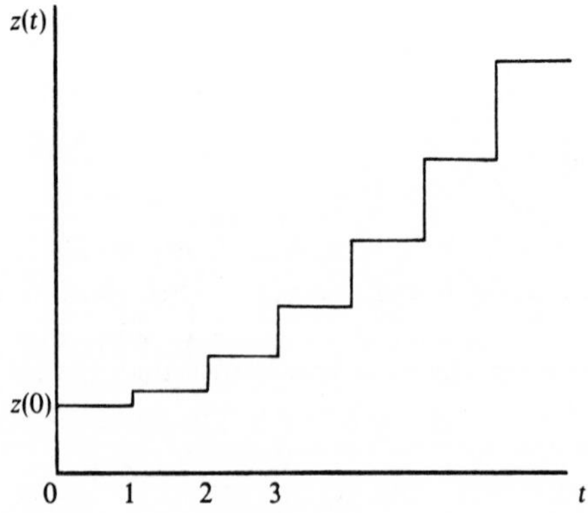

Figure 9.1

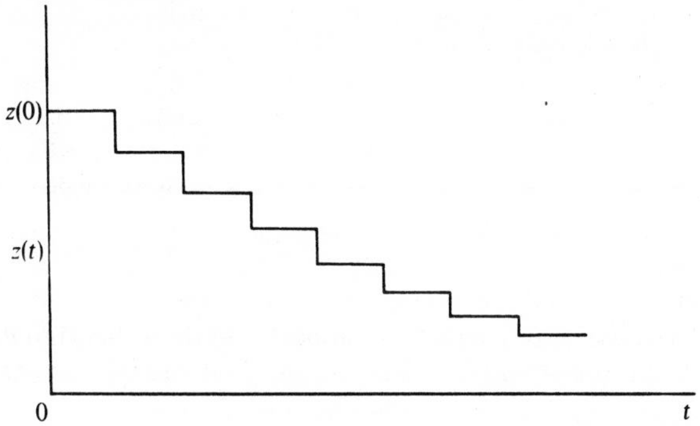

Figure 9.2

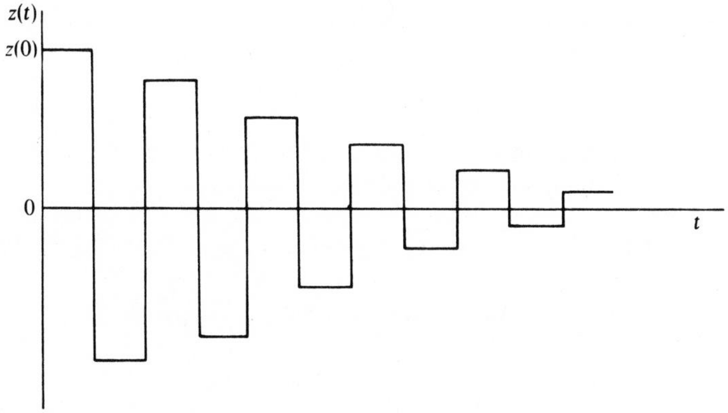

Figure 9.3

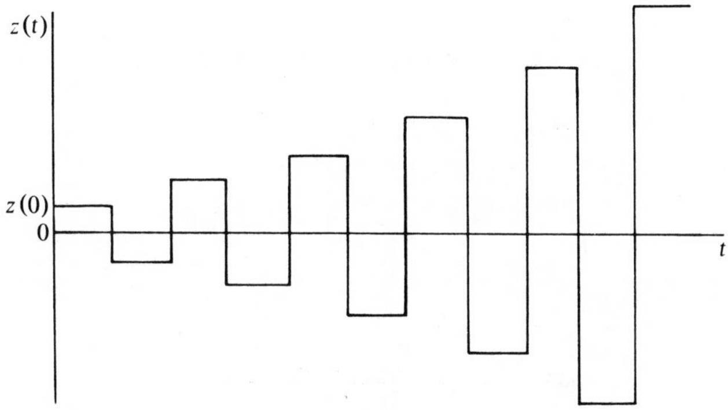

Figure 9.4

(4) $\alpha < -1$, then we have increasing cycles with a period of two time periods (see Figure 9.4).

Notice that in cases (2) and (3) the $z(t)$ settles towards the value $z=0$; and, whatever initial value is specified, $z(t)$ will eventually become 'close' to the value $z=0$. Now, the value $z^*=0$ is known as an *equilibrium point* because, in *all four* cases, if $z=0$ is specified as an initial value then $z(t)$ will always stay at zero. However, in cases (1) and (4), if $z(0)$ is only very slightly different from z^* then $z(t)$ will never return to it, but will move away at an ever-increasing rate, and we say that the equilibrium point is *unstable*. On the other hand, in cases (2) and (3) $z(t)$ gets closer to z^* as time progresses, no matter how far away $z(0)$ is, and we say that the equilibrium is *globally stable*. The word 'globally' is included because it is easy to see that there may be situations in more complicated models where an equilibrium is stable if the initial point is close to it, but unstable if the initial point is a long way away, in which case we can only claim *local* stability.

(*b*) The linear, *non*homogeneous, first-order equation can sometimes be dealt with by transforming it into a homogeneous equation and then using the same solution technique. This is so if it has the form

$$y(t) = \alpha y(t-1) + b$$

where b is a constant. In the more general case b may be a function of time, and then special techniques are required.

As before, let y^* be the equilibrium value of y; that is, a value such that if y were fixed at y^* then it would stay there for ever more. In other words, such that

$$y(t-1) = y^* \quad \text{and} \quad y(t) = y^* \;\; \forall t.$$

Hence

$$y^* = \alpha y^* + b$$

or

$$y^* = \frac{b}{1-\alpha} (\alpha \neq 1).$$

Now let $z(t) = y(t) - y^*$, the deviation of y from y^*. Then

$$y(t) = z(t) + y^*$$

and, substituting in the original equation,

$$z(t) + y^* = \alpha\{z(t-1) + y^*\} + b$$

or

$$z(t) = \alpha z(t-1),$$

which is linear homogeneous with solution

$$z(t) = \alpha^t z(0).$$

Hence, the solution for $y(t)$ is given by

$$\begin{aligned} y(t) &= z(t) + y^* \\ &= \alpha^t\{y(0) - y^*\} + y^* \\ &= \alpha^t y(0) + (1 + \alpha^t)\frac{b}{(1-\alpha)}. \end{aligned}$$

Much the same stability analysis as in case (*a*) now applies, since the critical term is again α^t, but the equilibrium is now $b/(1-\alpha)$ rather than zero as it was before.

We now apply this analysis to the *cobweb* model of fluctuation in prices–particularly agricultural prices such as those of wheat. We suppose that farmers plan to supply an amount of wheat which is directly proportional to the ruling price, but that it takes a year to grow. The demand for wheat is assumed to be a linear function of the current price,

$$D(t) = a_1 p(t) + b_1 \quad a_1 < 0, b_1 > 0$$

$$S(t) = a_2 p(t-1) \quad a_2 > 0.$$

The market clearing price must be such that

$$D(t) = S(t) \quad \forall t$$

that is

$$a_1 p(t) + b_1 = a_2 p(t-1).$$

Rewriting,

$$p(t) = \left(\frac{a_2}{a_1}\right) p(t-1) - \left(\frac{b_1}{b_2}\right)$$

which is of the standard form (*b*) above, with solution

$$p(t) = \left(\frac{a_2}{a_1}\right)^t \{p(0) - p^*\} + p^*$$

where $p^* = p(t) = p(t-1)$

or

$$p^* = \frac{b_1}{(a_2 - a_1)},$$

which is the point where demand and supply curves intersect; the *static* equilibrium. Remember that the demand curve slopes downwards, $a_1 < 0$ and the supply curve slopes upwards $a_2 > 0$. So the ratio (a_2/a_1) is negative, giving oscillating prices which will be stable if $0 > a_2/a_1 > -1$, or if $a_2 > |a_1|$. In other words, prices will settle to an equilibrium level once disturbed, if consumers are more responsive to price changes than are farmers. You should interpret this condition and carry out the graphical analysis (which gives the model its name). It will be found in many elementary texts. Smith (1982) is a good example.

We now come to the solution of a *simultaneous system* of two of these equations. The particular example chosen here is an extension of the cobweb model, and is a model of two interdependent markets (the so-called *Corn–hog* model). This model, like the simple corn model, assumes that farmers have no foresight or expectations (or else they might try to act countercyclically), and that there is no government intervention to try to stabilize prices.

We are given the price of corn $p_c(0)$ and the price of hogs $p_h(0)$ at time 0, and we assume that

$$D_c(t) = a_{11}p_c(t) + b_1 \tag{1}$$

$$S_c(t) = a_{21}p_c(t-1) + b_2 \tag{2}$$

$$D_h(t) = a_{31}p_h(t) + b_3 \tag{3}$$

$$S_h(t) = a_{41}p_h(t-1) + a_{42}p_c(t-1) + b_4 \tag{4}$$

Equations 1 and 2 are very similar to the model already discussed. Equations 3 and 4, representing the market for hogs are again much the same, except that the supply of hogs is taken to depend on the price of corn in the previous period since it is used as fodder, as well as on the previous price of hogs.

Now, $D_c = S_c$ and $D_h = S_h$ for equilibrium, so we may rewrite thus:

$$a_{11}p_c(t) = a_{21}p_c(t-1) + b_2 - b_1$$

$$a_{31}p_h(t) = a_{41}p_h(t-1) + a_{42}p_c(t-1) + b_4 - b_3$$

Now, these equations may be written using a 2×2 matrix:

$$\begin{bmatrix} p_c(t) \\ \\ p_h(t) \end{bmatrix} = \begin{bmatrix} \dfrac{a_{21}}{a_{11}} & 0 \\ \\ \dfrac{a_{42}}{a_{31}} & \dfrac{a_{41}}{a_{31}} \end{bmatrix} \begin{bmatrix} p_c(t-1) \\ \\ p_h(t-1) \end{bmatrix} + \begin{bmatrix} \dfrac{b_2 - b_1}{a_{11}} \\ \\ \dfrac{b_4 - b_3}{a_{31}} \end{bmatrix}.$$

The general form of this is

$$\boldsymbol{p}(t) = \mathbf{A}\boldsymbol{p}(t-1) + \boldsymbol{b}$$

where $\boldsymbol{p}(t)$ and $\boldsymbol{b}$ are column vectors and $\mathbf{A}$ is a matrix. The following theory, which we shall use to solve this system, applies equally to systems of any size.

(*c*) *Systems of simultaneous*, nonhomogeneous, linear, first-order difference equations of the general form

$$y(t) = \mathbf{A}y(t-1) + \boldsymbol{b}.$$

Once again we solve for the equilibrium, y^*;

$$y^* = \mathbf{A}y^* + b$$

$$y^* = [\mathbf{I} - \mathbf{A}]^{-1}b.$$

Let

$$z(t) = y(t) - y^*$$

or

$$y(t) = z(t) + y^*.$$

Then

$$z(t) + y^* = \mathbf{A}\{z(t-1) + y^*\} + b$$

or

$$z(t) = \mathbf{A}z(t-1)$$

which is the homogeneous form. To solve this we make a further transformation to diagonalize $\mathbf{A}$. Let

$$w(t) = \mathbf{Q}^{-1}z(t)$$

or

$$z(t) = \mathbf{Q}w(t)$$

where $\mathbf{Q}$ is the matrix of eigenvectors of $\mathbf{A}$. Then

$$\mathbf{Q}^{-1}z(t) = \mathbf{Q}^{-1}\mathbf{A}z(t-1)$$

or transforming from z to w,

$$w(t) = \mathbf{Q}^{-1}\mathbf{A}\mathbf{Q}w(t-1).$$

Now, assuming $\mathbf{Q}^{-1}\mathbf{A}\mathbf{Q}$ to be of pure diagonal form, the solution for each of the ws is very simple, because each element, $w_i(t)$ depends only on $w_i(t-1)$ and not on any $w_j(t-1), j \neq i$. In fact

$$w_i(t) = \lambda_i w_i(t-1)$$

and from Section 9.5(a) above

$$w_i(t) = \lambda_i^t w_i(0).$$

Performing the reverse transformation to get back to the zs,

$$z(t) = \mathbf{Q}w(t)$$

or

$$z_i(t) = x_{i1}\lambda_1^t w_1(0) + x_{i2}\lambda_2^t w_2(0) + \ldots + x_{in}\lambda_n^t w_n(0)$$

$$= \sum_{j=1}^{n} x_{ij}\lambda_j^t w_j(0), \quad i = 1, 2, \ldots, n$$

where x_{ij} is the ith element of the jth eigenvector. Hence we see that $z_i(t)$ is a linear combination of the tth powers of the eigenvalues. Transforming back to the original ys,

$$y(t) = z(t) + y^*$$

or

$$y_i(t) = x_{i1}w_1(0)\lambda_1^t + x_{i2}w_2(0)\lambda_2^t + \ldots + x_{in}w_n(0)\lambda_n^t + y_i^*, \quad i = 1, 2, \ldots, n$$

which could be rewritten,

$$y_i(t) = k_{i0} + k_{i1}\lambda_1^t + k_{i2}\lambda_2^t + \ldots + k_{in}\lambda_n^t$$

where the k_{ij} are constants, which in practice are calculated directly from the initial values of the ys.

It should now be clear that the development over time of the ys will depend entirely upon the eigenvalues. In particular, assuming real roots, the system will be stable if and only if *every* eigenvalue is less than unity in absolute value. If complex roots occur, then they must all lie within the unit circle. The possibility of complex roots is particularly interesting here because it is shown in Section 14.3 that, if they occur, the solution will exhibit cycles which need not be restricted to a period of two time periods; the period might be ten, twenty or one hundred years, depending on the values of the parameters. For this reason models of this type have been used to provide interesting explanations of trade cycles, inventory cycles and various other periodic phenomena.

The very close formal similarity between the theories of systems of difference equations, of transition matrices and Leontief inverses should be obvious.

To return to our corn-hog model, the two eigenvalues are simply $\lambda_1 = a_{21}/a_{11}$ and $\lambda_2 = a_{41}/a_{31}$ since then $[\mathbf{A} - \lambda\mathbf{I}]$ has respectively a row or a column of zeros. Both prices are stable *iff*

$$\max\left(\left|\frac{a_{21}}{a_{11}}\right|, \left|\frac{a_{41}}{a_{32}}\right|\right) < 1$$

in other words, *iff* both markets are independently stable.

For completeness, we show how second and higher-order equations can be handled.

(d) Linear, homogeneous, *second*- (and higher)-order difference equations. These have the general form

$$z(t) + bz(t-1) + cz(t-2) = 0$$

and can be reduced to a system of first-order equations by the following device. Let

$$w(t) = z(t-1),$$
$$w(t-1) = z(t-2).$$

Then we have the system

$$z(t) = -bz(t-1) - cw(t-1)$$
$$w(t) = z(t-1)$$

or, in matrix notation,

$$\begin{bmatrix} z(t) \\ w(t) \end{bmatrix} = \begin{bmatrix} -b & -c \\ 1 & 0 \end{bmatrix} \begin{bmatrix} z(t-1) \\ w(t-1) \end{bmatrix}.$$

This may now be solved using the techniques of (*c*) above. The eigenvalues are the solutions to the characteristic equation,

$$(-b-\lambda)(-\lambda) + c = 0$$

or

$$\lambda^2 + b\lambda + c = 0.$$

(In the theory of differential and difference equations this is known as the *auxiliary equation* (see Section 19.5). Note the correspondence between its coefficients and those of the original equation.) the solution is then

$$z(t) = k_1\lambda_1^t + k_2\lambda_2^t$$

where k_1 and k_2 are found using given values of $z(0)$ and $z(1)$. Higher-order systems can be solved by using the same trick. The nonhomogeneous system is transformed into a homogeneous one by the same technique as before.

Note the equivalence between a *second*-order difference equation and a system of *two* first-order simultaneous difference equations. This is a general equivalence, so that an *n*th order difference equation can be solved by transforming it to a system of *n* first-order simultaneous difference equations, and vice versa.

It should be emphasised that if the term making these equations nonhomogeneous is not a simple constant, then some extra technique will be necessary to obtain a complete solution, although the solution to the homogeneous equations will still have to be found, and stability is likely to depend on the stability of the solution to this.

The program given earlier in this chapter illustrates (line 180 should now be deleted). The value of x for each t is calculated from the two previous values in line 310. In other words the program carries out a direct simulation rather than relying on a known solution. The result is graphed in lines 330 to 460 so that you can see the nature of the behaviour implied by the equation you have specified. The constant in line 410 determines the width of the graph across the page. You may find it necessary to alter this value to suit your particular machine.

By setting $A(1, 2) = 0$ (that is $c = 0$) you will have the first-order equation discussed in section 9.5(*a*) with $\alpha = -A(1, 1)$, that is, $\alpha = -b$. By taking a nonzero value for $A(1, 2)$ you will have the second-order homogeneous system discussed in this section. As examples try plotting 400 points with

$A(1,1)=0.99$ and $A(1,2)=0$
$A(1,1)=-0.99$ and $A(1,2)=0$
$A(1,1)=1.8$ and $A(1,2)=-0.98$
$A(1,1)=1.8$ and $A(1,2)=-1.02$
$A(1,1)=-1.8$ and $A(1,2)=-0.98$.

By trying other values you will discover other modes of behaviour. The analysis of all these modes is given in Section 14.3. You could also experiment with nonhomogeneous equations by adding a constant or some function of time to the right-hand side of line 310: for instance 0.5*SIN(T).

9.6 Relationship between eigenvalues and determinants

As a final application of diagonalization, we prove the following theorem.

Theorem 9.6 The determinant of a symmetric matrix is equal to the product of all its eigenvalues.

Proof. We have that

$$\mathbf{A} = \mathbf{Q}\Lambda\mathbf{Q}^{-1}$$

where Λ is the diagonal matrix of eigenvalues. Taking determinants

$$\begin{aligned}|\mathbf{A}| &= |\mathbf{Q}\Lambda\mathbf{Q}^{-1}| \\ &= |\mathbf{Q}||\Lambda||\mathbf{Q}^{-1}|.\end{aligned}$$

But

$$|\mathbf{Q}^{-1}| = \frac{1}{|\mathbf{Q}|},$$

and so

$$|\mathbf{A}| = |\Lambda| = \lambda_1 . \lambda_2 . \lambda_3 \ldots \lambda_n \quad \blacksquare$$

In proving this theorem we have used two minor results which the reader might like to confirm for himself; that $|\mathbf{AB}| = |\mathbf{A}||\mathbf{B}|$ and that $|\mathbf{A}^{-1}| = 1/|\mathbf{A}|$.

9.7 Problems

1. Calculate the eigenvalues and a set of eigenvectors of the matrix

$$\mathbf{A} = \begin{bmatrix} 1 & 1 & 5 \\ 4 & 1 & 3 \\ 0 & 0 & 1 \end{bmatrix}.$$

(Hint: Expand the characteristic determinant along the last row.)

If the eigenvalues are diagonal elements of Λ, and $\mathbf{D}$ is a matrix whose columns are the corresponding eigenvectors, $|\mathbf{D}| \neq 0$, verify that $\Lambda = \mathbf{D}^{-1}\mathbf{A}\mathbf{D}$ or, more easily, $\mathbf{D}\Lambda = \mathbf{A}\mathbf{D}$.

2. Repeat question 1 for the matrix

$$\mathbf{B} = \begin{bmatrix} 5 & 0 & 0 \\ 0 & 1 & -2 \\ -3 & 1 & 2 \end{bmatrix}.$$

3. Find the eigenvalues of the matrices,

(*a*) $\begin{bmatrix} -1 & -2 & 0 \\ 3 & 4 & 0 \\ 3 & 1 & -1 \end{bmatrix}$ (*b*) $\begin{bmatrix} 2 & 9 & 2 \\ 0 & 3 & 2 \\ 0 & 2 & 3 \end{bmatrix}$

and an eigenvector associated with the largest eigenvalue in each case. Normalize so that it has unit length (leave the square roots in your answers).

10 Quadratic forms

10.1 Introduction

Our last topic in linear algebra is not included for its intrinsic interest, or for direct application, but because it is important in the formulation of tests for maxima and minima in the multivariate calculus chapters.

Let $\mathbf{A}$ be a 2×2 matrix and $\boldsymbol{x}$ be any two-element column vector. Then

$$\begin{aligned}\boldsymbol{x}'\mathbf{A}\boldsymbol{x} &= a_{11}x_1^2 + a_{12}x_1x_2 + a_{21}x_2x_1 + a_{22}x_2^2\\ &= a_{11}x_1^2 + (a_{12} + a_{21})x_1x_2 + a_{22}x_2^2\end{aligned}$$

as can be verified by direct matrix multiplication.

An expression of this type is known as a *quadratic form* in $\boldsymbol{x}$. It is a *scalar* whose value depends upon the particular vector $\boldsymbol{x}$ chosen. For a general $n \times n$ matrix,

$$F(\boldsymbol{x}) = \boldsymbol{x}'\mathbf{A}\boldsymbol{x} = \sum_{i=1}^{n}\sum_{j=1}^{n} a_{ij}x_ix_j.$$

The matrix $\mathbf{A}$ is known as the matrix of the quadratic form. This will always be assumed to be symmetric, since if $a_{ij} \neq a_{ji}$ a new, symmetric matrix can be defined, which will always yield the same value of $F(\boldsymbol{x})$, by taking $\tilde{a}_{ij} = \tilde{a}_{ji} = \frac{1}{2}(a_{ij} + a_{ji})$. For example, in the 2×2 case above,

$$\begin{aligned}F(\boldsymbol{x}) &= a_{11}x_1^2 + (a_{12} + a_{21})x_1x_2 + a_{22}x_2^2\\ &= a_{11}x_1^2 + 2\,.\tfrac{1}{2}(a_{12} + a_{21})x_1x_2 + a_{22}x_2^2\\ &= a_{11}x_1^2 + 2\tilde{a}_{12}x_1x_2 + a_{22}x_2^2\end{aligned}$$

which is the quadratic form with symmetric matrix

$$\begin{bmatrix} a_{11} & \tilde{a}_{12} \\ \tilde{a}_{12} & a_{22} \end{bmatrix}.$$

10.2 Definite matrices

D10.1 A symmetric matrix $\mathbf{A}$ is said to be *positive definite* if $x'\mathbf{A}x > 0$ for all $x \neq \mathbf{0}$.

In this definition, notice that the quadratic form must be strictly positive for *every possible*, nonzero vector x. Do not confuse the concepts of a positive matrix, a matrix with all elements positive, and a positive definite matrix. For example, if

$$\mathbf{A} = \begin{bmatrix} 1 & -1 & 0 \\ -1 & 3 & 1 \\ 0 & 1 & 1 \end{bmatrix}$$

then

$$\begin{aligned} x'\mathbf{A}x &= x_1^2 - 2x_1x_2 + 3x_2^2 + 2x_2x_3 + x_3^2 \\ &= (x_1 - x_2)^2 + (x_2 + x_3)^2 + x_2^2 \\ &> 0 \\ &\forall\, (x_1, x_2, x_3)' \neq (0, 0, 0)' \end{aligned}$$

so that $\mathbf{A}$ is positive definite.

Similarly,

D10.2 $\mathbf{A}$ is positive semidefinite if $x'\mathbf{A}x \geqslant 0$, $\forall x$.

D10.3 $\mathbf{A}$ is negative semidefinite if $x'\mathbf{A}x \leqslant 0$, $\forall x$.

D10.4 $\mathbf{A}$ is negative definite if $x'\mathbf{A}x < 0$, $\forall x \neq \mathbf{0}$.

If a matrix is not definite then it is said to be *indefinite.*

Since, in applying these definitions one has to show that the inequality holds for all possible vectors x they are, in general, not very easy to use. Hence, we now state two alternative criteria.

Theorem 10.1 A symmetric matrix is $\left\{\begin{matrix} \text{positive (semi)} \\ \text{negative (semi)} \end{matrix}\right\}$ definite *iff* all its eigenvalues are $\left\{\begin{matrix} >0 & (\geqslant 0) \\ <0 & (\leqslant 0) \end{matrix}\right\}$.

Proof. Let x be an arbitrary vector and let $x = \mathbf{Q}y$. Then

$$\begin{aligned} x'\mathbf{A}x &= y'\mathbf{Q}'\mathbf{A}\mathbf{Q}y \\ &= y'\Lambda y \\ &= \sum_{i=1}^{n} \lambda_i y_i^2 \end{aligned}$$

where Λ is the diagonalized form of $\mathbf{A}$. This proves the theorem, since $x'\mathbf{A}x > 0$ *iff* $\lambda_i > 0$, $\forall i$, (and similarly for the other cases). If, say $\lambda_1 < 0$, then we could choose x such that $y_1 = 1, y_2 = 0, \ldots, y_n = 0$, yielding

$$x'\mathbf{A}x = \lambda_1 < 0$$

violating the definition of positive definiteness. ∎

The second alternative criterion is given in the following theorem.

Theorem 10.2 $\mathbf{A} = (a_{ij})$ is positive definite *iff*

(*a*) $a_{11} > 0$

(*b*) $\begin{vmatrix} a_{11} & a_{12} \\ a_{21} & a_{22} \end{vmatrix} > 0$

(*c*) $\begin{vmatrix} a_{11} & a_{12} & a_{13} \\ a_{21} & a_{22} & a_{23} \\ a_{31} & a_{32} & a_{33} \end{vmatrix} > 0,$

⋮

(*n*) $|\mathbf{A}| > 0$.

For semidefiniteness, some zero determinants are allowed. $\mathbf{A}$ is negative definite *iff*

(*a*) $a_{11} < 0$

(*b*) $\begin{vmatrix} a_{11} & a_{12} \\ a_{21} & a_{22} \end{vmatrix} > 0$

(*c*) $\begin{vmatrix} a_{11} \ldots a_{13} \\ a_{21} \ldots a_{23} \\ a_{31} \ldots a_{33} \end{vmatrix} < 0$

⋮

(*n*) $|\mathbf{A}|$ has the same sign as $(-1)^n$; so that the principal minors alternate in sign starting negative.

It would be a useful exercise to apply these criterion to the above example. The reader might also think about the relationship between these last two criteria. Theorem 10.2 can in fact be proved very easily using Theorem 10.1, together with the fact that the determinant of a symmetric matrix (or submatrix) is equal to the product of its eigenvalues (Theorem 9.4).

10.3 Problems

1. Consider the determinantal conditions for positive definiteness for

(*a*)

$$\mathbf{A} = \begin{bmatrix} 1 & -1 & -2 \\ -1 & 2 & 3 \\ -2 & 3 & 10 \end{bmatrix}$$

(*b*)

$$\mathbf{A} = \begin{bmatrix} 1 & -1 & -1 \\ -1 & 1 & 1 \\ -1 & 1 & -3 \end{bmatrix}.$$

2. Consider the definiteness of the following matrices from first principles:

(*a*) $\mathbf{A} = \begin{bmatrix} 1 & 1 \\ 1 & 1 \end{bmatrix}$

(*b*) $\mathbf{A} = \begin{bmatrix} 1 & 2 \\ 2 & 1 \end{bmatrix}$

(*c*) $\mathbf{A} = \begin{bmatrix} 1 & 2 \\ 2 & 5 \end{bmatrix}.$

Check your results by considering the eigenvalues of the matrices.

3. Test the following matrix for definiteness using two different methods:

$$\begin{bmatrix} 1 & -1 & 0 \\ -1 & 3 & 1 \\ 0 & 1 & 1 \end{bmatrix}.$$

4. Show that a matrix $\mathbf{A}$ is positive (semi)definite if and only if $-\mathbf{A}$ is negative (semi)definite.

11 Elementary analysis; sets

11.1 Introduction

We begin with a few words on the theory of sets. We shall not make extensive use of this theory, but it is interesting because of the fact that the whole of mathematics uses it as a foundation. It is equivalent to the theory of formal logic. It would be useful for the interested reader to study this topic more fully in one of the Bibliography given at the end of the book.

11.2* Sets

D11.1 A *set* is a collection of definite and well-distinguished objects, which are called *elements.*

Observe that this is really a tautologous definition: a set is a collection, and a collection is a set. But any dictionary must either be circular or incomplete, and in setting up a formal theory, one has to start somewhere.

Although a set can be a set of anything, we shall be discussing sets of points in Euclidean spaces of various dimension.

Particular sets can be defined in two ways: by enumeration and by a relation:

Enumeration: $S = \{\text{list}\}$; for example, $S = \{1, 2, 3, 4\}$.
By a relation; for example: $S = \{x \mid x^2 < 1\}$.

These are examples of sets of points in E^1. The second statement is to be read: 'S is a set of numbers, denoted by x, such that $x^2 < 1$.'

D11.2 The *empty set*, denoted by $\emptyset$, is a set with no elements. For example,

$$\emptyset = \{x \mid x^2 < 0, x \text{ real}\}$$

$$\emptyset = \{x \mid x < 1 \text{ and } x > 2\}.$$

Be careful not to confuse $\emptyset$ and $\{0\}$.

D11.3 Two sets S and T are *equal iff* S and T have the same elements, in which case we write $S = T$.

D11.4 S is a *subset* of T if $x \in S \Rightarrow x \in T$, in which case we write $S \subseteq T$. ($\in$ means 'is an element of'.)

For example,

$$\{x \mid x^2 < \tfrac{1}{2}\} \subseteq \{x \mid x^2 < 1\}.$$

It is easily shown that $S = T$ *if* $S \subseteq T$ and $T \subseteq S$. Note that any set is a subset of itself, but if $S \subseteq T$, $S \neq T$ and $S \neq \emptyset$, we say that S is a *proper* subset of T.

D11.5 Let $S \cup T$ be the *union* of S and T. Then

$$S \cup T = \{x \mid x \in S \quad \text{or} \quad x \in T, \text{or both}\}.$$

Let $S \cap T$ be the *intersection* of S and T. Then

$$S \cap T = \{x \mid x \in S \quad \text{and} \quad x \in T\}.$$

The operations of taking unions and intersections correspond to the logical 'or' and 'and' operations.

We can illustrate the union and intersection in a *Venn* diagram (Figure 11.1) by taking shaded regions in E^2 as the sets of S and T. $S \cup T$ is the total shaded area. $S \cap T$ is the cross-hatched area.

If $S \cap T = \emptyset$ then we say that S and T are *disjoint* sets.

D11.6 $T \backslash S$, 'T without S' is given by

$$T \backslash S = \{x \mid x \in T \quad \text{and} \quad x \notin S\}.$$

The shaded area in Figure 11.2 is the *complement of S relative to T*.

The following is an example of an important set in E^2.

$$N = \{(x_1, x_2) \mid \sqrt{(x_1^2 + x_2^2)} < 1\}. \tag{1}$$

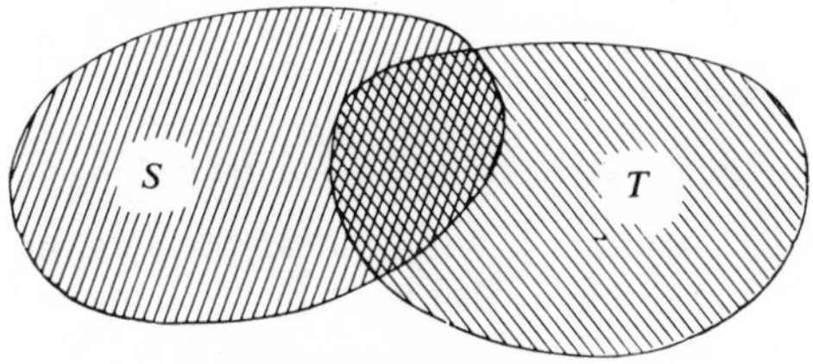

Figure 11.1

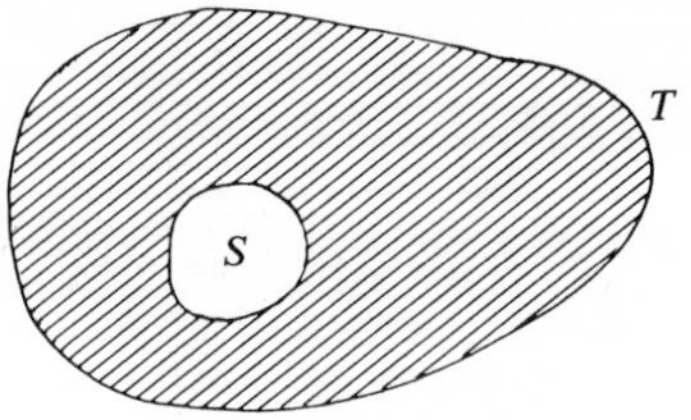

Figure 11.2

The analogous set in E^n would take the form:

$$N = \left\{ (x_1, \ldots, x_n) \,\middle|\, \sqrt{\left(\sum_{i=1}^{n} x_i^2 \right)} < 1 \right\} \tag{2}$$

(1) is a disc of radius 1, centre the origin. But it does not contain its 'boundary' points. Similarly (2) is a 'hypersphere' in E^n. This set has 'boundary' points on the circle of radius 1, centre the origin, but the boundary is not included in the set. This means the set is *open*–however close to the edge you are, you can always get closer. There is no point in the set 'farthest' from the origin along a given radius because the boundary is not contained in the set. By generalizing the radius and centre we have

D11.7 An *epsilon neighbourhood* of a point $\boldsymbol{p} \in E^n$ denoted by $N(\boldsymbol{p}, \epsilon)$, where $\epsilon > 0$, is given by

$$N(\boldsymbol{p}, \epsilon) = \{\boldsymbol{x} \mid \|\boldsymbol{x} - \boldsymbol{p}\| < \epsilon\}.$$

An alternative formulation is

$$\{\boldsymbol{x} \mid \sqrt{[\Sigma(x_i - p_i)^2]} < \epsilon\}.$$

This set is a sphere (or, in E^2, a disc) of radius ϵ, about the point $\boldsymbol{p}$. You will remember from Section 3.6 that $\|\boldsymbol{x} - \boldsymbol{p}\|$ is the Euclidean distance between $\boldsymbol{x}$ and $\boldsymbol{p}$, so that $N(\boldsymbol{p}, \epsilon)$ is a set of points less than ϵ away from $\boldsymbol{p}$.

D11.8 $\boldsymbol{x}$ is a *boundary point* of a set S if *every* neighbourhood of $\boldsymbol{x}$ contains at least one point in S and one point not in S. Here, 'every' means 'no matter how small is ϵ'. The set of boundary points of S, the *boundary* of S, is often denoted by ∂S.

An alternative statement of D11.8 is:

$$\forall \epsilon > 0, \quad \exists \boldsymbol{y} \in N(\boldsymbol{x}, \epsilon) \text{ s.t. } \boldsymbol{y} \in S, \text{ and } \exists \boldsymbol{z} \in N(\boldsymbol{x}, \epsilon) \text{ s.t. } \boldsymbol{z} \notin S.$$

Those points in S, but not in the boundary of S are in the *interior* of S, denoted Int S (see Figure 11.3). That is,

$$\text{Int } S = \{\boldsymbol{x} \mid \boldsymbol{x} \in S, \boldsymbol{x} \notin \partial S\}$$

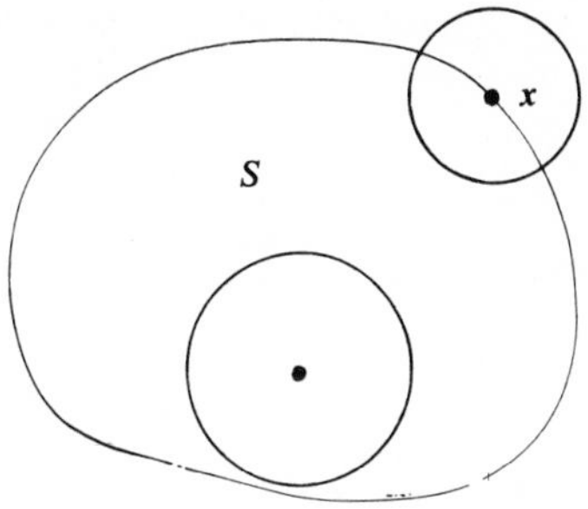

Figure 11.3

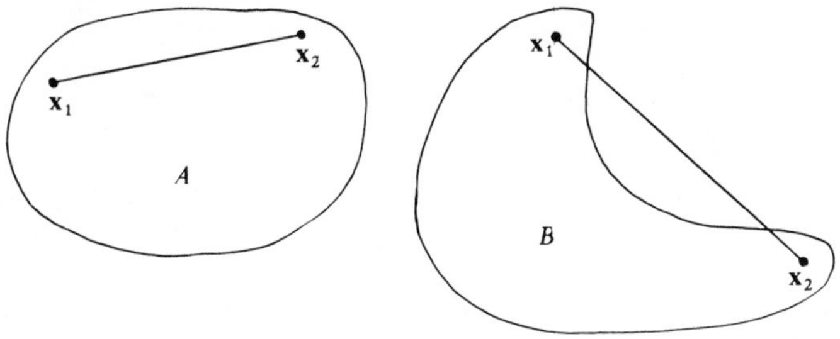

Figure 11.4

D11.9 A set is *closed* if it contains all its boundary points. Clearly a set may contain all, some, or none of its boundary points. Hence,

D11.10 A set is *open* if it is possible to find some neighbourhood about every one of its points, which is completely contained in the set. That is, S is open if

$$\forall \boldsymbol{x} \in S, \exists \epsilon > 0 \text{ s.t. } N(\boldsymbol{x}, \epsilon) \subseteq S.$$

In other words it does not contain any of its boundary points. For completeness we add

D11.11 A point $\boldsymbol{p}$ is a *point of accumulation* (or *limit point*) of S if *every* nbhd of $\boldsymbol{p}$ contains at least one point of S other than $\boldsymbol{p}$.

The interested reader should think out the relationship between these concepts. In texts you may find them defined in various different, but equivalent, ways.

11.3* Convexity

This topic is fairly simple and has become extremely important in economics and operations research. A set is said to be convex if the line joining *any* two points of the set lies entirely within the set. In Figure 11.4, for example, set

A is convex, but B is not. Now, by trying a few examples in E^2, you will easily see that if $\boldsymbol{x}_1$ and $\boldsymbol{x}_2$ are two vectors, then $\frac{1}{2}\boldsymbol{x}_1 + \frac{1}{2}\boldsymbol{x}_2$ is a point halfway along the line joining $\boldsymbol{x}_1$ to $\boldsymbol{x}_2$: if

$$\boldsymbol{x}_1 = \begin{bmatrix}1\\2\end{bmatrix}, \quad \boldsymbol{x}_2 = \begin{bmatrix}2\\1\end{bmatrix},$$

then

$$\tfrac{1}{2}\boldsymbol{x}_1 + \tfrac{1}{2}\boldsymbol{x}_2 = \begin{bmatrix}\frac{3}{2}\\\frac{3}{2}\end{bmatrix}.$$

Similarly, $\frac{1}{3}\boldsymbol{x}_1 + \frac{2}{3}\boldsymbol{x}_2$ is one-third of the way along the line, and $\alpha\boldsymbol{x}_1 + (1-\alpha)\boldsymbol{x}_2$, $0 \leqslant \alpha \leqslant 1$, is α of the way along the line. Such a point is called a *convex combination* of $\boldsymbol{x}_1$ and $\boldsymbol{x}_2$. Hence

D11.12 A set C is *convex* if for *every* pair of points $\boldsymbol{x}_1 \in C$ and $\boldsymbol{x}_2 \in C$, $\alpha\boldsymbol{x}_1 + (1-\alpha)\boldsymbol{x}_2$ is also an element of C, for every value of α, $0 \leqslant \alpha \leqslant 1$.

Some of the most important results which employ convexity are in the application of the so-called *separation theorem* which states that if S and T are two non-empty convex sets with non-intersecting interiors, it is possible to draw a straight line (or plane in many dimensions) which has all of S on one side and all of T on the other. If they are not convex then this may not be possible (see Figure 11.5).

As an application, recall that in Section 3.5 we mentioned the input and output vector $\boldsymbol{x}$ of a firm, with positive values for outputs and negative ones for inputs. If we now specify the set of technically possible choices for $\boldsymbol{x}$ as X then the profit-maximizing problem could be written as:

Maximize $\boldsymbol{p}'.\boldsymbol{x}$ with respect to $\boldsymbol{x}$, subject to the condition that $\boldsymbol{x} \in X$.

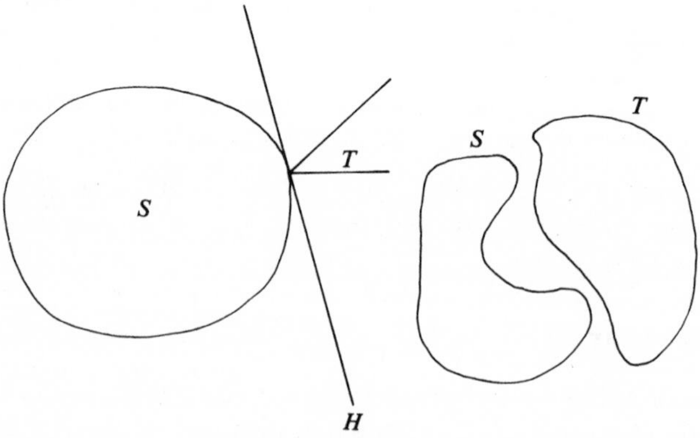

Figure 11.5

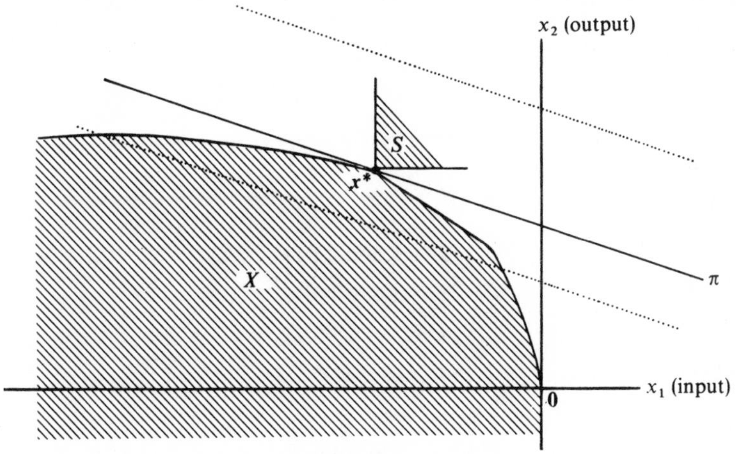

Figure 11.6

Then the assumption that X is convex corresponds to the assumption that the firm has diminishing returns to scale and diminishing returns to each factor. Such a set for a firm which can produce good 2, using good 1 as an input is sketched in Figure 11.6. (Cf. Problem 11.4.5 below.)

Notice that no efficient firm would produce in the interior of X, since then it could have more output for the same input. It can easily be shown that all points on a line like π yield the same profit, that the slope of π is determined by the given price vector $\boldsymbol{p}$, and that higher profits are earned on lines lying to the 'northeast'. Hence, the solution to the problem of finding an $\boldsymbol{x} \in X$ lying on the most northeasterly profit line is $\boldsymbol{x}^*$. Observe that at this point the line 'separates' the convex set X from the convex set S, of technically superior (more output for the same input) but unattainable points. Further, the line is tangential to X at $\boldsymbol{x}^*$. You will probably recognize that this is fairly typical of this type of analysis: indifference curves tangential to budget lines, tangential indifference curves on the Pareto optimal points of the 'Edgeworth box' and so on. The separation theorem applied here gives us a very important result from an economic point of view; that for any *efficient* production vector, $\boldsymbol{x}^*$ there exists a set of prices–that is a separating hyperplane–which would induce a profit-maximizing producer to choose that point. Hence a central planner could achieve any efficient set of inputs and outputs he wanted from the firm either by issuing an explicit directive or by quoting the appropriate set of prices to him and instructing him to maximize his profits. This result forms a vital part of some of the most fundamental results in economic theory. Note how it may break down if there are any 'dents' in the boundary of the production set; certain points may then only be attainable by direct instruction. Further, such points could never be a part of a competitive equilibrium–the market would 'fail' to produce them. 'Dents' correspond to local areas of increasing returns.

The fundamental role of convexity in optimization theory will become more apparent in Section 15.2.

11.4 Problems

1. Consider the sets:

$$A = \{x \mid x \geqslant 0\}$$
$$B = \{x \mid x \leqslant 0\}$$
$$C = \{x \mid x > 0\}$$
$$D = \{x \mid x < 0\}$$

What are the sets $A \cap B$, $C \cap D$, $A \cup B$, $C \cup D$, $B \cap (A \cup C)$, $(B \cap A) \cup C$, $A \cap B \cap C \cap D$?

2. If A and B are as specified below, find $A \cup B$ and $A \cap B$. In each case, $A \subseteq E^2, B \subseteq E^2$.

(*a*) $A = \{(x_1, x_2) \mid x_1 \geqslant 1\}$, $B = \{(x_1, x_2) \mid x_1 \leqslant 1\}$.
(*b*) $A = \{(x_1, x_2) \mid x_1 \geqslant 1\}$, $B = \{(x_1, x_2) \mid x_2 \geqslant 1\}$.
(*c*) $A = \{(x_1, x_2) \mid x_2 \geqslant x_1^2\}$, $B = \{(x_1, x_2) \mid x_2 = 0\}$.
(*d*) $A = N((0, 0), \epsilon_1)$ $B = N((0, 1), \epsilon_2)$

if (i) $\epsilon_1 = \epsilon_2 = \frac{1}{2}$,
(ii) $\epsilon_1 > \frac{1}{2}$, $\epsilon_2 > \frac{1}{2}$,
(iii) $\epsilon_1 \geqslant 1 - \epsilon_2$.

3. Find the boundary points of the following sets, and say whether they are open or closed;

(*a*) $\{x \mid 0 \leqslant x \leqslant 1\}$. (*b*) $\{x \mid 0 < x < 1\}$.
(*c*) $\{x \mid 0 < x \leqslant 1\}$. (*d*) $\{1, 2, 3, \ldots\}$.
(*e*) $N(\mathbf{0}, 1)$. (*f*) $\{1, \frac{1}{2}, \frac{1}{3}, \ldots, 1/n, \ldots\}$.

4. By using a suitable diagram convince yourself that

$$A \cap (B \cup C) = (A \cap B) \cup (A \cap C)$$

for any sets A, B and C. Now prove this analytically. (Note the analogy with $a \times (b + c) = (a \times b) + (a \times c)$ for real numbers.) Similarly show that

$$A \cup (A \cap B) = A = A \cap (A \cup B)$$

5*. A firm may either produce y_1 from y_2 or vice versa, and its production set is given by

$$Y = \{y_1, y_2 \mid (y_1 + 3)^2 + (y_2 + 4)^2 \leqslant 5^2\},$$

outputs being positive numbers, and inputs being negative. Sketch the set.

Are the following production plans (i) feasible; (ii) boundary points; (iii) 'efficient'?

(*a*) $y_1 = -2$, $y_2 = 1$. (*b*) $y_1 = 0$, $y_2 = 0$.

(*c*) $y_1 = -3$, $y_2 = -4$. (*d*) $y_1 = -3$, $y_2 = 1$.

(*e*) $y_1 = 2$, $y_2 = -4$. (*f*) $y_1 = 1$, $y_2 = -1$.

(*g*) $y_1 = 1$, $y_2 = -7$.

What is the economic significance of a point such as point (*g*)? If the price ratio $p_1/p_2 = \frac{1}{2}$, find the profit-maximizing production plan.

6. In E^2 consider the set

$$B = \{(x_1, x_2) | p_1x_1 + p_2x_2 = m;\ p_1 > 0, p_2 > 0\}.$$

What does this set look like? How does it depend upon the given values of m, p_1 and p_2?

Consider similarly

$$B' = \{(x_1, x_2) | p_1x_1 + p_2x_2 \leqslant m;\ p_1 > 0, p_2 > 0\}.$$

Can you give at least two economic interpretations of these sets?

7**. Show that the following sets are convex:

(*a*) The set B' in Problem 6.

(*b*) $\{x | \mathbf{A}x = b, \mathbf{A}(n \times n), \text{rank}(\mathbf{A}) < n\}$.

(*c*) The set Y in Problem 5.

8*. Prove that the intersection of two closed sets is a closed set, if it is nonempty.

12 Functions

12.1 Definitions

We have already alluded to the concept of a function on several occasions; it is fundamental in analysis.

D12.1 A *function* (*transformation*, *mapping*) is a rule (relation) which associates a *unique* element of a set R (the range) with *every* element of a set D (the domain).

The statement that 'f maps points in D into R' is often abbreviated to

$$f\colon D \to R$$

where, in the cases of interest to us,

$$R \subseteq E^m$$

$$D \subseteq E^n$$

and m and n are positive integers. In what follows we shall initially take both R and D to be subsets of E^1 and later the domain will be extended to subsets of E^n, to give respectively 'functions of a single variable' and 'functions of several variables'. In principle the specification of the domain and range of a function are important. However many functions are defined on all of (or most of) the space and so, in practice, domain and range are often left unspecified.

When $D \subseteq E^1$ and $R \subseteq E^1$ we can draw the *graph* of a function by marking the domain on the horizontal axis, the range on the vertical axis and plotting points with coordinates $(x, f(x))$, where $f(x)$ is the value of the function f at x.

As an example, take $D = E^1$, $R = \{x \mid x > 0\}$ and $f(x) = x^2$. This is a rule which says: 'To obtain $f(x)$ from x, multiply x by itself.' It has the graph shown in Figure 12.1.

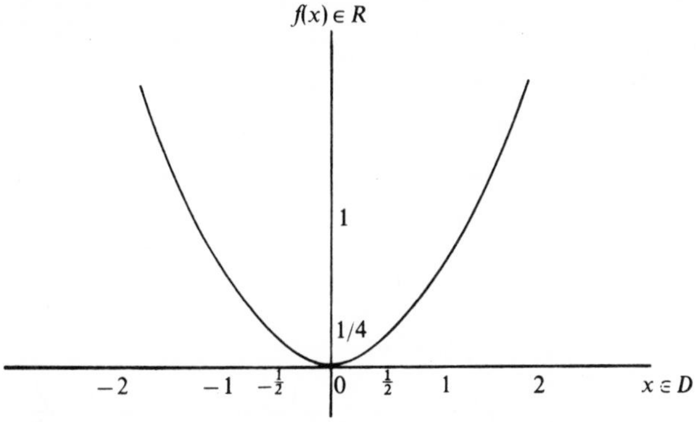

Figure 12.1

Two of the diagrams in Figure 12.2 illustrate examples of relations which do not qualify as functions on the marked domains. In (*a*), D12.1 is not satisfied since there are some points in D which are not given values by the function; had D been $\{x \mid a \leqslant x \leqslant c\}$, then we would have had a perfectly good function on that domain. In (*b*), the relation gives *two* values in R, for every value in D, and so the uniqueness requirement is not satisfied. In (*c*), we have a perfectly good function from D to R; $f\colon D \to R$. Note however, that the *inverse*, 'going the other way', $g\colon R \to D$ is not a function in this case.

D12.2 If $x_1 > x_2 \Rightarrow f(x_1) > f(x_2)$ then we say that $f(x)$ is strictly *monotonically increasing*. If $f(x_1) < f(x_2)$ then $f(x)$ is strictly monotonically decreasing.

For example, the function $f(x) = a + bx$ is monotonic increasing if $b > 0$ and monotonic decreasing if $b < 0$. (Cf. Problem 2.3.2.) $f(x) = x^2$ is not monotonic on $\{x \mid -1 < x < 1\}$.

It is intuitively clear that strict monotonicity together with a lack of sudden jumps (*continuity*) will ensure the existence of an inverse function.

Often the symbol $f(x)$ is replaced simply by y;

$$y = f(x).$$

Here the 'x' is suppressed on the left-hand side but it is still implicitly there. x is known as the *argument* of the function, or the *independent*, *exogenous*, *predetermined*, or *policy* variable, and y or $f(x)$ as the *dependent*, *endogenous* or *target* variable. When plotting functions it is conventional to use the horizontal axis for the independent variable (although economists confuse the issue when they write $q = f(p)$ for a demand function, and then plot price on the vertical axis).

12.2 Some examples

The following program will plot a graph of any function that you specify in line 200 between any two values of x.

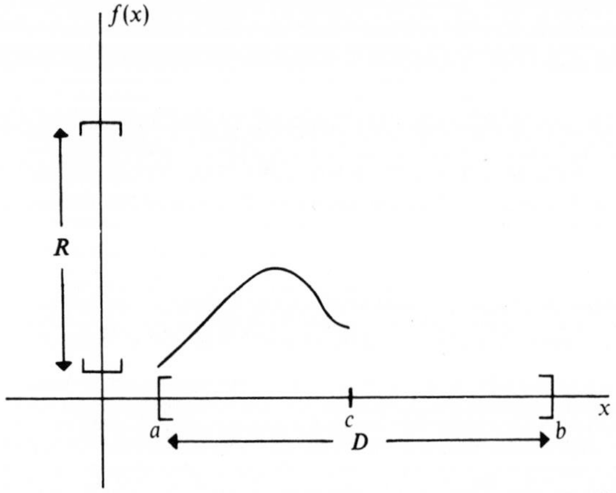

(a)

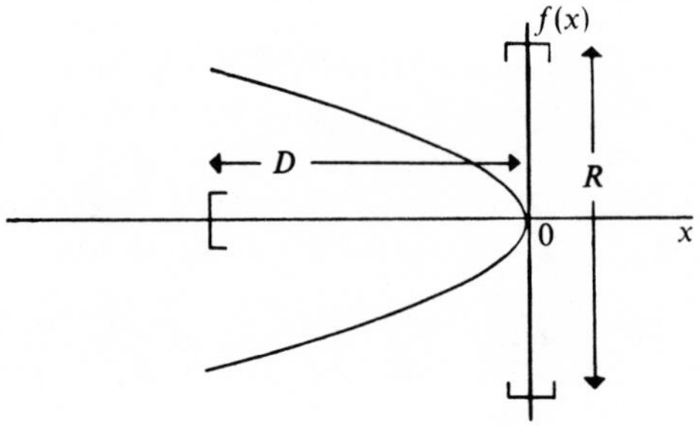

(b)

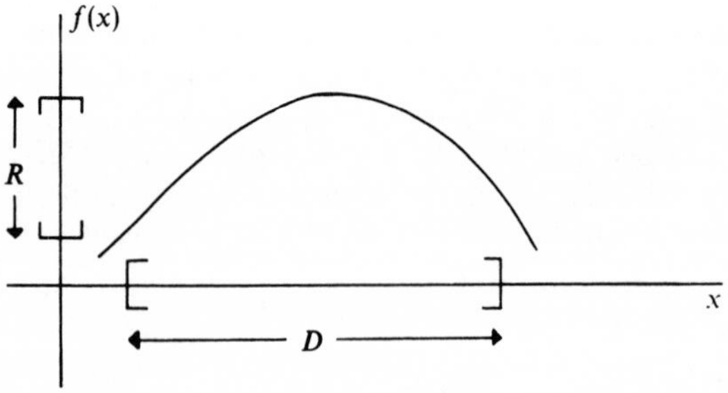

(c)

Figure 12.2

```
100  WIDE = 95
110  HIGH = 43
120  DIM Y(WIDE)
125  :
130  INPUT"SMALLEST VALUE OF X"; MIN(1)
140  INPUT"LARGEST VALUE OF X"; MAX(1)
150  IF MIN(1) > MAX(1) THEN PRINT"??": GOTO 130
155  :
200  DEF FNF(X) = 1 + 3*X
205  :
300  MIN(2) = 1.OE38 : REM A VERY LARGE NUMBER
310  MAX(2) = - 1.OE38
320  FOR I = 0 TO WIDE
330  X = (I/WIDE)*MAX(1) + (1-(I/WIDE))*MIN(1)
340  Y(I) = FNF(X)
350  IF Y(I) < MIN(2) THEN MIN(2) = Y(I)
360  IF Y(I) > MAX(2) THEN MAX(2) = Y(I)
370  NEXT I
375  :
380  RANGE(1) = MAX(1) - MIN(1) : REM INDEX 1 FOR X AND...
390  SCALE(1) = WIDE/RANGE(1)
400  RANGE(2) = MAX(2) - MIN(2) : REM ... INDEX 2 FOR Y
410  SCALE(2) = HIGH/RANGE(2)
415  :
500  CLS : REM CLEAR SCREEN
510  ZERO(1) = (1 - MAX(1)/(MAX(1) - MIN(1)))*WIDE
520  IF MIN(1) > 0 THEN ZERO(1) = 0
530  IF MAX (1) < 0 THEN ZERO(1) = WIDE
540  ZERO(2) = (1 - MAX(2)/(MAX(2) - MIN(2)))*HIGH
550  IF MIN(2) > 0 THEN ZERO (2) = 0
560  IF MAX(2) < 0 THEN ZERO(2) = HIGH
565  :
570  FOR I = 3 TO WIDE
580  SET (I,HIGH - ZERO(2)) : REM SET IS EQUIVALENT TO PLOT IN
     SOME BASICS
590  NEXT I
595  :
600  FOR I = 0 TO HIGH
610  SET (ZERO(1),I)
620  NEXT I
625  :
700  FOR I = 3 TO WIDE
710  SET( I, HIGH - SCALE(2)*(Y(I)-MIN(2)) )
720  NEXT I
730  END
```

Lines 100 and 110 determine the horizontal and vertical resolutions that you wish to use. They may need altering in order to suit the capabilities of your particular machine. Line 200 uses the facility in BASIC to define a function for later use; this is the function to be graphed. Lines 300-370 step along the horizontal axis and calculate the corresponding values of y for the vertical axis. They also find the maximum and minimum values of y. Lines 380-410 calculate scaling factors so that the graphs will always be plotted on a scale which just fills the screen. Lines 500-620 plot the horizontal (570-590) and vertical (600-620) axes. Lines 500-560 arrange that if the origin occurs somewhere on the screen then the axes will be appropriately positioned. If one axis or the other would be off the screen then it is plotted on an appropriate border. Note that the actual plotting statements (580, 610 and 710) vary in syntax from one version of BASIC to another. The graph is plotted in lines 700-720.

As you work through the remainder of this chapter you can, by altering line 200 and experimenting with the limits for x, plot graphs to illustrate the various functions discussed.

As we saw in Section 1.2 and in Problem 2.3.2,

$$f(x) = a + bx$$

is the 'equation of a straight line'. The *intercept* (that is, the value of $f(x)$ at $x = 0$, $f(0)$) is a and the *slope* is b. Commonly this is written in the form $y = mx + c$, so that $m = b$ and $c = a$. Problem 2.3.2 asks you to experiment with a few values of a and b.

x^2 is an example of a *quadratic* function, of which the general form is

$$f(x) = a + bx + cx^2$$

where $a, b, c \neq 0$ are any numbers. This is also known as a *polynomial of the second degree*. If $x = 0$, $f(x) = a$, and assuming $a < 0$, $b = 0$, $c > 0$ we have the graph given in Figure 12.3.

Changes in the constant a have the effect of shifting the whole function up or down. The constant c, affects the slope of the function. If $c > 1$, the slope of $f(x)$ will be greater than $f(x) = x^2$. Changes with respect to the constant b will have different effects depending on whether x is positive or negative. If one considers $f(x) = bx$, a straight line through the origin, the function

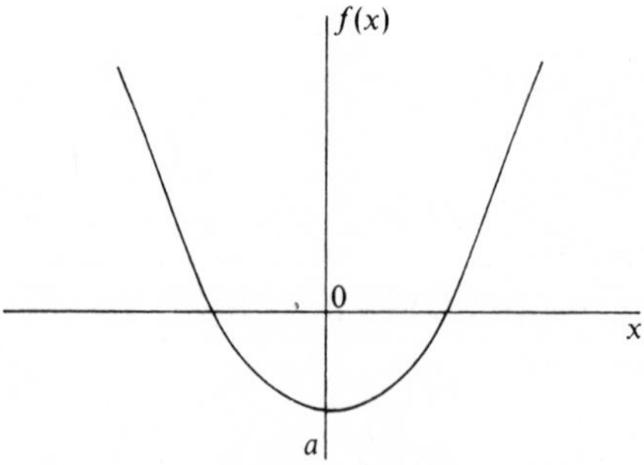

Figure 12.3

$f(x) = a + bx + cx^2$ $(b \neq 0)$ is obtained by adding this straight line to the function $a + cx^2$ and in fact the lowest point is moved to the point where $x = -b/2c$. If $c < 0$, the graph will be the other way up.

In the graphing program try changing line 200 to

```
200  DEF FNF(X) = -3 + 2*X*X
```

and plot between $x = -5$ and $x = 5$. Then repeat with the sign of the term in x squared changed.

An example of an application is as a cost function for production, where x is output level, and $f(x)$ is the minimum cost of producing that output, on the domain $D = \{x \mid x \geqslant 0\}$.

A cubic function of the form

$$f(x) = a + bx + cx^2 + dx^3,$$

a third-degree polynomial, has more possibilities; some are shown in Figure 12.4.

The graphing program will reproduce Figure 12.4(b) if line 200 is

```
200  DEF FNF(X) = -1 - 3*X + 4*X*X + 2*X*X*X
```

plotted between $x = -2.5$ and $x = 1.5$.

A general property of nth-degree polynomials is that they can have up to $(n-1)$ *turning points*, that is, points where the slope changes sign. For example, a third-degree polynomial may have two turning points. As a corollary, there can be up to n points where the function cuts the horizontal axis, that is, where $f(x) = 0$, and these points are the (real) *roots* of the polynomial. We have already come across this fact in Section 9.2, where we observed that the characteristic polynomial of an $n \times n$ matrix is a polynomial of the nth degree, with n roots.

You can confirm this by experimentation with the program by putting polynomials of higher degree in line 200.

The class of polynomial functions is a very important one, but there are many others. An example is $f(x) = 1/x$, on $D = \{x \mid x \neq 0\}$, which is graphed in Figure 12.5. The point $x = 0$ is excluded from the domain because $f(x)$ is not defined at that point for the following reason.

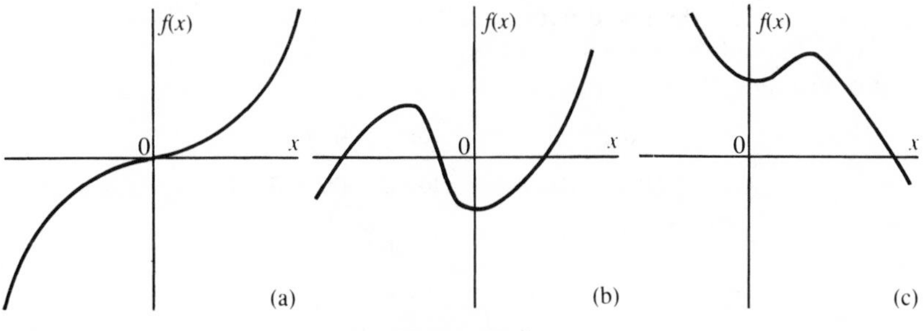

Figure 12.4

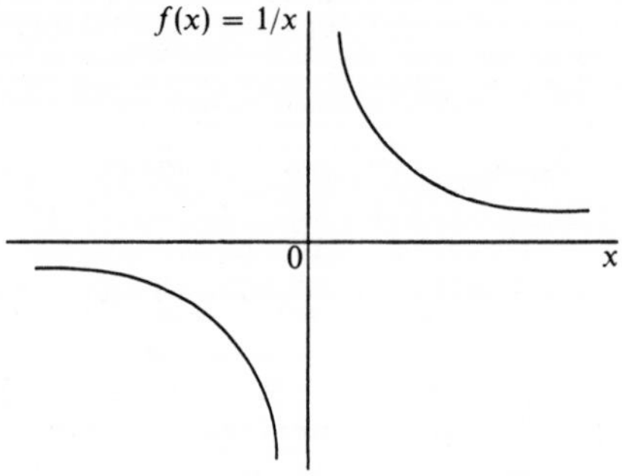

Figure 12.5

Consider the 'limit' of $f(x)$ as x tends towards zero from the right. When $x = 1, f(x) = 1$. Moving towards the origin from $x = 1$,

$$\text{at } x = \tfrac{1}{2}, \qquad f(x) = 2$$

$$\text{at } x = \tfrac{1}{4}, \qquad f(x) = 4$$

$$\text{and at } x = \tfrac{1}{100}, \qquad f(x) = 100$$

so that as x decreases, $f(x)$ gets bigger and bigger. When $x = -\frac{1}{2}$, $f(x) = -2$, and so on. Hence the function is unbounded above and below at $x = 0$. No meaning can be given to the expression $1/0$.

The use of fractional and negative indices greatly extends the number of functional forms available to us and, in particular, the two rules for indices given in the introduction are exploited in the definition of logarithms and in their use for calculation.

D12.3 The *logarithm to the base a* of a number of x is that power to which a must be raised in order to yield x, and is denoted as $\log_a x$.

That is, by definition,

$$x = a^{\log_a x}.$$

If one can keep this definition in one's mind, most of the properties of logarithms are easily remembered. Two bases are commonly used for logarithms, 10 and the natural constant e $(= 2{\cdot}7183\ldots)$, known respectively as common logarithms and natural or Napierian logarithms. Both kinds will be found in books of mathematical tables.

For example, since

$$100 = 10^2, \qquad \log_{10} 100 = 2$$

$$1000 = 10^3, \qquad \log_{10} 1000 = 3$$

$$10 = 10^1, \qquad \log_{10} 10 = 1$$

$$1 = 10^0, \qquad \log_{10} 1 = 0$$

$$0{\cdot}1 = 10^{-1} \qquad \log_{10} 0{\cdot}1 = -1$$

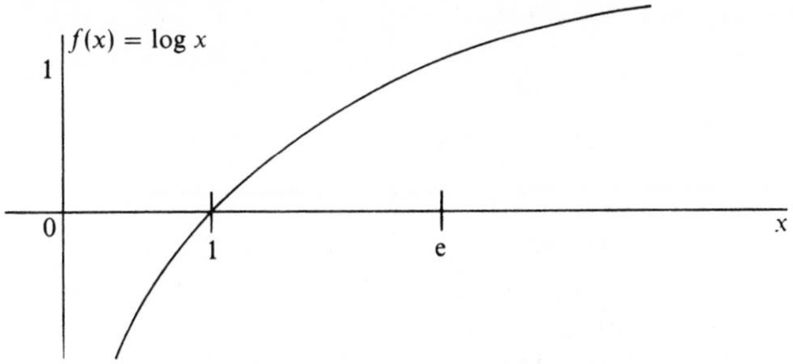

Figure 12.6

Observe that:

1 Since there is no way of raising a positive number to a power to yield a result less than or equal to zero, the log (to any base) of a negative number is not defined:
2 The log (to any base) of 1 is always 0.
3 The log of a number less than 1 is always negative.

The graph of $\log_e x$ is drawn in Figure 12.6.

Now, suppose we wish to multiply x by y using logs to the base 10. Then,

$$x = 10^{\log x}, \qquad y = 10^{\log y}$$

and by the rules for indices,

$$xy = 10^{\log x}.10^{\log y} = 10^{(\log x + \log y)}.$$

Hence, if we look up $\log_{10} x$ and $\log_{10} y$, and add the results, and then use a table of *antilogs* to evaluate $10^{(\log x + \log y)}$, then we have the product xy. This enables us to use addition to evaluate products. Also, it is clear that since

$$xy = 10^{\log xy} = 10^{(\log x + \log y)},$$

$$\log xy = \log x + \log y.$$

Similarly,

$$\log x^2 = \log x + \log x = 2 \log x$$

and in general

$$\log x^n = n \log x$$

for any n.

The facts that

$$\log xy = \log x + \log y$$

and

$$\log x^n = n \log x$$

are two useful properties of logarithms to any base. It follows that

$$\log 1/y = \log y^{-1} = -\log y$$

and

$$\log x/y = \log x - \log y.$$

With the easy availability of cheap calculators and computers, tables of logarithms have fallen into disuse. But you should find it easy to use a calculator to find logs and powers of a few numbers and to confirm the properties just outlined. Note that most calculators give both natural logs and logs to the base of 10. Some computers assume that LOG(X) means the natural logarithm. Others take LOG(X) to mean logarithm to the base 10 and use LN(X) to denote the natural logarithm. Natural logarithms are used exclusively in analysis for reasons which will become clear in Sections 13.3(5) and 14.2(*d*).

We shall not be concerned with the use of logarithms for numerical computation, but with the logarithm as a functional form. This has two main uses, one of which is given in Section 13.5(*a*). The other is in the linearization of certain nonlinear functions. Consider, for example, the famous Cobb–Douglas production function,

$$X = \gamma L^{\alpha} \quad (\alpha > 0, \gamma > 0)$$

(which reappears in various guises below), giving the maximum amount of output X available when labour is used in amount L. It might be necessary to use statistical techniques which could only deal with linear functions to estimate this, or one might want to incorporate the function into a linear model. Then all that is necessary is to take logarithms of both sides, yielding

$$\log X = \log \gamma + \alpha \log L$$

and defining new variables

$$x = \log X, c = \log \gamma \text{ and } l = \log L$$

we have

$$x = c + \alpha l$$

which is a linear function. This illustrates how nonlinear functions can sometimes be transformed to make them linear (and in particular, how the logarithmic transformation makes functions involving products of terms into sums of terms).

This can all be illustrated with the plotting program in the following way. First put

```
200  DEF FNX(X) = 2*X↑0.5
```

and plot from $x = 0{\cdot}1$ to $x = 2$. Now put

```
200  DEF FNF(X) = LOG(2) + 0.5*LOG(X)
```

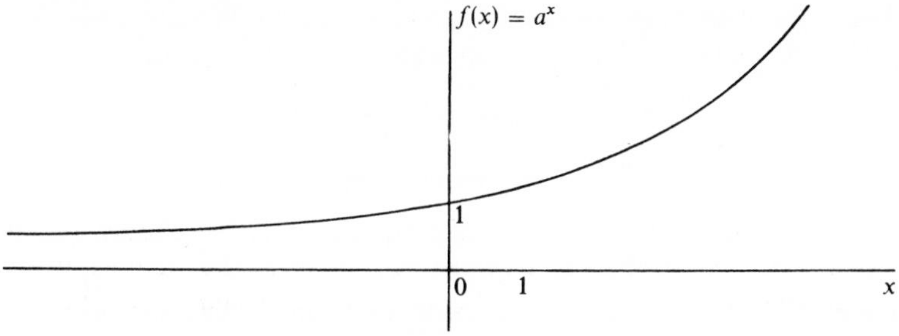

Figure 12.7

and plot between the same limits. Now change line 340:

```
340   Y(I) = FNF(EXP(X))
```

The result should be a straight line.

Another important class of functions is of the form

$$f(x) = a^n$$

where $a > 0$, (n.b., here *the index* is changing) which have the graph shown in Figure 12.7 if $a > 1$.

As x increases, $f(x)$ increases very rapidly, and as x increases negatively, it declines more and more slowly. In particular, if $a = \mathrm{e}$, the base of natural logarithms, then we have the 'exponential' function.

Any economic variable which exhibits constant proportional growth (a constant *percentage* every period, as opposed to a constant absolute amount) will behave like the exponential function, as we show in Chapter 19. Examples are population growth, funds earning compound interest, 'radio-active' depreciation (a negative rate of growth). The exponential function is also vital in statistical theory because of its use in defining the normal distribution.

The exponential function may be graphed by putting

```
200   DEF FNF(X) = EXP(X)
```

We now need to develop a concept that will enable us to distinguish a function which is smooth from a function which has jumps in it, because at such points the function does not have a slope. To illustrate a discontinuous function take

```
200   DEF FNF(X) = – 1 + 3*X
```

and add the line

```
345   IF X > 1 THEN Y(I) = Y(I) + 1
```

Now graph this between $x = -1$ and $x = 2$ and you will see a discontinuity at the point $x = 1$. If you now change the new line to

```
345   IF X > 1 THEN Y(I) = Y(I) + 1 + 3*X
```

you will find a discontinuity which is more complex in that rather than a simple parallel shift, the slope has changed as well (from 3 to 6).

12.3* The limit of a function

A complete grasp of this rather abstract material is not absolutely essential. The main ideas can probably be gained by looking at the pictures. We first define the two concepts of a limit as x becomes large, and a limit at a point.

D12.4 $f(x)$ has a limit, L, as $x \to \infty$, if

$$\forall \epsilon > 0, \exists \bar{x} \text{ s.t. } x > \bar{x} \Rightarrow |f(x) - L| < \epsilon$$

where '$x \to \infty$' means that x increases without bound.

Two examples are sketched in Figure 12.8. In (*a*), $f(x)$ has no limit as $x \to \infty$; it just increases without bound. Examples are e^x, x^2 or $\log x$. In (*b*), $f(x)$ has a limit, since, as x gets larger, $f(x)$ gets closer and closer to L; for example, $f(x) = 1 - 1/x$ has the limit $L = 1$.

To test if some number L satisfies the definition of a limit, we take any positive number ϵ and add it to and subtract it from L. We then ask if we can find a number $\bar{x}$ such that whenever x is greater than $\bar{x}$, the distance between $f(x)$ and L is less than the ϵ chosen; that is, $f(x)$ falls in the interval $L - \epsilon$ to $L + \epsilon$. If this can always be done, no matter how small ϵ, then L is the limit of the function and we write

$$\lim_{x \to \infty} f(x) = L$$

and say that $f(x)$ 'tends to the limit L'. The function may be of the type which oscillates above and below a limit; an example was the cobweb (Section 9.4) where $p(t)$ oscillated about an equilibrium price p^* (see Figure 12.9). We asked whether the limit of $p(t)$ as $t \to \infty$ was p^*. If this was so, then the model was said to be stable.

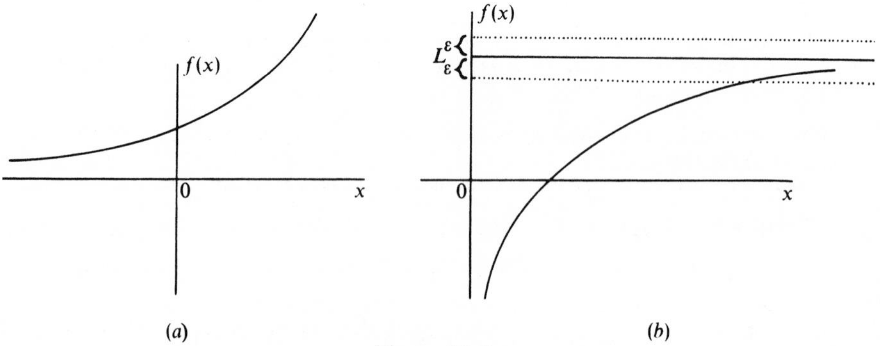

Figure 12.8

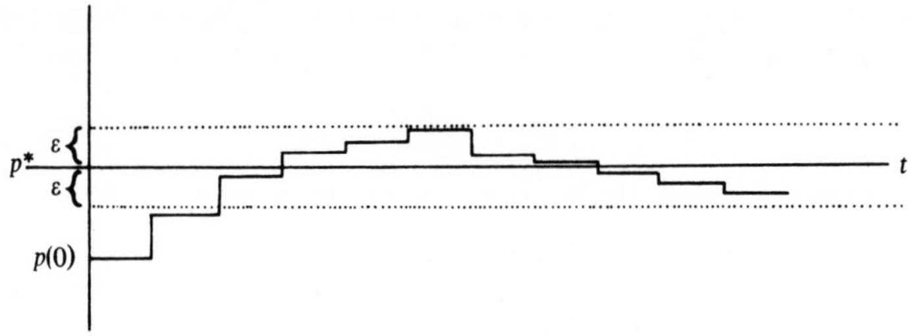

Figure 12.9

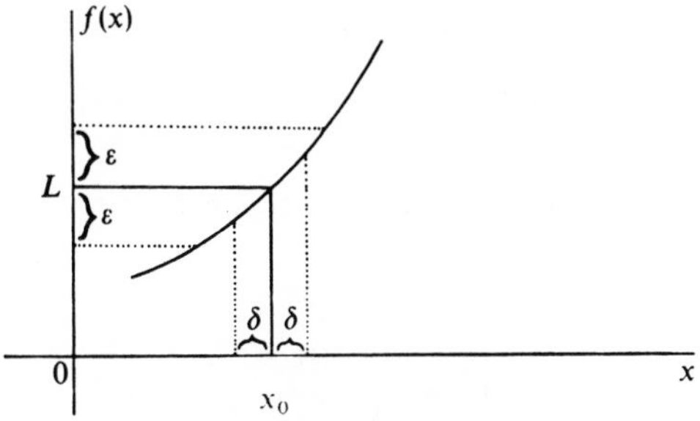

Figure 12.10

The limit as $x \to -\infty$ is analogously defined; note that e^x has a limit as $x \to -\infty$, namely 0, but that x^2 has not.

D12.5 $f(x)$ has a *limit*, L *at the point* x_0, if

$$\forall \epsilon > 0, \exists \delta > 0 \text{ s.t. } 0 < \|x - x_0\| < \delta$$
$$\Rightarrow \| f(x) - L \| < \epsilon.$$

Or alternatively

$$\forall \epsilon > 0, \exists \delta > 0 \text{ s.t. } x \in N(x_0, \delta)\, x \neq x_0$$
$$\Rightarrow f(x) \in N(L, \epsilon).$$

The question here is: As x gets closer to *a point* x_0, does $f(x)$ get closer to some number, L?

It is quite obvious that it does in the example, sketched in Figure 12.10, and we write

$$\lim_{x \to x_0} f(x) = L.$$

In general we fix an ϵ arbitrarily and draw a band on either side of L. We then try to find a value of δ with the property that when the distance between

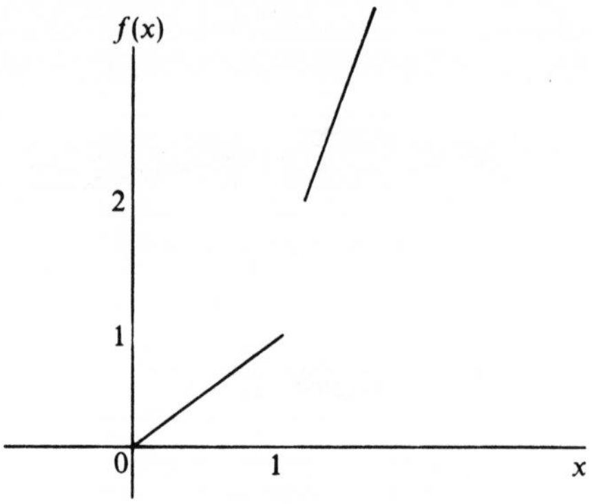

Figure 12.11

x_0 and any other point x is less than δ, the distance between $f(x)$ and L is less than ϵ.

Consider now

$$f(x) = \begin{cases} x \; (x < 1) \\ 2x \; (x \geqslant 1) \end{cases}$$

where $D = \{x \mid x \geqslant 0\}$.

This function has the graph shown in Figure 12.11.

Starting from the origin, $f(x)$ increases in proportion as x increases (along the 45° line) until it gets close to the point 1. $f(x)$ will never actually get to 1, because as soon as x becomes 1, $f(x)$ jumps to $2x$, that is, the value 2, and then goes on increasing with twice the slope. The limit of $f(x)$ as $x \to 1$ 'from the left' is 1, although $f(x) = 2$ when $x = 1$, and this is also the limit of the function as $x \to 1$ 'from the right'. Clearly this function has no limit at the jump point, $x = 1$, and this is how we identify points of discontinuity.

12.4* Continuity

A function is continuous if there are no jumps in it. Formally:

D12.6 $f(x)$ is *continuous* at the point x_0 if

(*a*) $f(x_0)$ exists;

(*b*) $\lim_{x \to x_0} f(x)$ exists;

(*c*) $\lim_{x \to x_0} f(x) = f(x_0)$.

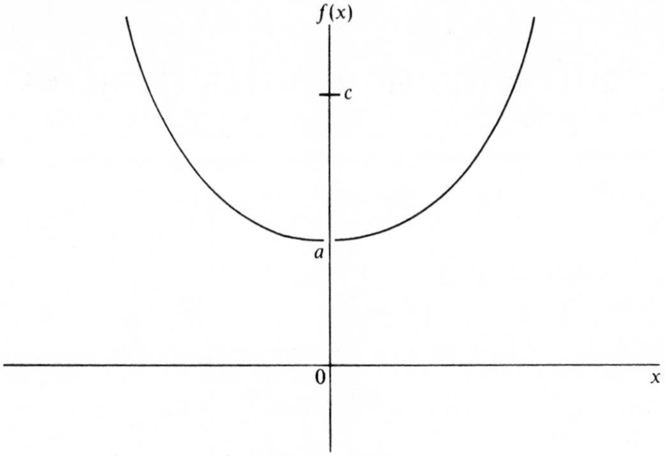

Figure 12.12

For example, if

$$f(x) = \begin{cases} a + bx^2 (x \neq 0) \\ c \neq a \quad (x = 0), \end{cases}$$

$$\lim_{x \to 0} f(x) = a$$

but

$$f(0) = c$$

(see Figure 12.12).

13 Differentiation and derivatives

13.1 Introduction

The process of differentiation is simply the process of finding the slope of a function. Before making formal definitions we start with an example. Suppose that the minimum cost of producing an output of x units per unit time of some good is

$$c(x) = a + bx^2$$

where $a > 0$, $b > 0$. The problem is to choose x so as to maximize the firm's profit, given the selling price (a fixed parameter). The profit is given by revenue net of costs:

$$\begin{aligned}\pi(x) &= px - c(x)\\ &= px - a - bx^2\end{aligned}$$

or

$$\pi(x) = -a + px - bx^2.$$

Hence the profit earned is a function of the number of units produced, with the graph shown in Figure 13.1.

When x is 0, $\pi(x) = -a$. As x increases by one unit, profits increase by p and decrease by bx^2. Supposing we are at a level of output x_0, and we are interested in the *rate* at which profit is changing as output changes. If we increase x by one unit, suppose we observe that the change of profit we get is $\Delta_1\pi(x_0)$, where the symbol Δ_1 means the change in π, $\pi(x_0 + 1) - \pi(x_0)$. We now increase output by another unit to give a total change in profit $\Delta_2\pi(x_0)$. These changes are not directly comparable because they were obtained by different changes in x. What we want is the *rate* at which $\pi(x)$ changes, rather than the absolute amount; in other words the change in profit *per unit* change in output. Dividing by the change in output, we obtain, in each case, the

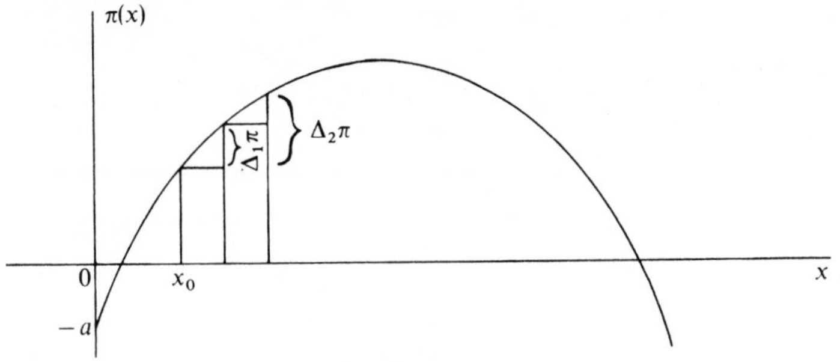

Figure 13.1

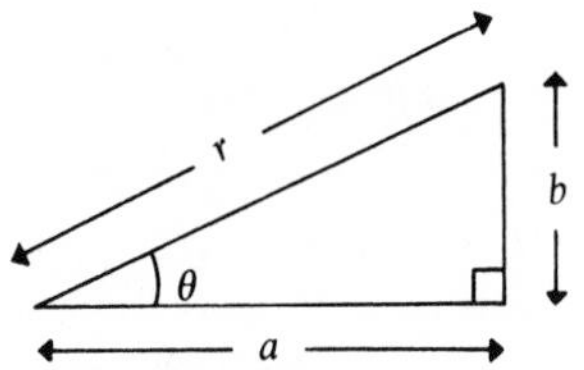

Figure 13.2

desired rate at which profit is increasing with respect to changes in output. For example, if $\Delta_1\pi(x_0) = £10$ and $\Delta_2\pi(x_0) = £19$, then

$$\frac{\Delta_1\pi(x_0)}{\Delta_1 x} = \frac{10}{1} = £10 \quad \text{and} \quad \frac{\Delta_2\pi(x_0)}{\Delta_2 x} = \frac{19}{2} = £9{\cdot}5.$$

Now, these two rates of change are not actually quite equal because of the curvature of the function. The problem is how to define this rate of change of profit with respect to changes in output *unambiguously*. At the moment it depends on how big the change in output is. To overcome this, we take changes in output level which are successively smaller, and consider

$$\lim_{\Delta x \to 0} \frac{\Delta\pi(x_0)}{\Delta x}.$$

Consider first a general right-angled triangle (Figure 13.2). The *slope* of the hypotenuse r is the ratio b/a, which determines the angle θ. Hence, in Figure 13.3,

$$\frac{\Delta\pi(x_0)}{\Delta x}$$

is the slope of the chord shown. As Δx is reduced, the slope gets closer and closer to the slope of the *tangent* to $\pi(x)$ at $x = x_0$. This is what we mean by the *slope of the function at* x_0; that is, the rate at which profit is changing with respect to an infinitesimal change in output. This limit (if it exists) is

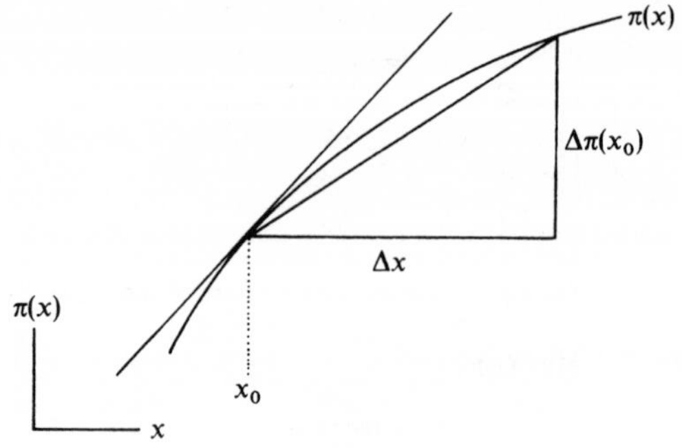

$$\frac{\Delta\pi(x_0)}{\Delta x}$$

Figure 13.3

known as the *derivative of* $\pi(x)$ *at* x_0 *with respect to* x, and is denoted $d\pi(x_0)/dx$. Before giving a formal definition, let us actually find the slope of $\pi(x)$ at x_0, and hence the profit-maximizing output: now, the profit at x_0 is given by

$$\pi(x_0) = -a + px_0 - bx_0^2$$

and at some other output x by

$$\pi(x) = -a + px - bx^2.$$

But

$$\Delta x = x - x_0$$

and

$$\Delta\pi = \pi(x) - \pi(x_0) = p(x - x_0) - b(x^2 - x_0^2).$$

Hence

$$\frac{\Delta\pi}{\Delta x} = \frac{p(x - x_0) - b(x^2 - x_0^2)}{x - x_0}$$

$$= p - \frac{b(x^2 - x_0^2)}{x - x_0}.$$

Taking the limit,

$$\frac{d\pi(x_0)}{dx} = \lim_{\Delta x \to 0} \frac{\Delta\pi}{\Delta x}$$

$$= p - \lim_{x \to x_0} \frac{b(x^2 - x_0^2)}{x - x_0}$$

(since $\lim_{\Delta x \to 0} p = p$, and since, if $f(x) = g(x) + h(x)$, then

$$\lim_{x \to x_0} f(x) = \lim_{x \to x_0} g(x) + \lim_{x \to x_0} h(x)).$$

But

$$(x^2 - x_0^2) = (x - x_0)(x + x_0).$$

Therefore

$$\frac{\mathrm{d}\pi(x_0)}{\mathrm{d}x} = p - \lim_{x \to x_0} b(x + x_0).$$

As $x \to x_0$ we get

$$x + x_0 \to 2x_0,$$

so the final result is

$$\frac{\mathrm{d}\pi(x_0)}{\mathrm{d}x} = p - 2bx_0.$$

This is the slope of the profit function at any point x_0.

For maximum profits, it is clear that the profit function should be flat: that its slope should be zero: $\mathrm{d}\pi(x_0)/\mathrm{d}x = 0$. Hence we must find a point x_0^* such that

$$p - 2bx_0^* = 0$$

or

$$p = 2bx_0^*.$$

Hence

$$x_0^* = \frac{p}{2b}.$$

Since we can now evaluate the derivative at any point, we can define a new function,

$$\frac{\mathrm{d}\pi(x)}{\mathrm{d}x} = p - 2bx$$

which is obtained by differentiating the original function. Effectively we have just dropped the 0 from x_0.

Note that the derivative of this polynomial of the second degree is a polynomial of the first degree, and we shall see that in general the derivative of a polynomial of degree n will be a polynomial of degree $(n - 1)$. We plot the graph of the derivative function in Figure 13.4.

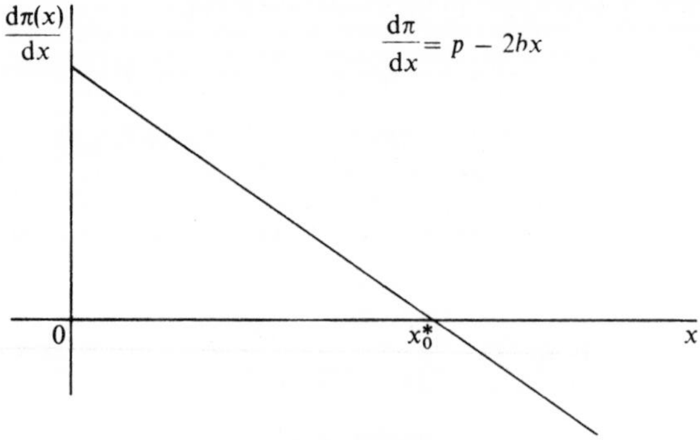

Figure 13.4

Some observations about the economics of this result are that:

1. At the maximum we adjust output so as to make the derivative of the cost function equal to the given price. But the derivative of the cost function is the extra cost incurred in producing one more unit; that is, the marginal cost; so we have the rule that at the optimum, it is necessary that price equal marginal cost. It is easy to justify this result intuitively, by supposing that price were not equal to marginal cost, and observing that profit could then be increased by either increasing or decreasing output.
2. a is eliminated, so that the optimum output is independent of it. a, here, could represent a lump-sum tax, or other fixed cost.
3. We are tacitly assuming that the maximum profit is nonnegative; otherwise the firm would not produce at all.
4. If marginal costs per unit of output ($2b$) increase because say, of a wage increase, then output decreases.
5. In a purchase tax of 100t per cent is applied, the remaining revenue is $p(1-t)$. So $x_0^* = p(1-t)/2b$, allowing one to investigate the response of output to changes in purchase tax.

The following additions to the program given in the last chapter will illustrate the limiting process involved in defining derivatives. It first plots a graph of the function as before. It then calculates successively more accurate estimates of the slope at x_0, a point specified in line 160. It will sketch a straight line passing through the function evaluated at x_0 using the current estimate of the slope. Then the increment in x is halved and the process is repeated. In this way you can watch the slope of the line become closer and closer to the slope of the tangent to the curve.

In line 690 the initial increment in x is set at the distance between x_0 and the right-hand extreme of the graph. In lines 1010 to 1040 the positions of x_0 and x_1 are calculated and marked on the horizontal axis by making a gap in it. In lines 1050 and 1060 the slope is calculated as the ratio of the change in y to the change in x. In lines 1070 to 1100 a part of the chord joining the

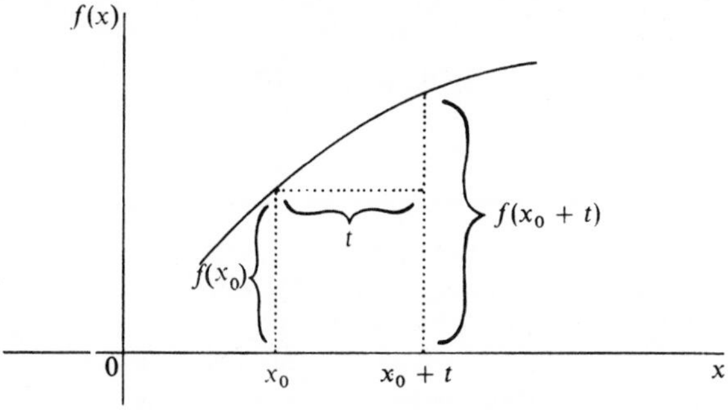

Figure 13.5

function evaluated at x_0 to the function evaluated at x_1 is drawn (x_1 corresponds to x_0+t in Figure 13.5). In lines 1120 to 1150 the chord is deleted so that it does not become confused with the one to be drawn on the next iteration. The increment in x is halved in line 2000. A record of the slope is kept in line 2010 and then the whole process is repeated by going back to line 700. In line 1110 a test is made to see if the slope has changed rather little since the last iteration. If so it is concluded that a limit has been found, control passes to line 2030 where the derivative (i.e. the slope) is printed and the program ends.

```
160  INPUT "DERIVATIVE TO BE FOUND AT"; X0
200  DEF FNF(X) = - 1 - 3*X + 4*X*X + 2*X*X*X : REM A CUBIC
690  XDEL = MAX(1) - X0 : REM CHANGE IN X
1000 X1 = X0 + XDEL
1010 I0 = SCALE(1)*(X0 - MIN(1)) : REM POSITION ON
                                   HORIZONTAL OF X0
1020 I1 = SCALE(1)*(X1 - MIN(1)) : REM POSITION ON
                                   HORIZONTAL OF X1
1030 RESET(I0,HIGH-ZERO(2)) : REM MARK X0 AND...
1040 RESET(I1,HIGH-ZERO(2)) : REM...X1 ON HORIZONTAL AXIS
1050 YDEL = FNF(X1) - FNF(X0) : REM CHANGE IN Y
1060 SLOPE = YDEL/XDEL : REM SLOPE OF CHORD
1070 FOR I = I0 - 20 TO I0 + 20
1080 Z = SCALE (2)*(Y(I0) - MIN(2) - SLOPE*(I0 - I)/SCALE(1))
1090 SET(I,HIGH - Z) : REM DRAW CHORD
1100 NEXT I
1110 IF ABS(SLOPE - OLDSLOPE) < 1E-3 THEN GOTO 2030 : REM
                                                FINISHED?
1120 FOR I = I0 - 20 TO I0 + 20
1130 Z = SCALE(2)*(Y(I0) - MIN(2) - SLOPE*(I0 - I)/SCALE (1))
1140 RESET(I,HIGH - Z) : REM DELETE CHORD
1150 NEXT I
2000 XDEL = XDEL/2 : REM HALVE CHANGE IN X
```

```
2010  OLDSLOPE = SLOPE : REM KEEP A RECORD OF SLOPE THIS
                          TIME
2020  GOTO 700 : REM GO ROUND AGAIN
2030  PRINT "DERIVATIVE AT X = "; X0" IS "; SLOPE
2040  END
```

As a test plot the function given in line 200 between −2·5 and 1·5 and find the derivative at −1·5. Now find the derivative at −1·6385: you should find that there is something special about this point.

This program may be used with other functions but it may require some modification to prevent an error occurring because plotting the chord causes an attempt to plot outside the boundary of the screen. Note that line 1120 specifies that the chord should be plotted at 20 points either side of x_0 and this can be changed if necessary. Note also that the accuracy of the final answer is limited by the value specified in line 1110. This limit may be tightened, but at the risk that the process will fail to converge because of the limited computational accuracy of your machine. For speed and simplicity you may want to use the program to calculate derivatives without plotting them, in which case you can omit all the statements associated with plotting.

13.2* Formal definitions

D13.1 The *derivative* of a function $f(x)$ at a point x_0 is given by

$$\frac{df(x_0)}{dx} = \lim_{t\to 0} \frac{f(x_0+t)-f(x_0)}{t}$$

if this limit exists, in which case $f(x)$ is *differentiable* at x_0. The process of finding a derivative is known as *differentiation*. (See Figure 13.5.)

Often one abbreviates the symbol by

$$\frac{df(x_0)}{dx} = f'(x_0)$$

For the limit to exist, it is necessary that the function be continuous at that point:

Theorem 13.1 If f is differentiable at x_0, then f is continuous at x_0.

Proof. By D12.6, we need to show that as $x \to x_0$, $f(x) \to f(x_0)$.

But

$$f(x_0+t)-f(x_0) = \left\{\frac{f(x_0+t)-f(x_0)}{t}\right\} t.$$

But, since f is differentiable,

$$\left\{\frac{f(x_0+t)-f(x_0)}{t}\right\} \to \text{finite limit as } t \to 0.$$

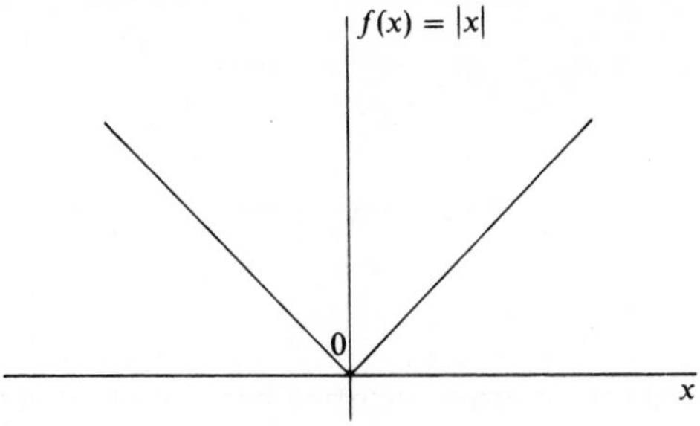

Figure 13.6

Therefore

$$\left\{\frac{f(x_0+t)-f(x_0)}{t}\right\}t \to 0 \text{ as } t \to 0$$

so that

$$f(x_0+t)-f(x_0) \to 0$$

or

$$f(x_0+t) \to f(x_0). \ ■$$

But continuity is not sufficient because a function like the one graphed in Figure 13.6 has no unambiguous slope at $x_0 = 0$, and is not differentiable. There is an important class of economic problems which cannot be solved by the use of the calculus because of a lack of differentiability—for instance, because of indivisibilities in the production of something like aircraft or nuclear power, or because of 'kinks' as illustrated above.

13.3 Rules for differentiating various functional forms

These fundamental rules follow from the definition of a derivative, but most proofs are omitted. They are given in, for example, Courant and John, 1965, and Binmore, 1983.

Each one of the rules that follows can be, and if possible should be, confirmed by the use of suitable examples with the program given earlier.

(1) If $f(x) = c$, where c is a constant, then

$$\frac{\mathrm{d}f(x_0)}{\mathrm{d}x} = 0.$$

Obviously, if $f(x)$ is a constant, in other words is independent of x, then the rate of change of $f(x)$ with respect to x is zero.

(2) If $f(x) = x^2$, then

$$\frac{df(x_0)}{dx} = \lim_{t \to 0} \left[\frac{(x_0 + t)^2 - x_0^2}{t} \right]$$

$$= \lim_{t \to 0} \left[\frac{(x_0^2 + 2tx_0 + t^2 - x_0^2)}{t} \right]$$

$$= \lim_{t \to 0} (2x_0 + t)$$

$$= 2x_0.$$

(3) A generalization of rule (2). If $f(x) = x^n$, for any index $n \neq 0$, then

$$\frac{df(x)}{dx} = nx^{n-1}.$$

Note that we are here stating the derivative for general values of x. Some examples:

$$f(x) = x^7, \qquad f'(x) = 7x^6$$

$$f(x) = x^{-3}, \qquad f'(x) = -3x^{-4}$$

$$f(x) = x^{1/4}, \qquad f'(x) = \tfrac{1}{4}x^{-3/4}.$$

(4) If $f(x) = c\,.\,g(x)$, then $df(x)/dx = c\,.\,dg(x)/dx$ where c is a constant. For example,

$$\frac{d}{dx}(c\,.\,x^n) = cnx^{n-1}$$

(5) The derivative of the sum of two functions is the sum of their derivatives: If

$$f(x) = h(x) + g(x)$$

then

$$\frac{df(x)}{dx} = \frac{dh(x)}{dx} + \frac{dg(x)}{dx}.$$

For example,

$$f(x) = 2x^2 + 3x^{-2} \Rightarrow f'(x) = 4x - 6x^{-3}.$$

Generally, if

$$f(x) = b_0 + b_1x + b_2x^2 + \ldots + b_nx^n$$

then

$$f'(x) = b_1 + 2b_2x + 3b_3x^2 + \ldots + nb_nx^{n-1}$$

so that we can differentiate term by term.

There is a particularly interesting function which is differentiated using this rule:

$$f(x) = 1 + \frac{x}{1!} + \frac{x^2}{2!} + \frac{x^3}{3!} + \ldots + \frac{x^n}{n!} + \ldots$$

where $n! = n(n-1)(n-2)\ldots 2.1$, so $4! = 4.3.2.1 = 24$.

$$f'(x) = 1 + \frac{2x}{2!} + \frac{3x^2}{3!} + \ldots + \frac{nx^{n-1}}{n!} + \ldots$$

$$= 1 + \frac{x}{1!} + \frac{x^2}{2!} + \frac{x^3}{3!} + \ldots + \frac{x^{n-1}}{(n-1)!} + \ldots.$$

So

$$f(x) = \frac{\mathrm{d}f(x)}{\mathrm{d}x}.$$

The function with this property is unique, and we shall see later that it is the exponential function, e^x. In particular, putting $x = 1$ yields

$$f(1) = \mathrm{e} = 1 + 1 + \tfrac{1}{2} + \tfrac{1}{6} + \ldots$$
$$= 2{\cdot}7183\ldots$$

This may be confirmed using the program by putting

```
200  DEF FNF(X) = EXP(X)
```

plotting between -1 and 3 and evaluating the derivative at 1. The result is 2·718. Evaluating at 2 gives the square of this, 7·389.

Note that rules (4) and (5) are the homogeneity and additivity properties of the operation of taking the derivative of a function. Hence the operation of applying $\mathrm{d}/\mathrm{d}x$ to a function $f(x)$ is a linear operation, just as multiplying a vector $\boldsymbol{x}$ by a matrix $\mathbf{A}$ was a linear operation. Sometimes the differential operator is denoted by D:

$$\mathrm{D}(x^3) = 3x^2.$$

(6) The product of two functions. Let

$$f(x) = h(x) . g(x),$$

then

$$f'(x) = h(x) . \frac{\mathrm{d}g(x)}{\mathrm{d}x} + g(x) . \frac{\mathrm{d}h(x)}{\mathrm{d}x},$$

'the first times the derivative of the second, plus the second times the derivative for the first'.

For example, let $f(x) = x^3.x^4$. This can be differentiated either by rule (3) or rule (6).

By rule (3):

$$f(x) = x^7, \text{ so } f'(x) = 7x^6.$$

By rule (6):

$$\text{Let } h(x) = x^3,\ g(x) = x^4;$$

$$f'(x) = x^3 . 4x^3 + 3x^2 . x^4$$

$$= 4x^6 + 3x^6 = 7x^6, \quad \text{as before.}$$

Similarly, if $f(x) = 5x^2 . \mathrm{e}^x$

$$f'(x) = 5(x^2 . \mathrm{e}^x + \mathrm{e}^x . 2x)$$

$$= 5x . \mathrm{e}^x (x + 2).$$

So the slope of this function is zero when $x = 0$, and when $x = -2$. But we do not yet know whether these points are maxima or minima, or 'points of inflexion'. The graphing program will settle this if you take

```
200  DEF FNF(X) = 5*X*X*EXP(X)
```

and plot between, say -3 and 1 with the derivative evaluated at either -2 or 0. This function is further analysed in Section 15.1.

(7) The chain rule. This rule tells us how to deal with a fairly common situation where, say, some variable y depends on z, and z depends on x, and we wish to find the rate of change of y with respect to changes in x. For instance if

$$y = g(z) \quad \text{and} \quad z = h(x), \quad \text{so} \quad y = g\{h(x)\},$$

we have that z, the argument of g, it itself a function, so that y is a 'function of a function'. If $y = f(x) = g(h(x))$, then

$$\frac{\mathrm{d}f(x)}{\mathrm{d}x} = \frac{\mathrm{d}g\{h(x)\}}{\mathrm{d}x} . \frac{\mathrm{d}h(x)}{\mathrm{d}x} .$$

'the derivative of the outside with respect to the inside, times the derivative of the inside'. Suppose that

$$f(x) = \mathrm{e}^{(3x+2)}.$$

Then take

$$h(x) = 3x + 2$$

and

$$g\{h(x)\} = \mathrm{e}^{h(x)} = \mathrm{e}^{(3x+2)}.$$

Then

$$\frac{\mathrm{d}g\{h(x)\}}{\mathrm{d}h} = \frac{\mathrm{d}\mathrm{e}^h}{\mathrm{d}h} = \mathrm{e}^h$$

and

$$\frac{dh(x)}{dx} = \frac{d(3x+2)}{dx} = 3.$$

So

$$\frac{df(x)}{dx} = e^h . 3 = 3e^{3x+2}.$$

Similarly

$$\frac{d}{dx}\{(x^3+6)^9\} = 9(x^3+6)^8 . 3x^2.$$

(8) The ratio of two functions. Rule (6) tells us how to deal with a product; we now use it together with rule (7) to show how to deal with ratios. If

$$f(x) = \frac{g(x)}{h(x)}$$
$$= g(x)\{h(x)\}^{-1}.$$

then

$$\frac{df(x)}{dx} = \frac{dg(x)}{dx}\{h(x)\}^{-1} + g(x)\left\{-h(x)^{-2}.\frac{dh}{dx}\right\}$$
$$= \frac{g'(x)}{h(x)} - \frac{g(x).h'(x)}{h^2(x)}$$
$$= \frac{g'(x)h(x) - g(x)h'(x)}{\{h(x)\}^2},$$

'the bottom times the derivative of the top minus the top times the derivative of the bottom, all over the bottom squared'. For example, let

$$f(x) = \frac{x^2}{x^5}.$$

Using rule (3):

$$f(x) = x^{-3}, \quad f'(x) = -3x^{-4}.$$

Using rule (8):

$$f'(x) = \frac{x^5 . 2x - x^2 . 5x^4}{(x^5)^2} = \frac{2x^6 - 5x^6}{x^{10}}$$
$$= -3x^{-4}, \quad \text{as before.}$$

Also, if

$$f(x) = \frac{(x^2 + 3)}{(x + 2)^3}$$

then

$$f'(x) = \frac{2x(x + 2)^3 - 3(x^2 + 3)(x + 2)^2}{(x + 2)^6}$$

$$= \frac{-x^2 + 4x - 9}{(x + 2)^4}.$$

(9) If $f(x) = \log x$, then, $f'(x) = 1/x$. See also Sections 13.4 and 13.5(a) below.

13.4 Implicit functions

All the functions we have met so far have been defined explicitly; for example,

$$f(x) = \frac{1}{(1 + x^2)},$$

or if we call y the variable whose values are given by $f(x)$,

$$y = \frac{1}{(1 + x^2)} = (1 + x^2)^{-1}.$$

Note that by calling $f(x)$ 'y', we have changed nothing; we have $y = f(x)$, which just means that y and $f(x)$ are one and the same thing. y is just as much a function of the variable x as $f(x)$ is, although x is not explicitly written as an argument of y. We have

$$\frac{\mathrm{d}y}{\mathrm{d}x} = -(1 + x^2)^{-2}.2x = \frac{-2x}{(1 + x^2)^2}$$

or, remembering the definition of y,

$$\frac{\mathrm{d}y}{\mathrm{d}x} = \frac{-2xy}{(1 + x^2)}.$$

However, the original definition of y could have been written

$$x^2y + y - 1 = 0.$$

If we had been given this last equation in the first place, we would have recognized that it defines a relationship between the variable y and the variable x *implicitly*. Given a value for x, chosen as the independent variable, there is a value for y (or possibly several values) consistent with the statement that the left-hand side is zero. Hence y is *implicitly* related to x. In this particular case, it is very easy to solve and find y as a function of x explicitly, but very often this is inconvenient, or impossible. It is still possible to find the derivative $\mathrm{d}y/\mathrm{d}x$ directly from the *implicit* definition of the function: we simply differentiate both sides of the equation, remembering to count y as a function of x. The resulting equation will always be *linear* in $\mathrm{d}y/\mathrm{d}x$, and so easily solved. From the example we have (using the product rule for x^2y)

$$2xy + x^2 \frac{\mathrm{d}y}{\mathrm{d}x} + \frac{\mathrm{d}y}{\mathrm{d}x} = 0$$

or

$$\frac{\mathrm{d}y}{\mathrm{d}x}(1 + x^2) = -2xy$$

so

$$\frac{\mathrm{d}y}{\mathrm{d}x} = \frac{-2xy}{(1 + x^2)},$$

which we obtained from the explicit version. The result often involves y, which in general we do not know. However, it is still useful if we know something about y; its sign for instance.

As another example, let us find the derivative of $\log_e x$. By definition

$$x = \mathrm{e}^{\log x} \quad \text{or} \quad x = \mathrm{e}^{y}$$

which defines y ($= \log x$) implicitly. Differentiating and using the chain rule,

$$1 = \frac{\mathrm{d}y}{\mathrm{d}x}\mathrm{e}^{y}$$

or

$$1 = \frac{\mathrm{d}y}{\mathrm{d}x}x$$

so

$$\frac{\mathrm{d}y}{\mathrm{d}x} = \frac{1}{x} \quad (x \neq 0);$$

hence,

$$\frac{\mathrm{d}\log(x)}{\mathrm{d}x} = \frac{1}{x}, \quad \text{which is rule 13.3 (9).}$$

Similarly, consider

$$(x - 3)^2 + (y - 4)^2 = 25.$$

Then

$$2(x-3)+2(y-4)\frac{dy}{dx}=0$$

or

$$\frac{dy}{dx}=-\frac{(x-3)}{(y-4)};$$

so that if, for example,

$$x=0, \quad y=0,$$

$$\frac{dy}{dx}=-\frac{3}{4}.$$

There are two minor difficulties with this technique.

(*a*) It is clear that y may not be unique for a given value of x and so not strictly a function. This can usually be overcome by selecting relevant parts of the range of the relation. The last illustration is a case in point. Values of x and y such that $(x-3)^2+(y-4)^2=25$ lie on a circle, radius 5, centre $x=3$, $y=4$ (see Figure 13.7) so that each value of x gives two values of y. We can calculate the value of dy/dx from the above formula, depending on which bit of the circle interests us.

(*b*) There may be *no* values of y consistent with the given implicit relation, although one might well calculate perfectly reasonable looking (but meaningless) derivatives. Consider

$$y^2+e^x=0.$$

Then

$$2y\frac{dy}{dx}+e^x=0$$

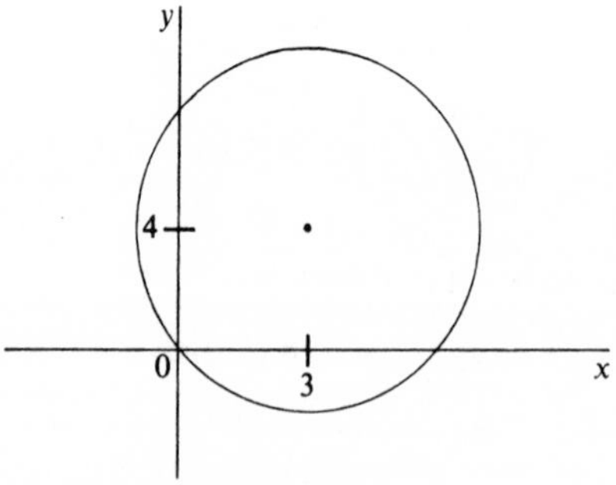

Figure 13.7

and

$$\frac{dy}{dx} = \frac{-e^x}{2y} \quad (y \neq 0).$$

However, $y^2 \geqslant 0$ and $e^x > 0$, so that there is no way of choosing y so as to make the sum zero. The 'derivative' on the other hand is perfectly well defined. $\log x$ is another example if $x \leqslant 0$. We know that in this case $\log x$ is undefined, but the 'derivative' x^{-1} *is* defined. Actually, these are points of some importance in some economic models; as we shall see in the following section on applications, it is quite easy to find the rate of change of the equilibrium value of some variable with respect to another when there is no guarantee that the equilibrium exists, or if it does that it is unique.

13.5 Applications

(*a*) *Logarithmic differentiation and elasticities*

Assume a demand function $q = f(p)$, giving the quantity q of some good that people would like to consume per unit time, if the price were p. The *elasticity* of demand ϵ, is colloquially defined by

$$\begin{aligned}\epsilon &= \frac{\text{Percentage change in quantity}}{\text{percentage change in price}}\\ &= \frac{\Delta q}{q} \times 100 \Big/ \frac{\Delta p}{p} \times 100\\ &= \frac{\Delta q}{\Delta p} \cdot \frac{p}{q}.\end{aligned}$$

We can write this more precisely as

$$\epsilon = \frac{dq}{dp} \cdot \frac{p}{q} = \frac{df(p)}{dp} \cdot \frac{p}{f(p)}.$$

However,

$$\begin{aligned}\frac{d \log f(p)}{dp} &= \frac{d \log f(p)}{df} \cdot \frac{df(p)}{dp}, \quad \text{by rule (7)}\\ &= \frac{1}{f(p)} \cdot \frac{df(p)}{dp}\end{aligned}$$

so that differentiating $\log f(p)$ rather than $f(p)$ itself, has the effect of 'putting an extra $f(p)$ on the bottom'. Similarly, differentiating with respect to $\log p$, rather than with respect to p has the effect of 'putting an extra p

on top'. Hence we have an alternative, and rather neater definition:

$$\epsilon = \frac{\mathrm{d}\log f(p)}{\mathrm{d}\log p}.$$

For example, if

$$f(p) = kp^{\delta} \quad (k > 0, \delta < 0, \text{constants}),$$
$$\log f(p) = \log k + \delta \log p$$

so immediately,

$$\epsilon = \delta.$$

This particular function is said to have constant elasticity of demand. In particular, if $\delta = -1$, we have

$$f(p) = kp^{-1} = \frac{k}{p},$$

a rectangular hyperbola giving unit elasticity for all prices.

(*b*) *Implicit production functions*

In, say, a 'Keynesian' short-run model, with fixed capital stock, we are used to writing output Y as an explicit function of labour employed

$$Y = F(L).$$

This may be written

$$Y - F(L) = 0$$

or, in the implicit form,

$$T(Y, L) = 0$$

which means the same thing. More generally, one might find (particularly in the theory of international trade)

$$T(X, Y, K, L) = 0,$$

which *implicitly* specifies the maximum amount of good Y which can be produced if an amount X of another good is produced, given specified quantities of capital and labour–a so-called *transformation relation*.

(*c*) *Elementary comparative statics: example*

Suppose the government levies a tax of t pence per unit sold on some good (say petrol), so that the producer receives $p - t$ if the consumer paid p pence. If the market is in equilibrium and the tax is increased, how will the price, quantity and tax revenue change once the new equilibrium has been attained?

Assume the demand and supply functions

$$d = f(p)$$
$$s = g(p - t).$$

By an 'equilibrium price' we mean one at which consumers want to buy exactly what suppliers want to sell; that is, one such that

$$f(p) = g(p - t).$$

This equation implicitly defines the equilibrium p as a function of t. Obviously we cannot find p explicitly without specifying the functions f and g, but we *can* say quite a bit about the derivative of p with respect to t. If, as an example, we take $f(p) = kp^{\epsilon}$ and $g(p - t) = (p - t).c$, $c > 0$, a constant, then we have

$$kp^{\epsilon} = (p - t).c$$

as our implicit relationship.

We now assume that there *exists* a *unique*, nonnegative solution to this implicit relationship, so that the functions can be graphed as in (*a*) in Figure 13.8, and not as in (*b*), (*c*) or (*d*). (See also Problem 2.3.4.)

Now let $\hat{p}$ be price net of tax; then we have the implicit relations in p,

$$f\{p(t)\} = g\{\hat{p}(t)\}, \quad \hat{p}(t) = p(t) - t.$$

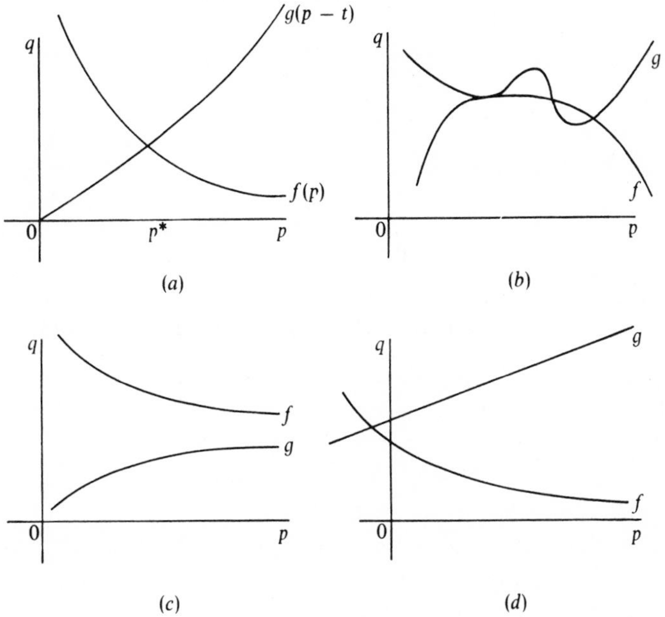

Figure 13.8

Differentiating by the chain rule,

$$\frac{df(p)}{dp}\cdot\frac{dp}{dt}=\frac{dg(\hat{p})}{d\hat{p}}\cdot\frac{d\hat{p}}{dt}$$

$$=\frac{dg(\hat{p})}{d\hat{p}}\left(\frac{dp}{dt}-1\right).$$

So

$$\frac{dp}{dt}=\frac{-dg/d\hat{p}}{(df/dp-dg/d\hat{p})}.$$

Now, assuming simply that $df/dp<0$ and $dg/d\hat{p}>0$, we immediately have that

$$0<\frac{dp}{dt}<1,$$

so that the price goes up, but by an amount less than the tax. Further,

$$\frac{dp}{dt}=\frac{-(1/g)(dg/d\hat{p})}{(1/g)(df/dp)-(1/g)(dg/d\hat{p})}$$

$$=\frac{-(1/g)(dg/d\hat{p})}{(1/f)(df/dp)-(1/g)(dg/d\hat{p})},\quad \text{since } f(p)=g(\hat{p}).$$

But

$$\frac{p}{f(p)}\frac{df(p)}{dp}=\epsilon,\quad \frac{\hat{p}}{g}\frac{dg}{d\hat{p}}=\mu,\quad \text{say}$$

where ϵ and μ are the elasticities of demand and supply, respectively. So

$$\frac{dp}{dt}=\frac{\mu/\hat{p}}{\mu/\hat{p}-\epsilon/p}.$$

This tells us a great deal; for instance, if $\epsilon=0$, $dp/dt=1$. In other words, if the demand is completely inelastic the whole tax is passed on. Similarly

$$\lim_{\mu\to\infty}\frac{dp}{dt}=1,\quad \lim_{\mu\to 0}\frac{dp}{dt}=0,$$

$$\lim_{t\to 0}\frac{dp}{dt}=\frac{\mu}{\mu-\epsilon},\quad \text{a rather neat result.}$$

The reader should be able to interpret these results easily by a graphical analysis.

Tax revenue is given by

$$R=tf\{p(t)\}$$

so using rules (6) and (7)

$$\frac{\mathrm{d}R}{\mathrm{d}t} = f(p) + t\,\frac{\mathrm{d}f(p)}{\mathrm{d}p}\cdot\frac{\mathrm{d}p}{\mathrm{d}t}$$

$$= f(p)\left\{1 - \frac{t\epsilon}{p}\cdot\frac{\mu/\hat{p}}{(\epsilon/p - \mu/\hat{p})}\right\}.$$

In particular, if $\mu \to \infty$, it will be possible to both reduce consumption and simultaneously raise revenue if

$$1 + \frac{t\epsilon}{p} > 0, \quad \text{or} \quad \frac{t\epsilon}{p} > -1.$$

Revenue will be maximized if

$$\frac{t\epsilon}{p} = -1.$$

This is illustrated in Problem 13.6.4.

Notice particularly that these results do depend on the assumption that the new equilibrium is in fact attained. If the market was, for example, an 'unstable cobweb' (see Section 9.4) it would never be attained; even if stable it might take a 'long time' for the market to get close to an equilibrium. The actual dynamic path of adjustment is not considered. Since we are comparing one long-term equilibrium with another, the method is called *comparative statics*.

(*d*) *The I–S curve*

In the simple macroeconomic model of the commodity market one assumes something of the form,

desired savings $= S(Y)$, where Y is national income

desired investment $= I(r)$, where r is the rate of interest.

Then the I–S curve is the set of pairs of values of Y and r such that

$$S(Y) = I(r)$$

that is, giving equilibrium in the commodity market. Under certain assumptions this equation implicitly defines r as a function of Y (or vice versa) and we can differentiate to find the slope of the I–S curve, which is the graph of this implicit function (see Figure 13.9).

Since we are choosing Y as the independent variable we differentiate with respect to Y:

$$\frac{\mathrm{d}S(Y)}{\mathrm{d}Y} = \frac{\mathrm{d}I(r)}{\mathrm{d}r}\cdot\frac{\mathrm{d}r}{\mathrm{d}Y}$$

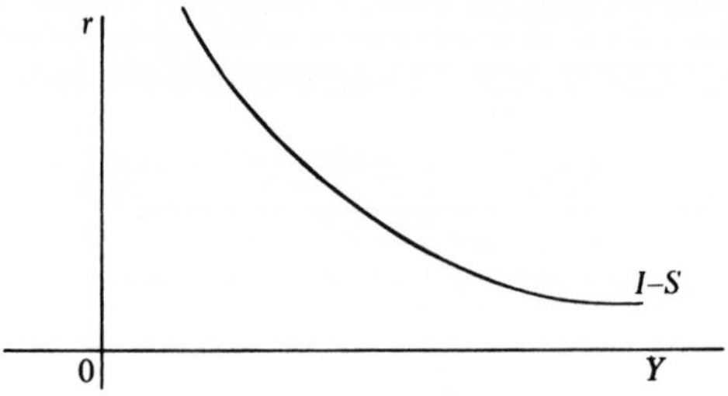

Figure 13.9

so

$$\frac{\mathrm{d}r}{\mathrm{d}Y} = \frac{\mathrm{d}S(Y)}{\mathrm{d}Y} \bigg/ \frac{\mathrm{d}I(r)}{\mathrm{d}r}$$

which is negative on the usual assumptions that

$$\frac{\mathrm{d}S}{\mathrm{d}Y} > 0 \quad \text{and} \quad \frac{\mathrm{d}I}{\mathrm{d}r} < 0.$$

Also

$$\frac{Y}{r}\frac{\mathrm{d}r}{\mathrm{d}Y} = \frac{Y/S\,.\,\mathrm{d}S/\mathrm{d}Y}{r/I\,.\,\mathrm{d}I/\mathrm{d}r}$$

so that the elasticity of the *I–S* curve is the ratio of the elasticity of the savings function to that of the investment function. This allows one to deduce, say, the implication of an inelastic investment function for the elasticity of the *I–S* curve.

Once again, we have presupposed that the equilibria exist, are unique and are attained. Of course this analysis yields a whole set of values of Y and r which are consistent with equilibrium in the commodity market. What values are also consistent with equilibrium in other markets (such as the money market) requires further analysis, which is partially specified in Problem 13.6.2. A more complete model is discussed in Chapter 18.

13.6 Problems

1. Differentiate the following functions with respect to x.

   (*a*) x^4 (*b*) x^6 (*c*) x^{n+1} (*d*) $x^{n/m}$ (*e*) $x^{-3/2}$ (*f*) $6x^5$

   (*g*) $\dfrac{x^{1-a-b}}{(a+b-1)}$ (*h*) $x^5(2x^2+1)$ (*i*) $(x^5+x^2)(x^3+x)$

(*j*) $(x+1)^3$ (*k*) $\dfrac{(x^2+1)}{x^3}$ (*l*) $\dfrac{3x+2}{4x^2+3}$ (*m*) e^{9x^2}

(*n*) $x^3e^{9x^2}$ (*o*) $(1+e^{-3x})^{-1}$ (*p*) a^{2x}

2. Repeat section 13.5 (*d*) for the *L–M* curve, defined by

$$\frac{M}{P} = L(r) + T(Y) \left(\frac{M}{P} \text{ a constant}\right)$$

$$\frac{dL(r)}{dr} < 0, \quad \frac{dT(Y)}{dY} > 0.$$

3. Find dy/dx from the following implicit relations:

(*a*) $2x - 3y = 6$ (*b*) $xy + y^2 = 4$ (*c*) $x^2 + 2xy + y^2 = 4$.

4. The elasticity of demand for cigarettes is $-1{\cdot}2$, the elasticity of supply is infinite. The price of a packet of cigarettes is 25p, of which 20p goes to the government in tax. The government wishes to both discourage smoking and raise its tax revenue. Is this possible? At what level of taxation would its tax revenue be maximized? Assume that cigarette taxation is of the form t pence per packet.

14 Taylor's theorem

We now introduce a rather remarkable theorem, which is exceptionally useful in many fields. Almost everything that we shall do from now on will make some use of it. First, we must extend our notion of a derivative.

14.1 Higher-order derivatives

We have seen many times that the derivative of a function is itself a function. Hence, there is no reason why we should not differentiate again to obtain the derivative of the derivative–or the *second derivative*. For example, if

$$f(x) = x^3$$

$$\frac{\mathrm{d}f(x)}{\mathrm{d}x} = 3x^2$$

and

$$\frac{\mathrm{d}}{\mathrm{d}x}\left\{\frac{\mathrm{d}f(x)}{\mathrm{d}x}\right\} = 3.2.x = 6x.$$

This is also denoted

$$\frac{\mathrm{d}^2f(x)}{\mathrm{d}x^2}, \quad \text{or } f''(x).$$

The process can be continued indefinitely:

$$\frac{\mathrm{d}^3f(x)}{\mathrm{d}x^3} = f'''(x) = 6$$

$$\frac{d^4 f(x)}{dx^4} = f^{(iv)}(x) = 0$$

$$\vdots$$

$$\frac{d^n f(x)}{dx^n} = f^{(n)}(x) = 0.$$

Note by the way, how the fourth- and higher-order derivatives of a third-order polynomial are all zero—a rule which generalizes.

14.2 Taylor's theorem

Stated baldly this theorem looks a little daunting, so we shall develop it in stages before making a formal statement.

Taylor's theorem can be thought of as a way of using the known value of a 'smooth' function at some point, together with its derivatives at that point to approximate the value of the function at some other point. Suppose we know $f(x_0)$ and the derivative, $f'(x_0)$, and we wish to estimate $f(x)$, where x is 'close' to x_0 (see Figure 14.1). Remember that $f(x_0)$ means the value of the function $f(x)$ at $x = x_0$. Now, $f'(x_0)$ is the slope of the function at x_0 and if we multiply this by the deviation in x, $(x - x_0)$, we get the increment obtained by moving along the tangent line. Adding this to $f(x_0)$ would give us a crude approximation to $f(x)$:

$$f(x) \approx f(x_0) + \frac{df(x_0)}{dx}(x - x_0).$$

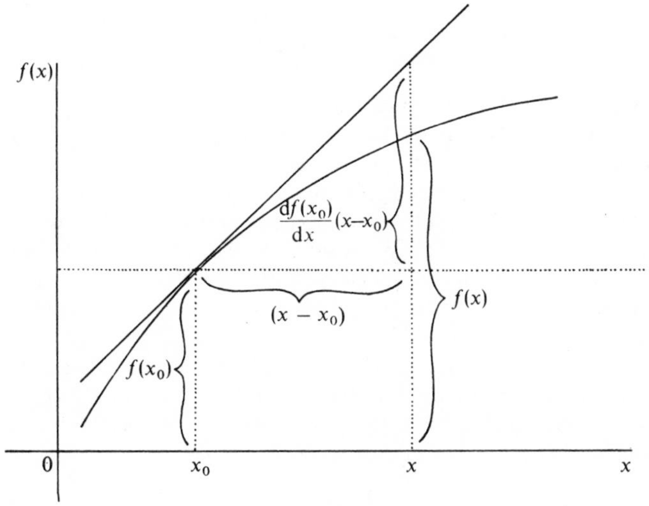

Figure 14.1

This is the approximation given by moving along the straight line remaining at the end of the differentiation program of the last chapter.

As Figure 14.1 is drawn this will clearly be an overestimate of $f(x)$, and this is because of the curvature of the function, which we should take into account if we want to improve our estimate. Now, the curvature is the rate of change of the slope; that is, the derivative of the derivative, the second derivative. The theorem tells us that a better approximation would be

$$f(x) \approx f(x_0) + \frac{\mathrm{d}f(x_0)}{\mathrm{d}x}(x - x_0) + \frac{1}{2!}\,\frac{\mathrm{d}^2 f(x_0)}{\mathrm{d}x^2}(x - x_0)^2.$$

In our case the slope is getting smaller as x increases, so the second derivative is negative. The square in $(x - x_0)^2$ ensures that it is always positive–even if $x < x_0$. So the complete new term is negative and it will reduce the estimate of $f(x)$, as it should do. We can get even closer by considering the rate of change of the curvature; that is, the third derivative, and so on. The presence of the factor of $1/n!$, which decreases very rapidly with n, ensures that we give less weight to higher-order terms. Formally,

Theorem 14.1 Let $f(x)$ be a function with continuous derivatives up to the $(n+1)$th order on the closed interval from x_0 to x, then

$$f(x) = f(x_0) + \frac{\mathrm{d}f(x_0)}{\mathrm{d}x}(x - x_0) + \frac{1}{2!}\,\frac{\mathrm{d}^2 f(x_0)}{\mathrm{d}x^2}(x - x_0)^2 + \dots$$

$$+ \frac{1}{n!}\,\frac{\mathrm{d}^n f(x_0)}{\mathrm{d}x^n}(x - x_0)^n + R_n$$

where R_n is the remaining error and is given by

$$R_n = \frac{1}{(n+1)!}\,\frac{\mathrm{d}^{(n+1)} f(\xi)}{\mathrm{d}x^{(n+1)}}(x - x_0)^{n+1}$$

for some point ξ such that $x_0 \leqslant \xi \leqslant x$ (or $x \leqslant \xi \leqslant x_0$, if $x \leqslant x_0$).

In stating the theorem we have made an exact statement rather than an approximation, and R_n is the remaining error if we stop after n terms. We even know how R_n can be expressed, but of course we do not in general know what ξ should be, so that we cannot evaluate R_n. This will not matter too much if we can show that R_n is small. In fact, in many cases we can show that $R_n \to 0$ as $n \to \infty$, in which case we can express $f(x)$ exactly as an *infinite series* of terms. We have already had an example of this as an illustration of rule 5, Section 13.3.

The expression as stated in the theorem would be known as the 'Taylor expansion of $f(x)$ *about the point* x_0', and note particularly that every one of the derivatives is also *evaluated at the point* x_0. A special case, sometimes known as Maclaurin's series, occurs when x_0 is taken as zero:

$$f(x) = f(0) + f'(0)x + \frac{1}{2!}f''(0)x^2 + \frac{1}{3!}f'''(0)x^3 + \dots + R_n.$$

We illustrate by expanding several common functions.

(*a*) Let $f(x) = (1 + x)^3$.

We know by direct multiplication that

$$(1 + x)^3 = 1 + 3x + 3x^2 + x^3$$

but we can confirm this by Taylor's expansion about $x_0 = 0$.

$$\begin{aligned} f(x) &= (1+x)^3 \quad &\text{so} \quad f(0) &= 1 \\ f'(x) &= 3(1+x)^2 \quad &\text{so} \quad f'(0) &= 3 \\ f''(x) &= 6(1+x) \quad &\text{so} \quad f''(0) &= 6 \\ f'''(x) &= 6 \quad &\text{so} \quad f'''(0) &= 6 \\ f^{(iv)}(x) &= 0 \quad &\text{so} \quad f^{(iv)}(0) &= 0 \end{aligned}$$

and higher derivatives are clearly all zero. Using Taylor's (in this case Maclaurin's) series yields

$$\begin{aligned} f(x) &= 1 + 3x + \frac{1}{2!}6x^2 + \frac{1}{3!}6x^3 \\ &= 1 + 3x + 3x^2 + x^3 \end{aligned}$$

as before. Here the remainder R_n is obviously zero if $n \geqslant 3$, and so the expansion is valid for all values of x. This would generalize to enable us to prove the *binomial theorem* that

$$(a + x)^n = \sum_{r=0}^{n} \binom{n}{r} a^{n-r} x^r \quad (n > 0)$$

where the binomial coefficients, $\binom{n}{r} = \frac{n!}{r!(n-r)!}$. Like the exponential function (Section 12.2) this expression is very important in statistical distribution theory.

The following program demonstrates this calculation.

```
100 INPUT "A";A
110 INPUT "X";X
120 INPUT "N";N
130 SUM = 0
140 ANMINUSR = A↑N : REM I.E. A POWER N MINUS R
150 XPOWERR = 1 : REM I.E. X POWER R
160 FOR R = 0 TO N
170 GOSUB 1000
180 SUM = SUM + B*ANMINUSR*XPOWERR
190 ANMINUSR = ANMINUSR/A
200 XPOWERR = XPOWERR*X
```

```
210  NEXT R
220  PRINT A+X; "TO THE POWER OF"; N; "IS "; SUM
230  GOTO 100
1000  B = 1
1010  FOR I = 1 TO R
1020  B = B*(N − I + 1)/I
1030  NEXT I
1040  IF R = 0 THEN B = 1
1050  PRINT "BINOMIAL COEFFICIENT WHEN N =";N;" AND
      R = ";R " IS"; B
1060  RETURN
```

The subroutine at 1000 is used to calculate and print the binomial coefficients. If you run this with $a = 1$ and $x = 1$ the results will be powers of 2. If you make N large (say 45) then you can check the result by calculation using a direct command such as

```
PRINT 2↑45
```

and you will be able to compare the speed of the computer's internal routine for exponentiation with that of the program.

(*b*) Let $f(x) = \dfrac{1}{(1-x)} = (1-x)^{-1}$, then $f(0) = 1$

$$f'(x) = (1-x)^{-2} \quad \text{so} \quad f'(0) = 1$$
$$f''(x) = 2(1-x)^{-3} \quad \text{so} \quad f''(0) = 2$$
$$f'''(x) = 3{\cdot}2(1-x)^{-4} \quad \text{so} \quad f'''(0) = 3!$$
$$\vdots \qquad\qquad\qquad \vdots$$

so

$$(1-x)^{-1} = 1 + x + \frac{2x^2}{2} + \frac{3!x^3}{3!} + \ldots + R_n$$

and if $-1 < x < 1$, $R_n \to 0$ *as* $n \to \infty$, so in this case

$$(1-x)^{-1} = 1 + x + x^2 + x^3 + \ldots.$$

Similarly,

$$(1+x)^{-1} = 1 - x + x^2 - x^3 + \ldots.$$

The expansion of $1/(1-x)$ gives a way of interpreting the simple multiplier in a closed economy. Suppose the marginal propensity to consume is x, and the government decides to increase investment by £1. Then £1 worth of extra investment goods are purchased, creating a total £1 of extra income for the workers, and shareholders of the suppliers. They will purchase an extra £x worth of goods to make a further contribution to the national income. The producers of these goods in turn spend a proportion x of their incremental income, a total of £$x.x$ = £x^2, and so the process goes on, to yield a total extra national income of

$$1 + x + x^2 + x^3 + \ldots$$

which we now know to be $1/(1-x)$; that is the inverse of the marginal propensity to save; a standard result.

(*c*) Let $f(x) = \log_e(1+x)$, then $f(0) = \log 1 = 0$.

$$\begin{array}{lll} f'(x) = (1+x)^{-1} & \text{so} & f'(0) = 1 \\ f''(x) = -(1+x)^{-2} & \text{so} & f''(0) = -1 \\ f'''(x) = 2(1+x)^{-3} & \text{so} & f'''(0) = 2 \\ \vdots & & \vdots \end{array}$$

so

$$\log_e(1+x) = x - \frac{x^2}{2} + \frac{x^3}{3} - \frac{x^4}{4} + \ldots \quad \text{for } x > -1.$$

(*d*) Let $f(x) = e^x$ and let us assume that $e^0 = 1$, and that f has the property that $f'(x) = f(x)$. Then

$$\begin{array}{lll} f(x) = e^x & \text{so} & f(0) = 1 \\ f'(x) = e^x & \text{so} & f'(0) = 1 \\ f''(x) = e^x & \text{so} & f''(0) = 1 \\ \vdots & & \vdots \end{array}$$

so

$$e^x = 1 + x + \frac{x^2}{2!} + \frac{x^3}{3!} + \ldots + \frac{x^n}{n!} + \ldots$$

which is the expression we had before, in Section 13.3.

So far we have used Taylor's theorem as a means of obtaining alternative ways of expressing various functions. Later we shall use it as a way of expanding nonlinear functions about equilibrium points to yield linear approximations to which we can then apply the methods of linear algebra.

14.3* Periodic functions, complex numbers

This section is somewhat subsidiary to the main arguments, and it is not absolutely necessary for an understanding of the rest of the book. It is essentially further application of the theory of series expansions, and introduces some simple trigonometrical results, together with some applications in the theory of complex numbers and dynamic systems.

Consider the diagram in Figure 14.2. The inscribed triangle is a right-angled triangle and so by Pythagoras's theorem, $r^2 = a^2 + b^2$. Let θ be the

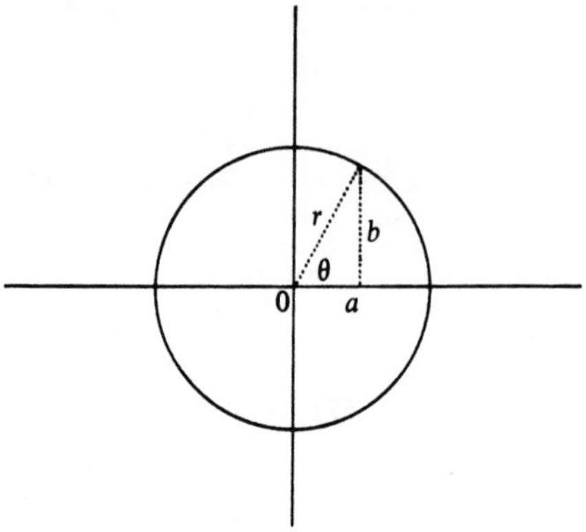

Figure 14.2

indicated angle, measured in degrees. Then, by definition of sine, cosine and tangent,

$$\sin\theta = \frac{b}{r}, \quad \cos\theta = \frac{a}{r}, \quad \tan\theta = \frac{\sin\theta}{\cos\theta} = \frac{b}{a}$$

or equivalently,

$$a = r\cos\theta, \quad b = r\sin\theta.$$

Note that $\tan\theta$ is the *slope* of r; cf. Section 13.1 above.

Several identities follow from these definitions (for example, $(\sin\theta)^2 + (\cos\theta)^2 = 1$), but we shall not consider these here. From the diagram, one can easily check that

$$\sin 0 = 0, \quad \sin 90 = 1, \quad \sin 180 = 0, \quad \sin 270 = -1, \quad \sin 360 = 0$$

$$\cos 0 = 1, \quad \cos 90 = 0, \quad \cos 180 = -1, \quad \cos 270 = 0, \quad \cos 360 = 1$$

and if we were to plot some intermediate values we would find that the graphs of these functions are as in Figure 14.3.

Now, the units in which angles are measured are entirely arbitrary, and it turns out to be much more convenient for our purposes to use *radians* rather than degrees. There are 2π radians in one complete rotation, and 360 degrees, so that

$$90^\circ = \tfrac{1}{2}\pi \text{ radians}, \quad 180^\circ = \pi \text{ radians}, \quad \text{and so on.}$$

Inspecting Figure 14.3, and remembering that the derivative of a function is its slope, it seems reasonable to *assume* that

$$\frac{d\sin x}{dx} = \cos x \quad \text{and} \quad \frac{d\cos x}{dx} = -\sin x$$

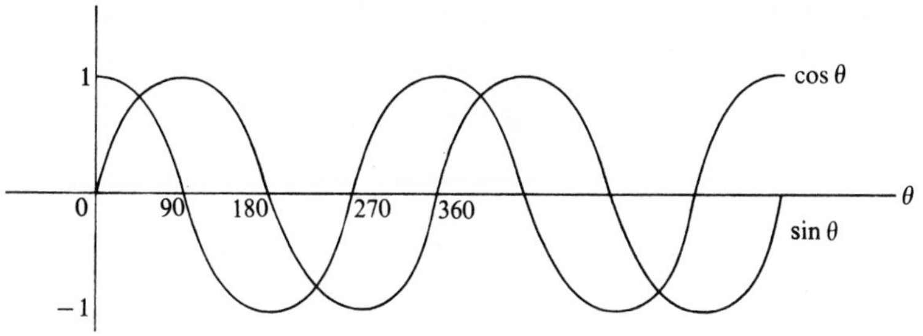

Figure 14.3

where x is measured in radians. We take this assumption as a starting point, but it can be justified. For instance, at $\frac{1}{2}\pi$, sin x has a zero slope, and $\cos\frac{1}{2}\pi = 0$. At $\frac{3}{2}\pi$, $\cos x$ has a slope of $+1$ and $\sin\frac{3}{2}\pi = -1$. You can confirm all of these properties by using the program for plotting and finding derivatives in the previous two chapters.

Given the properties that the derivative of the sine is the cosine and that the derivative of the cosine is minus the sine we can express $\sin x$ and $\cos x$ in terms of their Taylor series expansions:

$$\begin{aligned} f(x) &= \sin x & f(0) &= 0 \\ f'(x) &= \cos x & f'(0) &= 1 \\ f''(x) &= -\sin x & f''(0) &= 0 \\ f'''(x) &= -\cos x & f'''(0) &= -1 \\ &\vdots & &\vdots \end{aligned}$$

so

$$\sin x = x - \frac{x^3}{3!} + \frac{x^5}{5!} - \frac{x^7}{7!} + \frac{x^9}{9!} - \ldots,$$

a formula one can use to compute $\sin x$ to any required accuracy by taking the necessary number of terms. Similarly, the reader should confirm that

$$\cos x = 1 - \frac{x^2}{2!} + \frac{x^4}{4!} - \frac{x^6}{6!} + \frac{x^8}{8!} \ldots.$$

It is easy to verify from these series that the assumed rules for differentiating $\sin x$ and $\cos x$ are satisfied.

On several occasions we have come across complex numbers–in finding eigenvalues and in difference equations for instance. There is a close relationship between complex numbers, sines and cosines, and the exponential function which we can now explore.

Recall that in Section 9.2 we *defined* the symbol i by

$$\mathrm{i} = \sqrt{-1}, \quad \text{an imaginary number.}$$

From the definition,

$$i^2 = \sqrt{-1}.\sqrt{-1} = -1, \quad i^3 = i^2.i = -i, \quad i^4 = +1, \quad \text{etc.}$$

Now consider e^{ix}. Writing ix in place of x in the expansion of e^x, we have

$$e^{ix} = 1 + (ix) + \frac{(ix)^2}{2!} + \frac{(ix)^3}{3!} + \ldots$$

and using the properties of i,

$$e^{ix} = 1 + ix - \frac{x^2}{2!} - \frac{ix^3}{3!} + \frac{x^4}{4!} - \ldots.$$

Similarly,

$$e^{-ix} = 1 - ix - \frac{x^2}{2!} + \frac{ix^3}{3!} \ldots.$$

If we now take $e^{ix} + e^{-ix}$ we see that all the terms involving i will cancel out, to give

$$\frac{e^{ix} + e^{-ix}}{2} = 1 - \frac{x^2}{2!} + \frac{x^4}{4!} - \frac{x^6}{6!} + \ldots = \cos x.$$

Similarly,

$$\sin x = \frac{e^{ix} - e^{-ix}}{2i}.$$

These two expressions can be used as a way of *defining* $\sin x$ and $\cos x$; although they look as though they involve imaginary numbers, they do not because of the cancellation.

It also follows from this that

$$\cos x + i \sin x = e^{ix}$$

$$\cos x - i \sin x = e^{-ix}.$$

Recall that a complex number z has the general form

$$z = a + ib$$

where a is the real part, and b is the imaginary part. We can represent this on an *Argand diagram* by plotting the real part on the horizontal axis, and the imaginary part of the vertical axis (see Figure 14.4), where $r = \sqrt{(a^2 + b^2)}$ and x is the marked angle, known respectively as the *modulus* and the *argument* of z. (One can think of a complex number as a vector in E^2, with coordinates (a, b).) Referring to the beginning of this section, we see that

$$a = r \cos x, \quad b = r \sin x$$

so that we have

$$z = a + ib = r(\cos x + i \sin x) = r\, e^{ix},$$

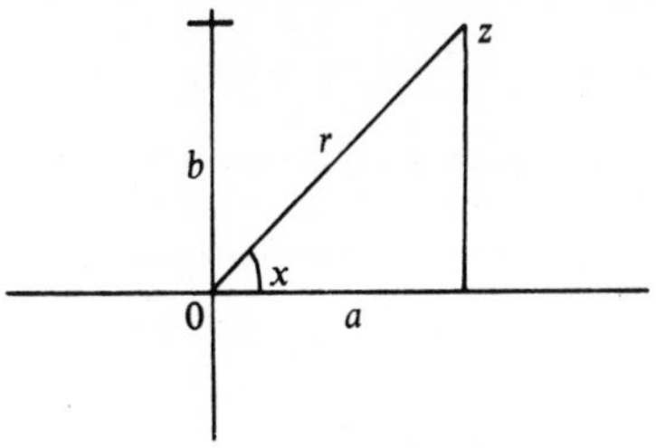

Figure 14.4

three equivalent ways of representing a complex number. The last of these gives us a way of multiplying two complex numbers z_1 and z_2, where

$$z_1 = a_1 + ib_1$$
$$z_2 = a_2 + ib_2.$$

But

$$z_1 = r_1 e^{ix_1}$$
$$z_2 = r_2 e^{ix_2}$$

so

$$\begin{aligned} z_1 z_2 &= r_1 r_2 e^{ix_1} e^{ix_2} = r_1 r_2 e^{i(x_1 + x_2)} \\ &= r_1 r_2 \{\cos(x_1 + x_2) + i \sin(x_1 + x_2)\}. \end{aligned}$$

That is, to multiply two complex numbers we add the arguments and multiply the moduli. In particular,

$$\begin{aligned} z^n &= \{r(\cos x + i \sin x)\}^n \\ &= r^n(\cos nx + i \sin nx) \end{aligned}$$

which is *De Moivre's theorem*.

As an application, consider the solution to the homogeneous second-order difference equation, or a system of two first-order equations which was (see Section 9.5)

$$z(t) = k_1 \lambda_1^t + k_2 \lambda_2^t$$

and suppose that λ_1 and λ_2 are *complex conjugates*, of the form

$$\lambda_1 = a + ib = r(\cos x + i \sin x)$$
$$\lambda_2 = a - ib = r(\cos x - i \sin x).$$

Then by De Moivre's theorem,

$$z(t) = k_1 r^t(\cos tx + i \sin tx) + k_2 r^t(\cos tx - i \sin tx)$$

or

$$z(t) = (k_1 + k_2)\, r^t \cos tx + \mathrm{i}(k_1 - k_2)\, r^t \sin tx.$$

But k_1 and k_2 are proportional to elements of the eigenvectors corresponding to λ_1 and λ_2, and will also be complex conjugates, say

$$k_1 = s(\cos \epsilon + \mathrm{i} \sin \epsilon), \quad k_2 = s(\cos \epsilon - \mathrm{i} \sin \epsilon)$$

so

$$z(t) = 2sr^t(\cos \epsilon)(\cos tx) - 2sr^t(\sin \epsilon)(\sin tx)$$

and, using the standard result that

$$\cos x \cos y - \sin x \sin y = \cos (x + y),$$

we have

$$z(t) = Ar^t \cos (tx + \epsilon)$$

where the constants A and ϵ are to be determined from the initial conditions. The cosine term always oscillates between -1 and $+1$ and so the term Ar^t is the *amplitude* of the cycle. If $|r| < 1$, that is, if the roots λ_1 and λ_2 lie within the unit circle, (cf. Sections 9.4 and 9.5), then the amplitude will be declining and the cycle is *damped* (see Figure 14.5). The time between peaks, the *period* of the cycle, is obviously $2\pi/x$. The constant ϵ determines the *phase*, that is the position in the cycle at the initial instant, $t = 0$. Hence we see that the solution to our equation can exhibit cycles of any period, whereas the first-order system could only give rather uninteresting two-period cycles. Clearly, if the roots are within the unit circle and the cycle is damped, then the system is globally stable. Otherwise it is unstable.

All of these properties can be illustrated by the program given in Chapter 9. In the case of complex eigenvalues for the characteristic equation of a second-order difference equation it calculates the modulus, the argument and the period of the cycles, and it also displays the nature of the motion implied.

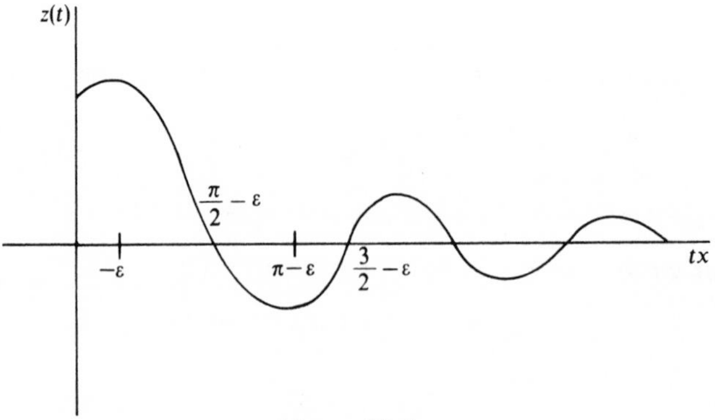

Figure 14.5

It can be shown that any regular motion can be represented by a sum of sinusoidal (or cosinusoidal) waves, no matter how complicated. Examples are the motion of weights on springs, pendulums, sound waves and cycles in economic activity. Try the plotting program of Chapter 12, between −10 and 10 with the following

```
200  DEF FNF(X) = SIN(X)
```

or

```
200  DEF FNF(X) = SIN(X) + 0.5*SIN(5*X)
```

or

```
200  DEF FNF(X) = SIN(X) + 0.5*SIN(3*X) + 0.25*SIN(5*X) +
     0.125*SIN(7*X)
```

It will be apparent that one could reproduce any waveform by the judicious choice of sine terms. Each term represents a unique frequency, each with its own amplitude or power. Thus a periodic pattern can be thought of as a spectrum of powers. This is the basis of the spectral, or harmonic, analysis of time series of data.

The following program may serve to illustrate this. It is adapted from Rogers (1980) and carries out what is known as a Fourier transform. No attempt is made here to explain in detail what this is, but broadly it takes a series of observations and analyses it to determine the power that is present at a spectrum of frequencies. The power spectrum is then plotted graphically. The points to be analysed are generated in lines 230 to 250 and then plotted in lines 260 to 430. There are many refinements you might like to make, such as more sophisticated plotting and labelling of the axes.

```
100  CLS : REM CLEAR SCREEN
110  WIDE = 95 : REM HORIZONTAL RESOLUTION
120  HIGH = 43 : REM VERTICAL RESOLUTION
130  INPUT "WHAT POWER OF 2";Q : REM 2 POWER Q POINTS
140  P = Q − 1
150  F = 0.1
160  R = INT(2↑Q+F)−1
170  DIM F(R),REAL(R),IMAGINARY(R),CO(R),SI(R),A(R)
175  REM ALL ARRAYS ASSUMED TO BE INITIALISED AT ZERO BY
     'DIM'
180  K = 2*3.14159265/(R+1)
190  FOR X = 0 TO R
200  CO(X) = COS(K*X)
210  SI(X) = SIN(K*X)
220  NEXT X
230  FOR X = 0 TO R
240  F(X)=SIN(K*X*5)
250  NEXT X
260  CLS
270  FOR X = 0 TO WIDE
```

```
280  SET(X,HIGH)
290  NEXT X
300  FOR X = 0 TO HIGH
310  SET(0, X)
320  NEXT X
330  MAX = − 1.0E38
340  MIN = 1.0E38
350  FOR X=0 TO R
360  IF F(X) < MIN THEN MIN = F(X)
370  IF F(X) > MAX THEN MAX = F(X)
380  NEXT X
390  PRINT "MAX = ";MAX;"MIN = ";MIN;
400  FOR X = 0 TO R
410  Z = (F(X) − MIN)/(MAX − MIN)
420  SET ((X/(2↑Q))*WIDE, HIGH*(1 − Z))
430  NEXT X
440  PRINT"FFT : BIT REVERSAL";
450  GOSUB 1000
460  GOSUB 1100
470  CLS
480  FOR X = 0 TO WIDE
490  SET(X, HIGH)
500  NEXT X
510  FOR X=0 TO R
520  A(X) = INT(SQR(REAL(X)*REAL(X) + IMAGINARY (X)*
     IMAGINARY(X)) )
530  NEXT X
540  MAX = 0
550  FOR X=0 TO R
560  IF A(X) > MAX THEN MAX = A(X)
570  NEXT X
580  PRINT"MAX POWER = ";MAX
590  Q2 = 2↑Q
600  FOR X = 0 TO R/2 STEP (Q2/WIDE)*3
610  FOR I = 0 TO A(X) STEP MAX/HIGH
620  SET (2*(X/Q2)*WIDE,(1 − I/MAX)*(HIGH − 4) + 4)
630  NEXT I
640  NEXT X
650  STOP
1000  FOR X = 0 TO R
1010  Y = 0
1020  FOR V = 0 TO P
1030  A = INT(2↑V+F)
1040  B = INT(2↑(P − V) + F)
1050  Y = Y + B*(X AND A)/A
1060  NEXT V
1070  REAL (Y) = F(X)
```

```
1080  NEXT X
1090  RETURN
1100  FOR S = 0 TO P
1110  PRINT"STAGE";S;
1120  T = INT(2↑S+F)
1130  D = INT(2↑(P − S) + F)
1140  FOR Z = 0 TO T − 1
1150  L = INT(D*Z + F)
1160  FOR I = 0 TO D − 1
1170  A = 2*I*T+Z
1180  B = A+T
1190  F1 = REAL(A)
1200  F2 = IMAGINARY(A)
1210  P1 = CO(L)*REAL(B)
1220  P2 = SI(L)*IMAGINARY(B)
1230  P3 = SI(L)*REAL(B)
1240  P4 = CO(L)*IMAGINARY(B)
1250  REAL(A) = F1 + P1 − P2
1260  IMAGINARY(A) = F2 + P3 + P4
1270  REAL(B) = F1 − P1 + P2
1280  IMAGINARY(B) = F2 − P3 − P4
1290  NEXT I
1300  NEXT Z
1310  NEXT S
1320  RETURN
```

The fast Fourier transform which is given here only works correctly if the number of points is a power of 2. The program begins by asking which power of 2 you wish to use. A reply of 7 implies 128 data points and 8 implies 256, etc. The more points used the more accurate the spectrum, but both memory requirements are computing time increase rapidly with the number of points.

The example given in line 240 is a simple sine wave with exactly 5 cycles over the sample period. Other examples are

```
240  F(X) = SIN(K*X*5.2)
240  F(X) = SIN(K*X*5.2) + SIN(K*X*6.2)
240  F(X) = EXP(−X*K)
240  F(X) = 2*RND(1) − 1
```

The last example uses a random number generator intrinsic to BASIC to create random numbers between −1 and +1. This is sometimes called white noise. It is instructive to experiment by adding increasing quantities of white noise to a sine wave and noting the extent to which the sine wave can be discerned in the plot of the resulting data points and the clarity with which its frequency shows up in the frequency spectrum. For example

```
240  F(X) = SIN(K*X*5.2) + 3*(2*RND(1) − 1)
```

Other series which have interesting spectra are square waves

```
240 F(X) = (-1)↑INT(X/10)
```

and regular trains of pulses

```
230 FOR X = 0 TO R STEP 10
240 F(X) = 1
250 NEXT X
```

14.4 Problems

1. Differentiate

(*a*) $(\sin x)^2$ (also written $\sin^2 x$) (*b*) $\cos(3x^2)$

(*c*) $e^x \sin x^3$ (*d*) $\tan(3x^2) = \dfrac{\sin(3x^2)}{\cos(3x^2)}$.

2. Find Taylor's expansion about zero of $(1+x/n)^n$ where n is a positive constant. By considering each term of this expansion, show that

$$\lim_{n\to\infty}\left(1+\frac{x}{n}\right)^n = e^x.$$

This result establishes the equivalence of two alternative definitions of the number e (and also justifies the use of e^r in continuous-compounding interest calculations, see Section 19.5).

3. Find the eigenvalues of the matrix

$$\begin{bmatrix} 1 & 0 & 0 \\ -2 & 1 & -7 \\ 4 & 1 & 2 \end{bmatrix}.$$

4. Under what conditions on the parameters b and c of a linear, homogeneous, second-order difference equation (see Section 9.4(*d*)) will the solution exhibit stable, long-period cycles?

15 Theory of maximization and minimization

15.1 Necessary conditions

D15.1 $f(x)$ has a *local* (or relative) *maximum* at x_0 if $f(x) \leqslant f(x_0)\ \forall\, x \in N(x_0, \epsilon)$ for some $\epsilon > 0$.

That is, if at some point x_0, the value of the function is no less than the value at every nearby point, then the function has a maximum at x_0. Taking an ϵ neighbourhood around x_0 in Figure 15.1, it is clear that the value of the function is less at any point other than x_0, which is therefore a local maximum. The same is true for x_0', because if ϵ is small enough there exists an $\epsilon > 0$ such that all points within that neighbourhood give a value of the function which is no greater than the value at x_0'.

The maximum is local in that it is only a maximum relative to nearby points. If the function is differentiable, these maxima all occur when the slope of $f(x)$ is zero, and hence the overall, or *global*, maximum on the domain cannot usually be distinguished just by looking at the slope. Note that the definition does not depend on differentiability, or even continuity

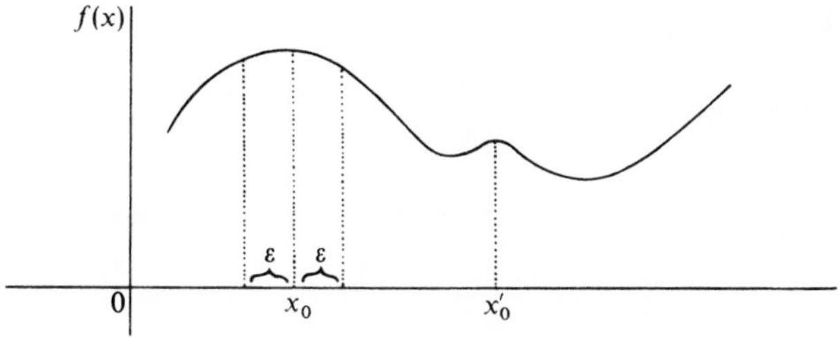

Figure 15.1

of the function. However, differentiability is necessary if we are to use the calculus to find optima. For minima, the inequality in D15.1 is the other way around; that is $f(x) \geqslant f(x_0)$.

Theorem 15.1 If f is differentiable at x_0, a point in the interior of the domain, then it is a *necessary* (or *first-order*) condition that

$$\frac{\mathrm{d}f(x_0)}{\mathrm{d}x} = 0$$

for x_0 to be a maximum or minimum.

Proof. Suppose x_0 is an interior maximum, but $f'(x_0) \neq 0$. Then either $f'(x_0) > 0$ or $f'(x_0) < 0$. If $f'(x_0) > 0$ we can increase x by an amount less than some ϵ, and still remain within the domain (since x_0 is an *interior point*; see D11.8), and so increase the value of the function, contradicting the definition of a maximum. Similarly, if $f'(x_0) < 0$, we can reduce x slightly. Hence the assumption that $f'(x_0) \neq 0$ is wrong, so that $f'(x_0) = 0$. ∎

The qualification that x_0 be in the interior of the domain is necessary since, as Figure 15.2 shows, a maximum may occur at the boundary or 'corner' of the domain with a nonzero slope. If it is assumed that the domain is the whole of the space, then this problem is eliminated, but this is not always possible in economics since, for example, one may want to restrict some variables like quantities of goods or prices to be nonnegative.

A zero slope is a necessary, but not sufficient condition for a maximum. The point might be a minimum or a point of inflection, which is illustrated at the point $x = 0$ by $f(x) = x^3$ in Figure 15.3. In the case of a maximum, as we move from the left of the maximizing point to the right of it, the slope is always decreasing, so the *second* derivative is negative. Hence, if we calculate $f''(x_0)$ and find that this is strictly negative (positive), then we can be sure that we have a maximum (minimum). This, together with $f'(x_0) = 0$ is a sufficient (or *second-order*) condition.

For example, take

$$f(x) = -x^2$$

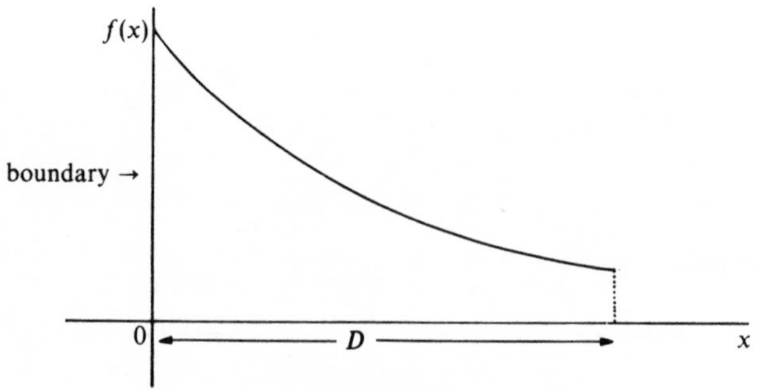

Figure 15.2

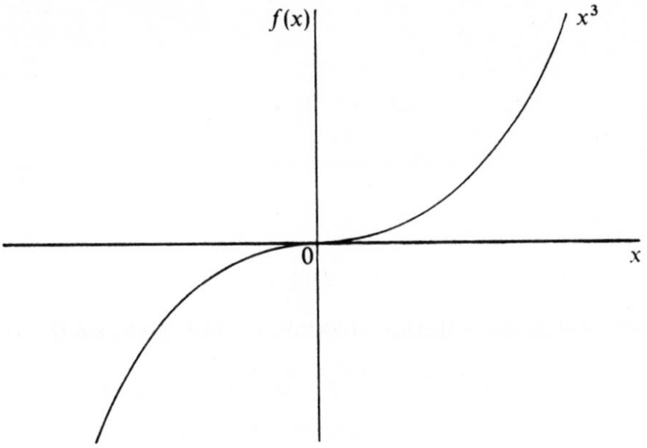

Figure 15.3

Then

$$f'(x) = -2x$$
$$= 0 \quad \text{if} \quad x = 0$$
$$f''(x) = -2 \quad \text{which is negative at } x = 0$$

(and everywhere else as it happens), so $x = 0$ is definitely a maximum.

As another illustration, consider

$$f(x) = 5x^2 \, e^x$$

In rule 6, Section 13.3, we found that

$$f'(x) = 5x \, e^x(x + 2)$$

so

$$f'(x) = 0 \quad \text{at } x = 0 \quad \text{and} \quad x = -2$$
$$f''(x) = 5\{e^x(2x + 2) + e^x(x^2 + 2x)\}$$

so

$$f''(0) = 5.2 = 10 > 0 \quad \text{and} \quad x = 0 \text{ is a minimum.}$$

Also

$$f''(-2) = 5.e^{-2}.-2 = -10e^{-2} < 0 \quad \text{and} \quad x = -2 \text{ is a maximum.}$$

Consider now

$$f(x) = x^3$$
$$f'(x) = 3x^2 \quad \text{and} \quad f'(x) = 0 \quad \text{if } x = 0$$
$$f''(x) = 6x \quad \text{and} \quad f''(0) = 0 \quad \text{also.}$$

Here we have a problem because $f''(0)$ is neither positive nor negative. In this case we cannot deduce the nature of the point from the second derivative. The procedure in such a case is to evaluate higher order derivatives at the point in question until the *first* non-zero derivative is obtained. If the order of this derivative is odd then we have a point of inflection. If it is even we apply the same rule as before—negative for a maximum and positive for a minimum.

In the case of x^3,

$$f'''(0) = 6 \neq 0$$

so 0 is a point of inflection. But if $f(x) = x^4$,

$$f'(0) = f''(0) = f'''(0) = 0$$
$$f^{(\text{iv})}(0) = 24 > 0$$

so $x = 0$ is a minimum.

Any value of x where the first derivative of the function is zero is known as a *stationary* point, and the value of the function at either a global maximum or a global minimum is called an *extreme* value.

15.2* Concavity and sufficient conditions

In Section 11.3 we defined the concept of a convex *set*. We now define *convex* and *concave functions.*

D15.2 A function f is said to be *concave* on the convex set D if

$$\{(z, x) \mid z \leqslant f(x), x \in D\}$$

is a convex set. For a *convex* function this inequality is reversed.

In cases (a) and (b) in Figure 15.4, the functions are respectively concave and convex, since the shaded area is a convex set. (c) is neither concave nor

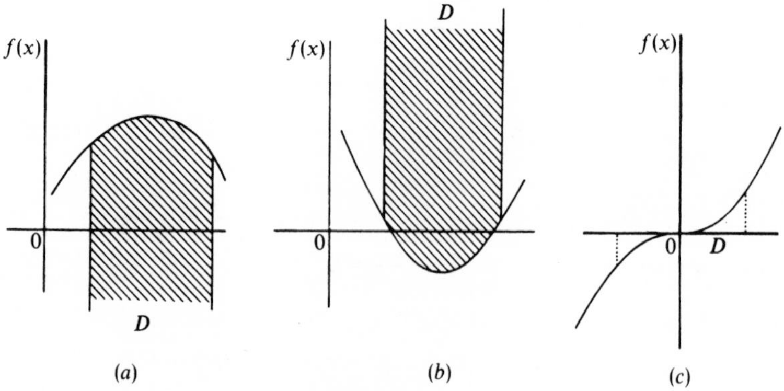

Figure 15.4

convex. It is clear that the tangent line to any point on a concave function will lie above the function. That is, if f is concave and differentiable

$$f(x) \leqslant f(x_0) + f'(x_0)(x - x_0),$$

for any x_0 and any other point x. But, by Taylor's theorem, if $(x - x_0)$ is so small that we can ignore third and higher-order terms (for example, if $(x - x_0) = 0{\cdot}1$, then $(x - x_0)^3 = 0{\cdot}001$),

$$f(x) = f(x_0) + f'(x_0)(x - x_0) + \frac{f''(x_0)}{2!}(x - x_0)^2.$$

Hence we see that if f is concave in the neighbourhood of any point x_0 then $f''(x_0)$ must be negative. So, as one might expect, the second-order condition for a maximum just says that the function should be concave in the neighbourhood of the point with zero slope; if $f'(x_0) = 0$

$$f(x) = f(x_0) + \frac{f''(x_0)}{2!}(x - x_0)^2,$$

so that if

$$f(x) \leqslant f(x_0)$$

for all x in a neighbourhood of x_0 it must be that

$$f''(x_0) \leqslant 0$$

and the definition of concavity is satisfied. Similarly, one can derive the rules for minima and points of inflection by appealing to Taylor's expansion.

The property of concavity plays an important part in economics. A general function may have a great many local maxima and minima and the process of choosing the true maximum from them can be very difficult. However, if one is able to assume that a function is concave at *every* point on its domain, one does not face this problem. If one has found *any* point with zero slope, it must be a maximum, so there is no need to check the second-order conditions. In addition, it must be the *global* maximum which will be *unique* unless the function has a 'plateau', in which case there may be a (convex) set of points all yielding the same maximum value.

To return to the profit example of Section 13.1, if $c(x)$ is the minimum cost of producing x units of a good per unit time then the profit function is given by

$$\pi(x) = px - c(x).$$

Now, at a stationary point,

$$\frac{d\pi(x)}{dx} = 0,$$

that is

$$p - \frac{dc(x)}{dx} = 0$$

or

$$p = \frac{\mathrm{d}c(x)}{\mathrm{d}x};$$

price is equal to marginal cost. We can be sure that this yields a global maximum if $\pi(x)$ is concave. But the sum of two concave functions is also concave and certainly px is concave since it is linear, and linear functions are both concave and convex. Hence we want $-c(x)$ to be concave, or equivalently, $c(x)$ to be convex, since if $f(x)$ is convex, $-f(x)$ is concave. But this is precisely the usual requirement of increasing marginal cost (that is, $c''(x)>0$) at the maximum, which follows from diminishing returns to scale in production or, equivalently, convexity of the production set drawn in Section 11.3.

15.3* Existence

We have already seen how a function may have a maximum at a corner, or at a nondifferentiable point, which we could not identify by the simple calculus. On the other hand, it is clear that it is quite possible to pose problems which simply have *no* solution. For instance the functions $f(x) = a + bx$ and $f(x) = x^2$ have no maxima on the domain $D = \{x \mid x \geqslant 0\}$. This is because D is unbounded, and one can go on increasing $f(x)$ indefinitely. It is no use attempting to say that these functions have maxima 'at infinity'–that is a meaningless statement. The situation is quite simple–there is *no* solution to that particular problem. Similarly e^x has no minimum on E^1.

Maxima can fail to exist for more subtle reasons. For instance

$$f(x) = x \quad \text{on} \quad D = \{x \mid 0 < x < 1\}$$

has no maximum because the domain does not contain any biggest element. This is because it is not closed. Also,

$$f(x) = \frac{1}{x} \quad \text{on} \quad D = \{x \mid -1 \leqslant x \leqslant 1\}$$

has neither maximum nor minimum, because, although the domain is closed and bounded, the function is not continuous. See Section 12.2 for a sketch of this function.

The examples given here are rather transparent, but occasionally it is difficult to be sure that a complex problem has a solution. Indeed, certain very reasonable looking maximization problems (particularly in the theory of growth and planning) have been found, on careful investigation, not to have solutions. Hence one is interested in having a set of conditions which will *guarantee* the existence of a maximum and a minimum of a function on a given domain. The examples given above failed to have solutions because of lack of boundedness, lack of closedness, and lack of continuity, respectively. The following definition and theorem rule out these possibilities.

D15.3 A set which is closed and bounded is said to be *compact*.

Theorem 15.2 A continuous function on a compact domain has both a maximum and a minimum on that domain.

Of course this theorem gives a *sufficient* set of conditions; if they are not all satisfied there may, or may not, be a solution.

15.4 Problems

1. Find the values of x for which the first derivatives of the following functions are zero, and find the sign of the second derivatives at these points for various values of a, b, and c.

(*a*) x^2 (*b*) $\frac{1}{2}ax^2 + b$ (*c*) $\frac{1}{3}ax^3 + \frac{1}{2}bx^2 + c$ (*d*) e^x (*e*) $ax + b$.

2. Find the turning points (if any) of the following functions and identify them as local maxima, local minima or points of inflection. In each case find the global maximum and global minimum where they exist when the domain is the whole of the real line.

(*a*) $f(x) = 4x^2 + 2$ (*b*) $f(x) = 9x^3 + 4x^2 + 2$

(*c*) $f(x) = 1/(x^2 + 1)$ (*d*) $f(x) = 3x + 1$

(*e*) $f(x) = \sin x$ (*f*) $f(x) = x^3$

(*g*) $f(x) = x^3 \mathrm{e}^{-x}$.

16 Functions of several variables

16.1 Introduction

All the functions we have discussed so far have had one independent variable. Since many things are determined by *several* variables we now wish to generalize. We now have

$$f: D \to R \quad (R \subseteq E^1, D \subseteq E^n)$$

and we write

$$f(x_1, x_2, x_3, \ldots, x_n) \text{ or just } f(\boldsymbol{x})$$

where $\boldsymbol{x}$ is now a vector. As examples, consider a production function which gives the maximum amount of some output y which can be obtained by using amounts x_1 and x_2 of two inputs

$$y = f(x_1, x_2).$$

This might have the Cobb-Douglas form

$$y = Ax_1^\alpha x_2^\beta \quad (\alpha, \beta, A \text{ positive constants}).$$

Most of the definitions of functions of one variable have been given in a form which apply equally to functions of several variables, when $\boldsymbol{x}$ is interpreted as a vector; for example, D12.1, the definition of a function itself. It might be useful to re-read the definitions in the last four chapters with this in mind.

Diagrammatically, for a function of two variables, the value of the function can be plotted on the vertical axis and values of the arguments on the horizontal plane. The graph of the function will be a surface in three-dimensional space, with each point on the surface corresponding to one point on the plane (see Figure 16.1).

We cannot usually use graphical techniques for four-dimensional space, which is where purely analytical techniques have the advantage since they can generalize results to any dimension.

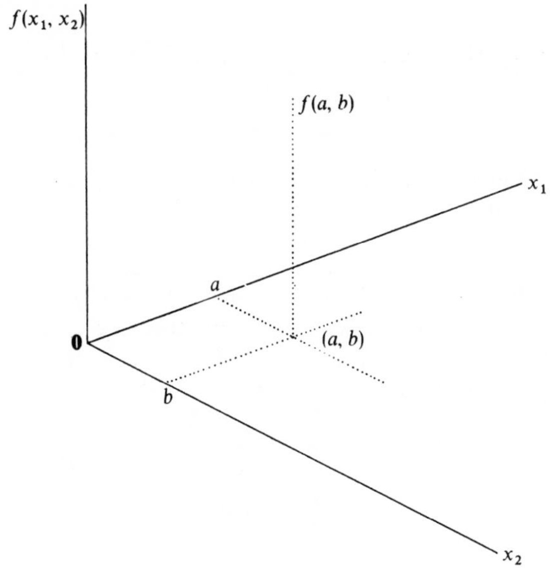

Figure 16.1

In E^3, the analogue of a straight line (in E^2) is a plane. A concave function might be an upturned bowl, in which case we could find the maximum as before by finding the point where the slope is zero. However, at any other point there is the problem of what is meant by the 'slope' at that point. Which way should we move? The change in y will depend on the direction of the change in $\mathbf{x}$. So we identify two slopes at every point; the slope when we move parallel to the x_1 axis (that is, the rate of change of f with respect to changes in x_1, *holding* x_2 *constant*) and the slope when we move parallel to the x_2 axis. These two slopes are called the *partial derivatives* of the function. It can be shown that the slope given by moving in any other direction can be written as a linear combination of these partial derivatives, assuming a regular, 'well-behaved' function.

It is sometimes convenient to use different letters for the different arguments of functions, rather than subscripted variables; for example,

$$w = f(x, y, z)$$

$$y = g(K, L).$$

16.2 Partial derivatives

Given a function of n variables,

$$f(x_1, x_2, \ldots, x_i, \ldots, x)$$

we now define the ith *partial derivative* at the point $\mathbf{x}^0$ (in other words, the partial derivative of f with respect to x_i):

D16.1

$$\frac{\partial f(x^0)}{\partial x_i} = \lim_{t \to 0} \frac{f(x_1^0, \ldots, x_i^0 + t, \ldots, x_n^0) - f(x_1^0, \ldots, x_i^0, \ldots, x_n^0)}{t}$$

if this limit exists.

That is, the value of the function when the ith element is changed by some small number t minus the value of the function at the original point, divided by the change in x_i. If you compare this with the definition of a simple derivative, D13.1, you will see that it is really just a simple derivative, with all the other variables regarded as constants.

It is important when writing derivatives to distinguish between the symbols d and ∂. The 'curly' ∂ indicates that there are variables being held constant. Both should also be distinguished from δ which is used as a parameter and for a different type of derivative in, for example, consumer theory. The ith partial derivative is often written $f_i(x)$, the subscript indicating that the differentiation is being carried out with respect to x_i.

As an example, consider the Cobb–Douglas production function

$$f(x_1, x_2) = Ax_1^\alpha x_2^\beta,$$

then

$$\frac{\partial f}{\partial x_1} = A\alpha x_1^{\alpha-1} x_2^\beta.$$

Similarly,

$$\frac{\partial f}{\partial x_2} = A\beta x_1^\alpha x_2^{\beta-1}.$$

These partial derivatives are the marginal products of the inputs x_1 and x_2, approximately interpreted as the extra output available if one input was increased by one unit, keeping other inputs constant (*ceteris parabus*).

As a second example, if

$$f(x_1, x_2) = x_1 + 2x_1x_2 + x_2^2$$

then

$$f_1(x) = 1 + 2x_2 + 0$$

and

$$f_2(x) = 0 + 2x_1 + 2x_2.$$

Second derivatives are obtained as before by differentiating a second time; but here there are more possibilities. We have

$$\frac{\partial}{\partial x_1}\left(\frac{\partial f(x)}{\partial x_1}\right) = \frac{\partial^2 f(x)}{\partial x_1^2} = f_{11}(x)$$

and

$$\frac{\partial}{\partial x_2}\left(\frac{\partial f(x)}{\partial x_2}\right) = \frac{\partial^2 f(x)}{\partial x_2^2} = f_{22}(x).$$

In the second example above

$$f_{11}(x) = 0$$

$$f_{22}(x) = 2.$$

But we could also differentiate first with respect to x_1 and second with respect to x_2 and vice versa to give

$$\frac{\partial}{\partial x_2}\left(\frac{\partial f(x)}{\partial x_1}\right) = \frac{\partial^2 f(x)}{\partial x_2 \partial x_1} = f_{12}(x)$$

and

$$\frac{\partial}{\partial x_1}\left(\frac{\partial f(x)}{\partial x_2}\right) = \frac{\partial^2 f(x)}{\partial x_1 \partial x_2} = f_{21}(x).$$

In this case we see that $f_{12}(x) = f_{21}(x) = 2$. The equality of *cross-partials* is a general property of differentiable functions. In general we have $f_{ij}(x) = f_{ji}(x)$ so that the order of differentiation does not matter. (There are a few 'pathological' functions for which f_{ij} and f_{ji} exist, but are not equal. We shall not come across any.) Since cross-partials carry two subscripts it is natural to consider them as elements of a matrix:

$$\mathbf{H}(x) = \begin{bmatrix} f_{11}(x) & f_{12}(x) \ldots & f_{1n}(x) \\ \vdots & \vdots & \vdots \\ f_{n1}(x) & f_{n2}(x) \ldots & f_{nn}(x) \end{bmatrix}.$$

This *Hessian* matrix is a square, symmetrical matrix, each of whose elements is (usually) a function of x, the point at which it is evaluated. We shall see later how this is used in considering second-order conditions for maxima and minima.

16.3 Taylor's expansion

Taylor's expansion generalizes in a straightforward way to functions of several variables. The formula looks daunting at first sight, but it is easily remembered if each term is understood and interpreted. We have that on certain assumptions

$$f(x) = f(x^0) + \frac{\partial f(x^0)}{\partial x_1}(x_1 - x_1^0) + \frac{\partial f(x^0)}{\partial x_2}(x_2 - x_2^0)$$

$$+ \ldots + \frac{\partial f(x^0)}{\partial x_n}(x_n - x_n^0) + \frac{1}{2!}\sum_{i=1}^{n}\sum_{j=1}^{n}\frac{\partial^2 f(x^0)}{\partial x_i x_j}(x_i - x_i^0)(x_j - x_j^0)$$

$$+ \text{higher-order terms,}$$

or

$$f(x) = f(x^0) + \sum_{i=1}^{n} f_i(x^0)(x_i - x_i^0)$$

$$+ \frac{1}{2!} \sum_{i=1}^{n} \sum_{j=1}^{n} f_{ij}(x^0)(x_i - x_i^0)(x_j - x_j^0) + \ldots .$$

As before, this says that the value of the function at some point $\boldsymbol{x}$ is the value at $\boldsymbol{x}^0$, plus the increment obtained by moving along the tangent plane to a point above $\boldsymbol{x}$, plus a term taking account of the curvature, plus higher-order terms. It is easy to confirm that in the special case where $n = 1$ we do indeed get the ordinary one-dimensional Taylor expansion.

In vector notation, let

$$\nabla f(\boldsymbol{x}^0) = \begin{bmatrix} f_1(\boldsymbol{x}^0) \\ f_2(\boldsymbol{x}^0) \\ \vdots \\ f_n(\boldsymbol{x}^0) \end{bmatrix} \text{ and } \mathbf{d}\boldsymbol{x} = \begin{bmatrix} x_1 - x_1^0 \\ x_2 - x_2^0 \\ \vdots \\ x_n - x_n^0 \end{bmatrix},$$

where $\nabla f(\boldsymbol{x})$ ('del $f(\boldsymbol{x})$') is known as the *gradient* of f, then we have

$$f(\boldsymbol{x}) = f(\boldsymbol{x}^0) + \mathbf{d}\boldsymbol{x}' . \nabla f(\boldsymbol{x}^0) + \frac{1}{2!} \mathbf{d}\boldsymbol{x}' \mathbf{H}(\boldsymbol{x}^0) \mathbf{d}\boldsymbol{x} + \ldots .$$

Notice that the third term is a quadratic form with matrix $\mathbf{H}(\boldsymbol{x}^0)$ (Chapter 10). One other point to notice about the result is that it says that in order to obtain the approximate change in f one simply adds the changes attributable to changes in each of the individual xs in turn, when all the others are held constant, so that the total change is resolved into a sum of independent effects. This is the substance of the following notion of a *differential*.

16.4 The differential

We know that if Taylor's expansion is valid, and if $\boldsymbol{x}$ is close to $\boldsymbol{x}^0$ then approximately

$$f(\boldsymbol{x}) \approx f(\boldsymbol{x}^0) + f_1(\boldsymbol{x}^0)\,\mathrm{d}x_1 + f_2(\boldsymbol{x}^0)\,\mathrm{d}x_2 + \ldots + f_n(\boldsymbol{x}^0)\,\mathrm{d}x_n$$

where

$$\mathrm{d}x_i = (x_i - x_i^0)$$

or

$$f(\boldsymbol{x}) - f(\boldsymbol{x}^0) \approx \sum_i f_i(\boldsymbol{x}^0)\,\mathrm{d}x_i.$$

The expression on the right is defined to be the *differential* of $f(\mathbf{x})$ at $\mathbf{x}^0$, denoted $\mathrm{d}f(\mathbf{x}^0)$:

D16.2 The *differential* of $f(\mathbf{x})$ at $\mathbf{x}^0$ is given by

$$\mathrm{d}f(\mathbf{x}^0) = \frac{\partial f(\mathbf{x}^0)}{\partial x_1}\,\mathrm{d}x_1 + \frac{\partial f(\mathbf{x}^0)}{\partial x_2}\,\mathrm{d}x_2 + \ldots + \frac{\partial f(\mathbf{x}^0)}{\partial x_n}\,\mathrm{d}x_n.$$

Note particularly that the definition is an exact statement.

For example, if we have output as a function of capital and labour:

$$Y = f(K, L)$$

then

$$\mathrm{d}Y = \frac{\partial f}{\partial K}\,\mathrm{d}K + \frac{\partial f}{\partial L}\,\mathrm{d}L,$$

or, if f has the Cobb-Douglas form,

$$Y = AK^{\alpha}L^{\beta}$$

then

$$\mathrm{d}Y = A\alpha K^{\alpha-1}L^{\beta}\,\mathrm{d}K + A\beta K^{\alpha}L^{\beta-1}\,\mathrm{d}K.$$

This seems a reasonable way of estimating the change in output when capital and labour change; to multiply the change in capital by the number of units of output obtainable with *one* unit of extra capital, holding labour constant (that is, the marginal product of capital, $\partial f/\partial K$), and to *add* this to the corresponding quantity for labour, holding capital constant. Incidentally, the process of finding the derivatives of a function is known as the process of 'differentiation', not to be confused with the process of 'taking a differential' of a function.

16.5 Optimization

The generalized theory of maxima and minima now follows easily. Definition 15.1 of a maximum applies to this case as it stands. It is necessary at interior maximum (minimum) that the tangent plane be horixontal; equivalently that the differential be zero for all $\mathbf{dx}$; equivalently that every first partial derivative be zero.

Definition D15.2, of a concave function, also applies here. Obviously, if the tangent plane lies *above* the surface in the neighbourhood of $\mathbf{x}^0$, where all partials are zero at $\mathbf{x}^0$, then $\mathbf{x}^0$ is a maximum (see Figure 16.2). In other words, it is sufficient that

$$f_i(\mathbf{x}^0) = 0, \quad i = 1, \ldots, n$$

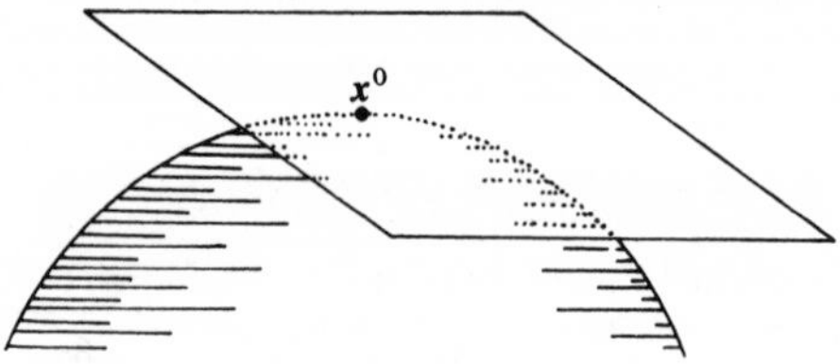

Figure 16.2

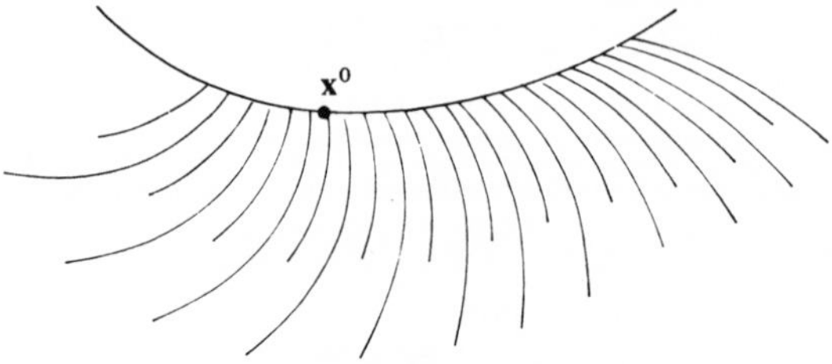

Figure 16.3

and

$$f(x) \leqslant f(x^0)$$

for all x in some neighbourhood of x^0. Since

$$f(x) \approx f(x^0) + \tfrac{1}{2}\, \mathbf{d}x' \mathbf{H}(x^0)\, \mathbf{d}x$$

this will be guaranteed if

$$\mathbf{d}x' \mathbf{H}(x^0)\, \mathbf{d}x < 0$$

for all vectors $\mathbf{d}x$. But this is just the definition of a negative definite matrix by D10.1. Hence to check the second-order condition for a maximum, one has to perform one of the tests given in Chapter 10 for negative difiniteness on the matrix $\mathbf{H}(x^0)$. Similarly, if the Hessian is positive definite we are sure of having a minimum. If it turns out to be indefinite, then we have either a point of inflection or a saddle point; so called because in three dimensions the surface would have the appearance of a saddle (Figure 16.3). In the special case where we have only one independent variable these results reduce to those we have had before, in which case $\mathbf{H}(x^0)$ is a scalar.

The assumption that $\mathbf{H}(x)$ is negative definite for all $x \in D$ implies that $f(x)$ is concave on D. The sufficiency theorem, 15.2, also applies in this case.

As an application we consider the theory of simple, ordinary least squares estimation. It is assumed that y_i, the ith observation of a variable y, is generated as a linear function of the corresponding value of an independent viarable x_i, with an additive random variable u_i:

$$y_i = \beta_0 + \beta_1 x_i + u_i.$$

Once values $\hat{\beta}_0$ and $\hat{\beta}_1$ have been fixed for β_0 and β_1, we can calculate the errors e_i by

$$e_i = y_i - \hat{\beta}_0 - \hat{\beta}_1 x_i.$$

The problem is to choose $\hat{\beta}_0$ and $\hat{\beta}_1$ so as to minimize the sum of the squares of the errors with respect to $\hat{\beta}_0$ and $\hat{\beta}_1$:

$$\min f(\hat{\beta}_0, \hat{\beta}_1) = \sum_{i=1}^{T} e_i^2$$

$$= \sum_{i=1}^{T} (y_i - \hat{\beta}_0 - \hat{\beta}_1 x_i)^2$$

where T is the number of observations. We solve by setting both partials to zero:

$$\frac{\partial f(\hat{\beta}_0, \hat{\beta}_1)}{\partial \hat{\beta}_0} = \sum_i -2(y_i - \hat{\beta}_0 - \hat{\beta}_1 x_i) = 0$$

$$\frac{\partial f(\hat{\beta}_0, \hat{\beta}_1)}{\partial \hat{\beta}_1} = \sum_i -2x_i(y_i - \hat{\beta}_0 - \hat{\beta}_1 x_i) = 0.$$

Rewriting yields the two *normal equations*,

$$\Sigma y_i - \Sigma \hat{\beta}_0 - \Sigma \hat{\beta}_1 x_i = 0$$

$$\Sigma x_i y_i - \Sigma \hat{\beta}_0 x_i - \Sigma \hat{\beta}_1 x_i^2 = 0$$

or

$$T\bar{y} - T\hat{\beta}_0 - \hat{\beta}_1 T\bar{x} = 0$$

$$\Sigma x_i y_i - T\hat{\beta}_0 \bar{x} - \hat{\beta}_1 \Sigma x_i^2 = 0$$

where

$$\bar{x} = \frac{1}{T}\Sigma x_i, \quad \bar{y} = \frac{1}{T}\Sigma y_i,$$

two simultaneous linear equations in $\hat{\beta}_0$ and $\hat{\beta}_1$ which can be solved to give the least squares estimates:

$$\hat{\beta}_0 = \bar{y} - \hat{\beta}_1 \bar{x}$$

$$\hat{\beta}_1 = \frac{\Sigma y_i x_i - T\bar{y}\bar{x}}{\Sigma x_i^2 - T\bar{x}^2}.$$

Also we have

$$\frac{\partial^2 f}{\partial \hat{\beta}_0^2} = \sum_i 2 = 2T, \quad \text{etc.}$$

and so the Hessian is

$$\begin{bmatrix} 2T & 2T\bar{x} \\ 2T\bar{x} & 2\Sigma x_i^2 \end{bmatrix}.$$

Using the alternating minor criterion (Theorem 10.2 (*a*) and (*b*)) we have

$$2T > 0$$

and

$$\begin{aligned} 4T\Sigma x_i^2 - 4T^2\bar{x}^2 &= 4T\{\Sigma x_i^2 - T\bar{x}^2\} \\ &= 4T\left\{\Sigma x_i^2 - \frac{1}{T}(\Sigma x_i)^2\right\} \\ &> 0 \end{aligned}$$

and so we have a minimum.

Simple programs in BASIC which employ these principles to fit linear regression lines can be found in a number of books, for example, Kemeny and Kurtz (1971), p. 114.

16.6 More on differentials. The chain rule and Euler's theorem

Differentials behave in very much the way we would expect them to behave; for instance, taking a differential is a linear operation and so the differential of a sum of two functions is the sum of their differentials:

$$f(\mathbf{x}) = g(\mathbf{x}) + h(\mathbf{x}) \Rightarrow \mathrm{d}f(\mathbf{x}) = \mathrm{d}g(\mathbf{x}) + \mathrm{d}h(\mathbf{x})$$

Similarly,

$$f(\mathbf{x}) = g(\mathbf{x})\,h(\mathbf{x}) \Rightarrow \mathrm{d}f(\mathbf{x}) = g(\mathbf{x})\,\mathrm{d}h(\mathbf{x}) + \mathrm{d}g(\mathbf{x})\,h(\mathbf{x})$$

$$f(\mathbf{x}) = \frac{g(\mathbf{x})}{h(\mathbf{x})} \Rightarrow \mathrm{d}f(\mathbf{x}) = \frac{h(\mathbf{x})\,\mathrm{d}g(\mathbf{x}) - g(\mathbf{x})\,\mathrm{d}h(\mathbf{x})}{\{h(\mathbf{x})\}^2}$$

They tell us how to deal with various situations. A common one is where a variable is determined by several others, each of which is in turn determined by one common variable:

$$y = g(t) = f\{x_1(t), x_2(t), \ldots, x_n(t)\}.$$

How should one differentiate f with respect to t? Taking differentials

$$\mathrm{d}g(t) = \frac{\partial f}{\partial x_1}\,\mathrm{d}x_1 + \frac{\partial f}{\partial x_2}\,\mathrm{d}x_2 + \ldots + \frac{\partial f}{\partial x_n}\mathrm{d}x_n.$$

But

$$\mathrm{d}x_1 = \frac{\mathrm{d}x_1(t)}{\mathrm{d}t}\mathrm{d}t, \quad \text{etc.}$$

hence

$$\mathrm{d}g(t) = \frac{\partial f}{\partial x_1}\frac{\mathrm{d}x_1}{\mathrm{d}t}\,\mathrm{d}t + \ldots + \frac{\partial f}{\partial x_n}\frac{\mathrm{d}x_n}{\mathrm{d}t}\,\mathrm{d}t$$

or, dividing by $\mathrm{d}t$,

$$\frac{\mathrm{d}g(t)}{\mathrm{d}t} = \frac{\partial f}{\partial x_1}\frac{\mathrm{d}x_1}{\mathrm{d}t} + \ldots + \frac{\partial f}{\partial x_n}\frac{\mathrm{d}x_n}{\mathrm{d}t}.$$

The quantity on the left is not the derivative of $g(t)$, but the ratio of two differentials. However, we can take the limit as $\mathrm{d}t \to 0$ to obtain an expression for the derivative. This is known as the *chain rule*.

To take a more complicated example, consider

$$Y = f\{K(r, w), L(r, w)\}$$

where r and w are respectively the rental on capital and the wage rate. Then

$$\begin{aligned} \mathrm{d}Y &= f_K\,\mathrm{d}K + f_L\,\mathrm{d}L \\ &= f_K\{K_r\,\mathrm{d}r + K_w\,\mathrm{d}w\} + f_L\{L_r\,\mathrm{d}r + L_w\,\mathrm{d}w\} \\ &= \{f_K K_r + f_L L_r\}\,\mathrm{d}r + \{f_K K_w + f_L L_w\}\,\mathrm{d}w. \end{aligned}$$

As a further illustration we consider the theory of *homogeneous* functions, which are quite important in economics. A homogeneous function has the property that multiplying all the arguments by some number, k, has the effect of multiplying the function by k raised to some power:

D16.3 $f(\mathbf{x})$ is *homogeneous of degree r* if

$$f(k\mathbf{x}) = k^r f(\mathbf{x}).$$

In particular, if $f(k\mathbf{x}) = kf(\mathbf{x})$, so $r = 1$, we have a function which is *homogeneous of degree 1*. This is the case, for example, of a production function where there are constant returns to scale. If all the inputs are multiplied by some (positive) scalar, then the output will be scaled up by the *same* amount. For example, when will $y = Ax_1^\alpha x_2^\beta$ be homogeneous of degree 1? We have

$$f(k\mathbf{x}) = A(kx_1)^\alpha (kx_2)^\beta$$

which is the value of the function when each argument (input) is multiplied by k; so

$$\begin{aligned} f(k\mathbf{x}) &= Ak^\alpha x_1^\alpha k^\beta x_2^\beta \\ &= Ak^{\alpha+\beta} x_1^\alpha x_2^\beta. \end{aligned}$$

But

$$f(\mathbf{x}) = Ax_1^\alpha x_2^\beta$$

and

$$f(k\mathbf{x}) = k^{(\alpha+\beta)} f(\mathbf{x})$$

so the function is homogeneous of degree $(\alpha + \beta)$. If $\beta = 1 - \alpha$, then we have constant returns to scale.

The demand function for a good is usually taken to be

$$x = f(p_1, p_2, \ldots, p_n, m)$$

where p_1, p_2, etc., are all the prices and m is income. If there is no 'money illusion', then doubling all prices and income will leave the demand unchanged. This is another way of saying that the function is homogeneous of degree zero. By the definition, if $f(\mathbf{x})$ is homogeneous of degree zero, then

$$f(k\mathbf{x}) = k^0 f(\mathbf{x}) = f(\mathbf{x})$$

since $k^0 = 1$. This property holds only if *all* the arguments are changed in the same proportion.

In general, by definition, a function homogeneous of degree n satisfies

$$f(kx_1, kx_2, \ldots, kx_n) = k^r f(\mathbf{x}).$$

Differentiating both sides with respect to k, and using the result derived above, on the left-hand side the derivative is the partial derivative of f with respect to its first argument times the derivative of the first argument with respect to k, and so on for each argument;

$$\frac{\partial f}{\partial (kx_1)} \frac{\mathrm{d}(kx_1)}{\mathrm{d}k} + \ldots + \frac{\partial f}{\partial (kx_n)} \frac{\mathrm{d}(kx_n)}{\mathrm{d}k} = rk^{r-1} f(\mathbf{x}).$$

But

$$\frac{\mathrm{d}(kx_1)}{\mathrm{d}k} = x_1 \quad \text{since } k \text{ is the variable and } x_1 \text{ is the constant}$$

and, putting $k = 1$, we are left with Euler's theorem:

Theorem 16.1 If $f(\mathbf{x})$ is homogeneous of degree r, then

$$\frac{\partial f}{\partial x_1} x_1 + \frac{\partial f}{\partial x_2} x_2 + \ldots + \frac{\partial f}{\partial x_n} x_n = rf(\mathbf{x}).$$

Applying this to our production function with two inputs, capital and labour, suppose a capitalist owns capital and is employing labour, paying the marginal product f_L. By Euler's theorem, assuming constant returns to scale

$$Y = f_L L + f_K K.$$

The wage bill will be $f_L L$, so the capitalist is left with

$$Y - f_L L = f_K K.$$

Dividing by K, the capitalist is left with exactly the marginal product per unit of capital he employs. So if he pays the competitive wage, every one gets his own marginal product, which might be held to be a 'fair' distribution of income. This result depends critically on the assumption of constant returns to scale. Without this, capital would get more, or less, than its marginal product in competitive equilibrium.

16.7 Problems

1. Find the local maxima and minima where they exist of the following functions:

(*a*) $x_1^2+x_2^2+x_1x_2+10x_1+10x_2$

(*b*) $3x_1^2+x_2^3-3x_1x_2$

(*c*) $2x_1^2-x_2^2-4x_1+8x_2$.

2. Find the local maxima and minima where they exist of the following functions:

(*a*) $2x_1^2+2x_2^2+9-6x_1-6x_2-2x_1x_2$

(*b*) $x_1^2-2x_1x_2+2x_2^2$

(*c*) $x_1^3-x_2^3$

(*d*) $x_1^2+3x_2^2+2x_3^2+5$

(*e*) $3x_1+2x_2-x_3+6$.

3. Find the differentials of the following functions:

(*a*) $f(r,m)$ (*b*) $f\left(r,\dfrac{M}{P}\right)$ (*c*) $e^r g\{r,h(r)\}$.

4. A firm using inputs capital K and labour L with the production function $F(K,L)$ sells its output at a constant price p and has to pay constant prices r and w respectively for the inputs. Investigate the first- and second-order conditions for maximization of profit, given by

$$\Pi(K,L)=pF(K,L)-rK-wL.$$

How will the optimum choices of K and L be affected by small increases in r and w? (Hint: Take the differentials of the first-order conditions.)

5. The constant elasticity of substitution (c.e.s.) production function is given by

$$F(K,L)=(aK^{-\beta}+bL^{-\beta})^{-1/\beta} \quad (a>0, b>0)$$

where a, b and β are constants. Show that it is homogeneous of degree one and verify that it satisfies Euler's theorem.

17 Constrained optimization

Very few problems in the social sciences can be formulated purely as ones of maximizing something by choosing the best values for the independent variables, without taking any other considerations into account. There are often restrictions or *constraints* on the values that the variables can take. An individual is assumed to behave so as to maximize his utility or satisfaction subject to the constraint imposed by his limited income; a firm is assumed to maximize its profit subject to the available technology (cf. Section 11.3); a country might be assumed to minimize unemployment subject to a restriction on the maximum allowable rate of inflation.

Consider the utility example with two goods, consumed in quantities x_1 and x_2 units per unit time purchased at fixed prices £p_2 and £p_2 per unit, by an individual with income £m per unit time. If the utility that he enjoys when he consumes these amounts is given by $u(x_1, x_2)$, then we might formulate the problem as

$$\max u(x_1, x_2)$$

subject to

$$m \geqslant p_1 x_1 + p_2 x_2, \quad x_1 \geqslant 0, \quad x_2 \geqslant 0;$$

expenditure must not exceed income, and negative consumption is not allowed. The specification of the constraints as inequalities, rather than equations, is typical. We do not mind if he does not spend all of his money and throws some of it away, if he becomes satiated. Unfortunately the solution of problems with inequality constraints is considerably harder than the solution of those where equations are specified. In Section 17.1 which follows, we very briefly consider the general case. Many will want to skip directly to Section 17.2 where the simple case is discussed in more detail.

17.1** The nonlinear programming problem and the Kuhn-Tucker theorem

This is the name given to the class of problems having the following form:

$$\max f(x) \text{ subject to } g(\boldsymbol{x}) \geqslant 0, \boldsymbol{x} \geqslant 0.$$

The utility-maximizing problem has this form, where in that case

$$g(\boldsymbol{x}) = m - p_1x_1 - p_2x_2.$$

The first step in solving such a problem is to introduce a new variable, which we shall call λ, known as a *Lagrangean* (or sometimes *undetermined*) *multiplier*. We use this to form a new function, known as the *Lagrangean function*, defined by

$$L(\boldsymbol{x}, \lambda) = f(\boldsymbol{x}) + \lambda g(\boldsymbol{x})$$

so that the argument list of L consists of the n independent variables x_i and the new variable λ. It turns out that the problem of solving our original problem is very close to the problem of finding a particular kind of saddle point for the new, Lagrangean function. (We came across saddle points in Section 16.5.) In this case we want a point $(\boldsymbol{x}^*, \lambda^*)$ at which $L(\boldsymbol{x}, \lambda)$ is maximized with respect to $\boldsymbol{x}$, and minimized with respect to λ with all $\boldsymbol{x}^*$s and λ^*s nonnegative.

In other words the solution is a point $\boldsymbol{x}^*, \lambda^*$ such that

$$f(\boldsymbol{x}) + \lambda^* g(\boldsymbol{x}) \leqslant f(\boldsymbol{x}^*) + \lambda^* g(\boldsymbol{x}^*) \leqslant f(\boldsymbol{x}^*) + \lambda g(\boldsymbol{x}^*)$$
$$\forall \boldsymbol{x} \text{ and } \lambda \text{ s.t. } x_1 \geqslant 0, x_2 \geqslant 0, \ldots, x_n \geqslant 0, \lambda \geqslant 0$$

which is known as the saddle-point condition.

The relevant theorem, a most remarkable one due to Kuhn and Tucker, can be split into two parts. The first part states that:

Theorem 17.1(a) If a point $(\boldsymbol{x}^*, \lambda^*)$ is found which is a saddle point of $L(\boldsymbol{x}, \lambda)$ with $\boldsymbol{x}^* \geqslant 0, \lambda^* \geqslant 0$, then $\boldsymbol{x}^*$ is a solution to the original problem.

Hence all we have to do to solve the problem is to form the Lagrangean and find a saddle point by any means that we choose. The critical thing to understand is that we can do this *without having to worry about whether the constraint is satisfied*; that is, we can vary $\boldsymbol{x}$ freely over the positive orthant and the variable λ will automatically guarantee that at a saddle point the constraint will be satisfied. For instance, we might well be able to use the calculus theory of unconstrained optimization developed in Chapter 16 to find the saddle point.

Of course the problem as specified may well not have a solution, and hence $L(\boldsymbol{x},\lambda)$ would not have a saddle point. This might be because of the reasons given in Section 15.3, or because the constraint is internally inconsistent. For example, there are no values of x_1 and x_2 such that

$$-x_1^2 - x_2^2 - 1 \geqslant 0.$$

However, the theorem has a second part which says that:

Theorem 17.1(b) If the functions f and g are concave (and if a certain extra weak and technical condition known as the *constraint qualification* is satisfied) and $\boldsymbol{x}^*$ solves the problem, then there exists a $\lambda^* \geqslant 0$ such that $(\boldsymbol{x}^*, \lambda^*)$ is a saddle point of the Lagrangean function.

This means that if we can assume concavity, we are justified in only looking for saddle points when trying to find a solution.

Notice that in the process of solving a problem by this technique we obtain a value for λ which on the face of it is of no interest since it did not appear in the original problem. However, we shall see later (Section 17.3) that it has a very natural and important interpretation, and it tells one a great deal about the problem. It is sometimes known as a *shadow price*, *accounting price* or a *dual variable*. For the moment we just point out one of its properties. From the right-hand inequality of the saddle-point condition we have

$$f(\boldsymbol{x}^*) + \lambda^* g(\boldsymbol{x}^*) \leqslant f(\boldsymbol{x}^*) + \lambda g(\boldsymbol{x}^*), \quad \forall \lambda \geqslant 0$$

or subtracting $f(\boldsymbol{x}^*)$ from both sides,

$$\lambda^* g(\boldsymbol{x}^*) \leqslant \lambda g(\boldsymbol{x}^*), \quad \forall \lambda \geqslant 0.$$

But since $\lambda^* \geqslant 0$ this implies that

$$g(\boldsymbol{x}^*) \geqslant 0$$

because λ may be made arbitrarily large and this would otherwise contradict the previous inequality. So certainly

$$\lambda^* g(\boldsymbol{x}^*) \geqslant 0.$$

In other words $\boldsymbol{x}^*$ must satisfy the constraint. On the other hand, the saddle-point condition must hold for every $\lambda \geqslant 0$ including, in particular, $\lambda = 0$. Hence we also have

$$\lambda^* g(\boldsymbol{x}^*) \leqslant 0$$

so taking these last inequalities together,

$$\lambda^* g(\boldsymbol{x}^*) = 0.$$

The implication of this is that if $g(\boldsymbol{x}^*) > 0$ then $\lambda^* = 0$ and conversely, if $\lambda^* > 0$ then $g(\boldsymbol{x}^*) = 0$. But if $g(\boldsymbol{x}^*) > 0$ we say that the constraint is *ineffective*, or *nonbinding*, or *slack*. In the utility-maximizing example, if not all of the income is spent then limited income is an ineffective constraint. In other words, the solution to the problem would not alter if we removed the constraint altogether. We have shown that if this happens then the associated shadow price is zero.

Very often there will be two or more constraints; imagine a producer with limited floor space, limited machine time, limited labour and limited amounts of certain resources. The way to cope with this is to introduce a new Lagrangean multiplier for each constraint. Suppose the m constraints are given by

$$g_1(\boldsymbol{x}) \geqslant 0, \quad g_2(\boldsymbol{x}) \geqslant 0, \ldots, \quad g_m(\boldsymbol{x}) \geqslant 0$$

then we take

$$L(\boldsymbol{x}, \boldsymbol{\lambda}) = f(\boldsymbol{x}) + \lambda_1 g_1(\boldsymbol{x}) + \lambda_2 g_2(\boldsymbol{x}) + \ldots + \lambda_m g_m(\boldsymbol{x}).$$

If we now define the vectors

$$\boldsymbol{\lambda} = (\lambda_1, \lambda_2, \ldots, \lambda_m), \quad g(x) = \begin{bmatrix} g_1(x) \\ g_2(x) \\ \vdots \\ g_m(x) \end{bmatrix}$$

and use the scalar product notation, we have

$$L(x, \lambda) = f(x) + \boldsymbol{\lambda}\cdot g(x).$$

All the results stated above now carry through to this case, with $\lambda g(x)$ interpreted as $\boldsymbol{\lambda}\cdot g(x)$, a scalar product, and each ineffective constraint will have a zero associated shadow price at the optimum.

A justification for the method (to be given in the next section) for dealing with strict equality constraints can now be seen. Suppose we wish to solve

$$\max f(x) \text{ subject to } g(x) = 0.$$

This is equivalent to the nonlinear programming problem

$$\max f(x) \text{ subject to } g(x) \geqslant 0$$
$$\textit{and } -g(x) \geqslant 0$$

since the two constraints imply

$$g(x) \geqslant 0 \textit{ and } g(x) \leqslant 0$$

so that

$$g(x) = 0.$$

To solve this we would write

$$L(x, \lambda_1, \lambda_2) = f(x) + \lambda_1 g(x) + \lambda_2\{-g(x)\}$$

or

$$L(x, \lambda_1, \lambda_2) = f(x) + (\lambda_1 - \lambda_2)\, g(x)$$

or

$$L(x, \lambda) = f(x) + \lambda g(x)$$

say, where $\lambda = (\lambda_1 - \lambda_2)$.

In other words we can proceed exactly as before, the only difference (apart from the fact that we have not required nonnegativity of the xs) is that we cannot be sure that the optimum value of the multiplier λ^* will be nonnegative. It might have either sign. We shall later see how this reflects the fact that the requirement that the constraint holds with *equality* may make the maximized value of the objective function lower, if the constraint would otherwise have been non-binding; a 'rich' consumer might have to consume more than he wants if we insist that he consume all his income.

It would be wrong to suggest that it is easy to solve nonlinear programming problems in practice. In fact it is only possible to solve a rather restricted set of such problems, and even then a large amount of expensive computing time is often necessary. As usual the assumption of linearity makes solution much simpler, and in fact, if all the gs are linear, and f is linear, a solution is always possible (if it exists), subject to the availability of computing time. In this case the problem can be written in the standard form

$$\max \boldsymbol{c}\cdot\boldsymbol{x} \text{ subject to } \mathbf{A}\boldsymbol{x} \leqslant \boldsymbol{b}, \boldsymbol{x} \geqslant 0$$

with $\boldsymbol{c}$, $\mathbf{A}$ and $\boldsymbol{b}$ given. Here $f(\boldsymbol{x}) = \boldsymbol{c}\cdot\boldsymbol{x}$ and $g_i(\boldsymbol{x}) = b_i - \boldsymbol{a}_i\cdot\boldsymbol{x}$, where $\boldsymbol{a}_i$ is the ith row of the matrix $\mathbf{A}$. This model has found an amazing number of applications in many diverse fields.

The interested reader will find a full development of both linear and nonlinear programming with application in economics in such books as Dorfman, Samuelson and Solow (1958), Intrilligator (1971), Gale (1960), Lancaster (1968) and Karlin (1959). Land and Powell (1973) give a set of computer programs in FORTRAN for solving them.

17.2 Optimization with an equality constraint

The first step in solving a problem of this kind is to rewrite the constraint in standard (implicit, cf. Section 13.4) form, with zero on the right-hand side:

$$g(\boldsymbol{x}) = 0.$$

Thus for the utility-maximizing example we would write the constraint

$$m - p_1x_1 - p_2x_2 = 0$$

where

$$g(\boldsymbol{x}) = m - p_1x_1 - p_2x_2.$$

Then we invent a new function by adding the function to be maximized or minimized (known as the *objective* function), to the product of a new variable λ and our function $g(\boldsymbol{x})$. The result is known as the *Lagrangean* function, denoted by $L(\boldsymbol{x}, \lambda)$:

$$L(\boldsymbol{x}, \lambda) = f(\boldsymbol{x}) + \lambda g(\boldsymbol{x}).$$

In our example this would be

$$L(\boldsymbol{x}, \lambda) = u(x_1, x_2) + \lambda(m - p_1x_1 - p_2x_2).$$

We then use the calculus to maximize (or minimize) the Lagrangean with respect to $\boldsymbol{x}$ and minimize (or maximize) it with respect to λ *as if there were no constraints to be considered*; the Lagrangean multiplier automatically takes account of the constraint. We can apply the ordinary theory of optimization developed in Chapter 16 to do this; the resulting first-order conditions will provide just the right number of equations to eliminate the apparently uninteresting variable, λ.

To see how this works consider the problem:

$$\max 6x_1 + 8x_2 - 8$$

subject to

$$(x_1-2)^2+(x_2-1)^2=25.$$

First rewrite the constraint:

$$(x_1-2)^2+(x_2-1)^2-25=0$$

and then form the Lagrangean

$$L(x_1,x_2,\lambda)=6x_1+8x_2-8+\lambda[(x_1-2)^2+(x_2-1)^2-25].$$

Differentiating,

$$\frac{\partial L}{\partial x_1}=6+2\lambda(x_1-2)$$

$$\frac{\partial L}{\partial x_2}=8+2\lambda(x_2-1)$$

$$\frac{\partial L}{\partial \lambda}=(x_1-2)^2+(x_2-1)^2-25.$$

Putting these derivatives equal to zero yields the three necessary conditions for a solution:

(*a*) $$6+2\lambda(x_1-2)=0$$

(*b*) $$8+2\lambda(x_2-1)=0$$

(*c*) $$(x_1-2)^2+(x_2-1)^2-25=0.$$

We see that we have three equations (in general, $n+1$ equations) to solve for the three variables, x_1, x_2 and λ (in general, $x_1,\ldots,x_n,\lambda$). Notice that one of these is just the original constraint; this is always the case.

From (*a*) we have

$$\lambda(x_1-2)=-3$$

and from (*b*)

$$\lambda(x_2-1)=-4.$$

Squaring,

$$\lambda^2(x_1-2)^2=9$$

and

$$\lambda^2(x_2-1)^2=16.$$

Adding,

$$\lambda^2(x_1-2)^2+\lambda^2(x_2-1)^2=25$$

or

$$\lambda^2\{(x_1-2)^2+(x_2-1)^2\}=25$$

and now using the constraint, (c),

$$\lambda^2.25 = 25$$

or

$$\lambda^2 = 1$$

so

$$\lambda = +1 \text{ or } -1.$$

Using first $\lambda = +1$, (a) and (b) give

$$x_1 = -1, \quad x_2 = -3.$$

If $\lambda = -1$, we have

$$x_1 = 5, \quad x_2 = 5.$$

Hence we apparently have two answers, $x_1 = -1$, $x_2 = -3$ and $x_1 = 5$, $x_2 = 5$. It is easy to confirm that both satisfy the constraint; in the second case we have

$$\begin{aligned}(5-2)^2 + (5-1)^2 &= 3^2 + 4^2\\ &= 9 + 16\\ &= 25, \quad \text{as required.}\end{aligned}$$

The mystery of the two solutions is cleared up by considering the geometry of the problem. We are maximizing a linear function, subject to the restriction that the xs lie on a circle in the domain, of radius 5 and centre (2,1). The linear function would be represented as a positively sloped plane in E^3, and clearly there is going to be one maximum *and* one minimum to the problem. The point $x_1 = -1$, $x_2 = -3$ is clearly the minimum. This illustrates that, as usual, the first-order conditions are only necessary conditions; to establish whether a given point is a maximum, minimum or something else, we must either look at appropriate second-order conditions (Section 17.7) or use other considerations, as we have done in this case.

Return now to the utility problem. The Lagrangean is

$$L(\mathbf{x}, \lambda) = u(x_1, x_2) + \lambda(m - p_1 x_1 - p_2 x_2).$$

Setting first partials to zero gives

$$\frac{\partial u}{\partial x_1} - \lambda p_1 = 0, \quad \frac{\partial u}{\partial x_2} - \lambda p_2 = 0, \quad m - p_1 x_1 - p_2 x_2 = 0.$$

Eliminating λ gives

$$\frac{\partial u}{\partial x_1} \bigg/ \frac{\partial u}{\partial x_2} = \frac{p_1}{p_2}.$$

Now the left-hand side is the marginal rate of substitution between the goods, which can easily be shown to be the negative of the slope of the indifference curves; these are defined as sets of points all yielding the same utility, k say. That is, points such that

$$k = u(x_1, x_2).$$

Taking differentials

$$dk = \frac{\partial u}{\partial x_1} dx_1 + \frac{\partial u}{\partial x_2} dx_2$$

but for movements along an indifference curve, $dk = 0$, so

$$\left(\frac{\partial u}{\partial x_1} \bigg/ \frac{\partial u}{\partial x_2}\right) dx_1 = dx_2$$

or dividing by dx_1 and taking the limit as $dx_1 \to 0$ we get

$$\frac{\partial u}{\partial x_1} \bigg/ \frac{\partial u}{\partial x_2} = -\frac{dx_2}{dx_1}.$$

In other words the left-hand side is minus the rate at which x_2 must be changed, as x_1 is changed, in order to hold utility constant; along an indifference curve. Similarly it is easy to show that p_1/p_2 is the negative of the slope of a budget constraint, so that our necessary conditions imply that the indifference curve must have the same slope as the budget constraint. The constraint itself implies that they must be actually *tangential* (cf. the tangency of profit line and the boundary of the production set in Section 11.3) a fact which is obvious from the usual diagram (see Figure 17.1). These equations are solved in Section 17.4 below, when an explicit form of the utility function is specified.

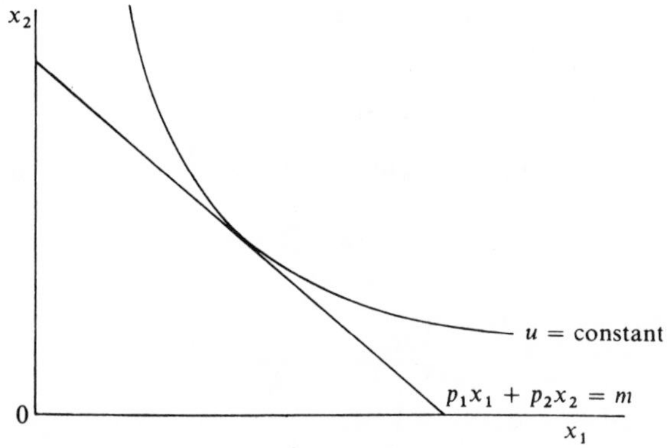

Figure 17.1

17.3* Interpretation of the Lagrangean multipliers

So far we have eliminated λ and forgotten it. However, it always has an interpretation, and this can be very useful. Consider the necessary conditions for utility maximization in the previous section. Multiplying each by its respective dx gives

$$\frac{\partial u}{\partial x_1} dx_1 = \lambda p_1 \, dx_1$$

$$\frac{\partial u}{\partial x_2} dx_2 = \lambda p_2 \, dx_2$$

Adding

$$\frac{\partial u}{\partial x_1} dx_1 + \frac{\partial u}{\partial x_2} dx_2 = \lambda(p_1 \, dx_1 + p_2 \, dx_2).$$

But this is the same as saying that

$$du = \lambda \, dm$$

or, dividing and taking the limit as $dm \to 0$ gives

$$\frac{\partial u}{\partial m} = \lambda.$$

Remembering that the partial derivatives $\partial u/\partial x_i$, and hence du, are evaluated at the maximizing choice, we see that this says that λ is the rate of increase of *maximized* utility with respect to an increase in income; that is the marginal utility of income. To put it another way, it is the cost in utility terms, of not having one more unit of income; the cost of having to observe the constraint.

This type of result can be shown to apply more generally. Consider the standard problem,

$$\max f(\mathbf{x}) \text{ subject to } g(\mathbf{x}) = 0.$$

Now suppose we relax the constraint slightly and write

$$g(\mathbf{x}) + a = 0$$

where a is small, and investigate the change in the maximized value of $f(\mathbf{x})$. Let

$$V(a) = \max_{x} \, [f(\mathbf{x}) + \lambda^*\{g(\mathbf{x}) + a\}],$$

the maximized value of the appropriate Lagrangean,

$$= f(\mathbf{x}^*) + \lambda^*\{g(\mathbf{x}^*) + a\}$$

so that the problem is solved at $\mathbf{x}^*$ for a given value of a. Clearly if a changes the solution will change, so that $\mathbf{x}^*$ is a function of a. In our utility example we are changing income, moving the budget line parallel to itself, and tracing out the *Engel* curve. Bearing this in mind we differentiate $V(a)$, using the chain rule (Section 16.6).

$$\frac{\mathrm{d}V(a)}{\mathrm{d}a} = \frac{\partial f}{\partial x_1}\frac{\partial x_1^*}{\partial a} + \frac{\partial f}{\partial x_2}\frac{\partial x_2^*}{\partial a} + \ldots + \frac{\partial f}{\partial x_n}\frac{\partial x_n^*}{\partial a}$$

$$+ \lambda^* \frac{\partial g}{\partial x_1}\frac{\partial x_1^*}{\partial a} + \lambda^* \frac{\partial g}{\partial x_2}\frac{\partial x_2^*}{\partial a} + \ldots + \lambda^* \frac{\partial g}{\partial x_n}\frac{\partial x_n^*}{\partial a} + \lambda^*.$$

Rewriting,

$$\frac{\mathrm{d}V(a)}{\mathrm{d}a} = \left(\frac{\partial f}{\partial x_1} + \lambda^* \frac{\partial g}{\partial x_1}\right)\frac{\partial x_1^*}{\partial a} + \ldots + \left(\frac{\partial f}{\partial x_n} + \lambda^* \frac{\partial g}{\partial x_n}\right)\frac{\partial x_n^*}{\partial a} + \lambda^*.$$

But each term in parentheses is zero by the first-order conditions, and so we are left with

$$\frac{\mathrm{d}V(a)}{\mathrm{d}a} = \lambda^*$$

which we can evaluate at $a = 0$ to show that λ^* is the rate of change of the maximized objective function, with respect to a small relaxation of the constraint.

For this reason λ is often known as a *shadow price*, or *accounting price*. Suppose we are maximizing a firm's profit subject to a constraint on factory floor space (or machine time, or labour or a limited resource), then the λ which emerges in the solution to the problem is the extra profit which could be earned if we had one more square metre of floor space (hour of machine time, man-hour of labour, unit of resource). It is therefore the maximum price we should be willing to pay in order to purchase that extra square metre, etc. It is also a sensible price to use in calculating the value of those assets which the firm does have (and, incidentally, must clearly be the price of this factor in any competitive equilibrium situation). As another example imagine a central authority wishing to maximize a social welfare function subject to the country's (convex) technology. Then the appropriate shadow prices would represent the maximum import prices at which it would be worthwhile to import pieces of capital equipment or technical knowledge to improve the technology.

17.4 Bus fares: an illustrative application

In this section we discuss a very simple model in order to illustrate the use of the theory of constrained optimization in a typical field of application. We wish to discuss the problem facing a 'city council' in choosing the socially optimum bus fare, in a town which is congested in the sense that the more private transport that is used, the more expensive it will become to provide a public service of a given standard. The criterion of social welfare to be used will become clear in due course. It should be emphasized from the start that although this particular model is highly simplified and contains many assumptions which people will find objectionable, the main conclusions can be obtained under very much weaker assumptions, with correspondingly more work.

We suppose that our city council has two quantities which it has to choose, the price of public transport and a rate of taxation to be levied on all inhabitants, a property tax, say. It has to choose these so as to maximize some suitable index of social welfare, subject to several constraints. One of these is one which says that the tax revenue must cover the losses incurred in running the bus services. Another is that individuals cannot be controlled directly; they must be free to choose how much public transport and how much private transport they are going to use, given the various costs of these. In addition, various possible additional policies are denied; such as taxes on private transport (petrol tax, road pricing, parking charges, etc.).

We assume for simplicity that there are k *identical* individuals in the town, each with the Cobb-Douglas utility function

$$u(x, y, z) = x^{\alpha} y^{\beta} z^{\gamma} \quad (\alpha + \beta + \gamma = 1)$$

where x, y and z are the quantities of three goods consumed per unit time; respectively consumpton good, private transport and public transport. (x can be thought of as 'everything else'.) The prices are respectively p_x, p_y and p_z, where p_z is to be chosen by the city council.

We first have to work out how much the consumer will choose to consume of each good, given values for p_z and the tax, t. We suppose that each consumer maximizes his utility subject to his budget constraint,

$$m - t = p_x x + p_y y + p_z z$$

where m is his income before tax. The Lagrangean is

$$L(x, y, z, \lambda) = x^{\alpha} y^{\beta} z^{\gamma} + \lambda(m - t - p_x x - p_y y - p_z z).$$

Putting the partials equal to zero gives

$$\alpha x^{\alpha-1} y^{\beta} z^{\gamma} - \lambda p_x = 0$$
$$\beta x^{\alpha} y^{\beta-1} z^{\gamma} - \lambda p_y = 0$$
$$\gamma x^{\alpha} y^{\beta} z^{\gamma-1} - \lambda p_z = 0$$

which correspond to the first-order conditions obtained in Section 17.2 above. Hence,

$$\lambda = \frac{\alpha x^{\alpha-1} y^{\beta} z^{\gamma}}{p_x} = \frac{\beta x^{\alpha} y^{\beta-1} z^{\gamma}}{p_y} = \frac{\gamma x^{\alpha} y^{\beta} z^{\gamma-1}}{p_z}.$$

Therefore,

$$p_y y = \frac{\beta p_x x}{\alpha}, \quad p_z z = \frac{\gamma p_x x}{\alpha}$$

and substituting $p_y y$ and $p_z z$ into the constraint,

$$m-t = p_x x + \frac{\beta p_x x}{\alpha} + \frac{\gamma p_x x}{\alpha}$$

$$= p_x x \left(1 + \frac{\beta}{\alpha} + \frac{\gamma}{\alpha}\right)$$

$$= \frac{p_x x}{\alpha}(\alpha+\beta+\gamma)$$

$$= \frac{p_x x}{\alpha}$$

since $\alpha+\beta+\gamma=1$ by assumption. Hence

$$x = \frac{\alpha(m-t)}{p_x}.$$

Similarly

$$y = \frac{\beta(m-t)}{p_y} \quad \text{and} \quad z = \frac{\gamma(m-t)}{p_z}.$$

Hence our consumers will always spend constant proportions α, β and γ of their net incomes on the three goods respectively. (This is a useful property of the Cobb-Douglas form of the utility function.) These equations are of course the equations of the demand curves for the three goods.

Substituting these optimum quantities into the utility function we get

$$u^* = \left\{\frac{\alpha(m-t)}{p_x}\right\}^{\alpha} \cdot \left\{\frac{\beta(m-t)}{p_y}\right\}^{\beta} \left\{\frac{\gamma(m-t)}{p_z}\right\}^{\gamma}$$

$$= \frac{\alpha^{\alpha}\beta^{\beta}\gamma^{\gamma}}{p_x^{\alpha}p_y^{\beta}} \cdot \frac{(m-t)}{p_z^{\gamma}}$$

An obvious index of social welfare in this case is the sum of all the maximized utilities. Since there are k identical individuals this is just

$$ku^* = \frac{K(m-t)}{p_z^{\gamma}}$$

where

$$K = \frac{k\alpha^{\alpha}\beta^{\beta}\gamma^{\gamma}}{p_x^{\alpha}p_y^{\beta}}$$

and u^* is the welfare level of each individual.

In order to specify the constraint which the council must observe we first specify the cost of running the bus service per individual as

$$c(y,z) \quad \text{with} \quad \frac{\partial c}{\partial y} > 0, \quad \frac{\partial c}{\partial z} > 0.$$

The first of these conditions reflects the fact that there is congestion; more private car journeys mean higher bus costs. The second just says that it costs more to run more buses. Then the total costs are $kc(y,z)$, and the problem is to

$$\max ku^* = \frac{K(m-t)}{p_z^{\gamma}} \text{ with respect to } p_z \text{ and } t$$

subject to

$$kt = kc(y,z) - kp_z z$$

or, since the ks cancel,

$$t = c(y,z) - p_z z.$$

The constraint just says that total tax revenue must equal the excess of operating costs over receipts from fares. Proceeding as usual

$$L(t, p_z, \mu) = \frac{K(m-t)}{p_z^{\gamma}} + \mu\{t - c(y,z) + p_z z\}$$

$$\frac{\partial L}{\partial t} = -\frac{K}{p_z^{\gamma}} + \mu\left\{1 - \frac{\partial c}{\partial y}\frac{\partial y}{\partial t} - \frac{\partial c}{\partial z}\frac{\partial z}{\partial t} + p_z \frac{\partial z}{\partial t}\right\} = 0$$

$$\frac{\partial L}{\partial p_z} = -\frac{\gamma K(m-t)}{p_z^{\gamma+1}} + \mu\left\{-\frac{\partial c}{\partial y}\frac{\partial y}{\partial p_z} - \frac{\partial c}{\partial z}\frac{\partial z}{\partial p_z} + z + p_z \frac{\partial z}{\partial p_z}\right\} = 0.$$

But, from the demand curves obtained above,

$$\frac{\partial y}{\partial t} = -\frac{\beta}{p_y}, \quad \frac{\partial z}{\partial t} = -\frac{\gamma}{p_z}, \quad \frac{\partial y}{\partial p_z} = 0, \quad \frac{\partial z}{\partial p_z} = -\frac{\gamma(m-t)}{p_z^2}$$

and

$$z + p_z \frac{\partial z}{\partial p_z} = z - \frac{\gamma(m-t)}{p_z} = 0$$

so, from the first-order conditions, we have,

$$\frac{K}{p_z^{\gamma}} = \mu\left\{1 + c_y \frac{\beta}{p_y} + c_z \frac{\gamma}{p_z} - \gamma\right\}$$

$$\frac{\gamma K(m-t)}{p_z^{\gamma+1}} = \mu\left\{c_z \frac{\gamma(m-t)}{p_z^2}\right\}$$

where

$$c_y = \frac{\partial c}{\partial y}, \quad \text{etc.}$$

Now we eliminate μ by dividing the first equation by the second

$$\frac{p_z}{\gamma(m-t)} = p_z^2 \frac{\left\{1 - \gamma + c_y \dfrac{\beta}{p_y} + c_z \dfrac{\gamma}{p_z}\right\}}{c_z \gamma(m-t)}$$

or

$$c_z(1-\gamma) = p_z(1-\gamma) + c_y \beta \frac{p_z}{p_y}$$

or

$$c_z = p_z + \frac{c_y \beta p_z}{(1-\gamma)\, p_y}.$$

If we were to specify the form of the cost function we could go on to obtain the explicit solutions for t and p_z. However, the most interesting result is immediately apparent in this last equation. Note first that if $c_y = 0$, so that there is no congestion, then the *social* optimum involves setting price equal to marginal cost. Second, we see that if there is congestion then the social optimum involves a bus fare which is below marginal cost, since the second term on the right-hand side is then positive. This is clearly because a lower bus fare makes car travel relatively more expensive, causes people to substitute bus journeys for car journeys, so relieving congestion, allowing everybody to get about more cheaply, and saving on everybody's tax bill. This is particularly interesting when one remembers that if the bus system was run so as to maximize its profit then, if a monopolist, it would in general set price *above* marginal cost. It is clear that this type of model can be used as a basis of an argument against operating urban transport systems on the basis of simplistic commercial principles. In this case we can interpret λ as the extra utility each individual gets if he has to pay one less unit of tax, and μ as the increase in the social welfare index if the council is allowed to overspend by one unit—because, say, of a grant towards transport services from central government. These arguments are further developed in Glaister (1981, 1984).

The particular approach used in this section is typical of the type of analysis used in the field of problems of public policy and taxation. Individuals have to be treated as free agents, so that policy must be formulated to take account of this, and various political and financial constraints must be observed.

17.5 The case of several constraints

If there is more than one constraint to be considered, then the technique of Lagrangean multipliers is easily generalized to handle this case. Suppose we have m constraints:

$$\max f(\boldsymbol{x}) \text{ subject to } g_1(\boldsymbol{x}) = 0$$
$$g_2(\boldsymbol{x}) = 0$$
$$\vdots$$
$$g_m(\boldsymbol{x}) = 0$$

Then we define one shadow price for each constraint and form the Lagrangean function,

$$L(\boldsymbol{x}, \lambda_1, \lambda_2, \ldots, \lambda_m) = f(\boldsymbol{x}) + \lambda_1 g_1(\boldsymbol{x}) + \lambda_2 g_2(\boldsymbol{x}) + \ldots + \lambda_m g_m(\boldsymbol{x})$$

and proceed as before. Once again we have the same number of equations from the first-order conditions as variables: $m + n$ in each case.

The only problem that we must be aware of is that, as before, if there is to be a solution it is necessary that the set of $\boldsymbol{x}$s satisfying the constraints be nonempty. Now, in a sense, we start with n degrees of freedom in the $\boldsymbol{x}$ space and lose one every time we add a constraint, and one would not expect more than n 'functionally independent' constraints on n variables to be consistent.

17.6 Solution by direct substitution

There is one alternative method of solution which we must mention, because it sometimes gives simpler results. Consider the case of one constraint:

$$g(\boldsymbol{x}) = 0.$$

Now it may be possible to 'solve' this equation to obtain one of the xs as a function of the remaining $n-1$ xs (cf. the discussion of implicit functions, Section 13.4). Suppose we succeed in solving for x_1, to give

$$x_1 = h(x_2, x_3, \ldots, x_n).$$

Then we can use this relation to eliminate x_1 from $f(\boldsymbol{x})$ and simply solve the unconstrained problem

$$\max f\{h(x_2, \ldots, x_n), x_2, x_3, \ldots, x_n\}$$

with respect to $x_2, \ldots, x_n$.

In practice this is not likely to be a useful idea unless the constraint happens to be linear, in which case it is easy to invert; the utility problem is a case in point. We have

$$\max u(x_1, x_2) \text{ subject to } m - p_1 x_1 - p_2 x_2 = 0.$$

Solving for x_1,

$$x_1 = \frac{m - p_2 x_2}{p_1} = h(x_2), \quad \text{say.}$$

Then we maximize $u\{h(x_2), x_2\}$ with respect to x_2 alone:

$$\frac{\partial u}{\partial x_2}\{h(x_2), x_2\} = \frac{\partial u}{\partial h}\frac{\mathrm{d}h}{\mathrm{d}x_2} + \frac{\partial u}{\partial x_2} = 0$$

or

$$\frac{\partial u}{\partial h} \bigg/ \frac{\partial u}{\partial x_2} = -1 \bigg/ \frac{\mathrm{d}h}{\mathrm{d}x_2}.$$

But $h(x_2) = x_1$, and

$$\frac{\mathrm{d}h(x_2)}{\mathrm{d}x_2} = -\frac{p_2}{p_1}$$

and so we have

$$\frac{\partial u}{\partial x_1} \bigg/ \frac{\partial u}{\partial x_2} = \frac{p_1}{p_2}$$

which is the condition obtained by eliminating λ from the necessary conditions obtained in Section 17.2.

Occasionally a complicated problem is best solved by a combination of the two methods. Variables which can easily be eliminated are eliminated, and then the method of Lagrangean multipliers is used.

17.7 Second-order conditions

As one might expect, these refer to the concavity or convexity properties of the objective function in the neighbourhood of points satisfying the first-order conditions. All the problems of distinguishing between local optima and global optima encountered before remain here.

The sufficiency conditions are usually stated in the form of conditions on the definiteness of the Hessian of the Lagrangean function, evaluated at the point of interest. Now,

$$L(\boldsymbol{x}, \lambda) = f(\boldsymbol{x}) + \lambda g(\boldsymbol{x})$$

so

$$\frac{\partial L}{\partial \lambda} = g(\boldsymbol{x})$$

$$\frac{\partial L}{\partial x_i} = \frac{\partial f}{\partial x_i} + \lambda \frac{\partial g}{\partial x_i}$$

and

$$\frac{\partial^2 L}{\partial \lambda^2} = 0, \qquad \frac{\partial^2 L}{\partial \lambda\, \partial x_i} = \frac{\partial g(x)}{\partial x_i} = \frac{\partial^2 L}{\partial x_i\, \partial \lambda}$$

$$\frac{\partial^2 L}{\partial x_i\, \partial x_j} = \frac{\partial^2 f}{\partial x_i\, \partial x_j} + \lambda \frac{\partial^2 g}{\partial x_i\, \partial x_j}.$$

The Hessian therefore has the form:

$$\begin{bmatrix} 0 & g_1 & g_2 & \cdots & g_n \\ g_1 & f_{11}+\lambda g_{11} & f_{12}+\lambda g_{21} & \cdots & f_{1n}+\lambda g_{1n} \\ g_2 & f_{21}+\lambda g_{21} & f_{22}+\lambda g_{22} & \cdots & f_{2n}+\lambda g_{2n} \\ \vdots & \vdots & \vdots & & \vdots \\ g_n & f_{n1}+\lambda g_{n1} & f_{n2}+\lambda g_{n2} & \cdots & f_{nn}+\lambda g_{nn} \end{bmatrix}$$

(cf. Section 16.2).

Because of the distinctive form of the first row and column this is known as a *bordered* Hessian. Since any rearrangement of the rows and columns gives an equivalent Hessian, it is written in a variety of ways, often with the border as the *last* row and column. The condition for a local maximum (minimum) is that, at a point which satisfies the necessary conditions, this Hessian be 'negative (positive) definite under constraint'. Now, there is clearly no point in checking the first two minors for sign, since they are bound to be respectively zero and nonpositive. Hence we start with the minor of order 3, and for a maximum this must be *positive* and higher-order minors must alternate in sign. For a minimum these minors must all be negative. Note that this is the opposite of the unbordered case.

The general rule, when there are m constraints, is that starting with the minor of order $(2m+1)$ they must alternate starting with sign $(-1)^{m+1}$ for a maximum, and must all have sign $(-1)^m$ for a minimum. However, these conditions get very complicated, and it is very difficult to apply them. If neither is obeyed then the matrix is indefinite and we have neither a maximum nor a minimum.

Consider the example in Section 17.2:

$$\frac{\partial L}{\partial x_1} = 6 + 2\lambda(x_1 - 2), \quad \frac{\partial L}{\partial x_2} = 8 + 2\lambda(x_2 - 1)$$

$$\frac{\partial L}{\partial \lambda} = (x_1 - 2)^2 + (x_2 - 1)^2 - 25$$

$$\frac{\partial^2 L}{\partial x_1^2} = 2\lambda, \quad \frac{\partial^2 L}{\partial x_1\, \partial x_2} = 0, \quad \frac{\partial^2 L}{\partial x_2^2} = 2\lambda$$

$$\frac{\partial^2 L}{\partial \lambda\, \partial x_1} = 2(x_1 - 2), \quad \frac{\partial^2 L}{\partial \lambda\, \partial x_2} = 2(x_2 - 1).$$

Evaluating these at $x_1 = 5, x_2 = 5$ and $\lambda = -1$, the Hessian is

$$\mathbf{H}(5,5) = \begin{bmatrix} 0 & 6 & 8 \\ 6 & -2 & 0 \\ 8 & 0 & -2 \end{bmatrix}.$$

There is only one minor to evaluate, the determinant of the whole matrix. This is 200, a positive number, and so we have a maximum. On the other hand

$$\mathbf{H}(-1,-3)=\begin{bmatrix} 0 & -6 & -8 \\ -6 & 2 & 0 \\ -8 & 0 & 2 \end{bmatrix}$$

with determinant -200; a minimum.

In practice it is often a good deal more sensible to rely on considerations of concavity or other considerations than to become involved in the evaluation of very ugly minors, in order to distinguish between the various types of solution.

17.8 Problems

1. Find the extreme value of

$$f(x_1, x_2, x_3) = x_1^2 + x_2^2 + 2x_3^2 + 3x_2x_3$$

subject to the constraint

$$x_1 + 2x_2 + 3x_3 = 1.$$

2. Verify that the function

$$f(x,y) = e^{(3y-4x^2)}$$

when constrained by

$$2x^3 + xy + y^2 = 0$$

has a stationary value at the point $x=-1$, $y=2$ and determine the nature of this stationary point.

3. (*a*) Find the solution to the problem

$$\text{maximize } \log x_1 + \log x_2 \text{ with respect to } x_1 \text{ and } x_2$$

when

$$(x_1 + 1) = \frac{4}{(x_2 + 1)}$$

confirming that your solution satisfies the second-order condition.

(*b*) Find the extreme values of the function

$$4x_1 + 2x_2 - 8$$

where

$$(x_1 - 2)^2 + (x_2 - 1)^2 = 36$$

and determine their nature.

4. Find the stationary values of the function

$$f(x_1,x_2,x_3)=x_1^2+2x_1x_2+x_1x_3-3x_1+2x_2^2+x_2x_3+2x_2+\tfrac{1}{2}x_3^2-x_3$$

and determine whether this is a maximum or a minimum point. Repeat the problem if x_1 and x_2 are to satisfy the constraint

$$x_1+x_2+3=0.$$

5. Find the extreme value of

$$f(x_1,x_2,x_3)=(x_1-2)^2+3(x_2-1)^2+2x_3-2(x_1-4)(x_2+1)$$

subject to the constraints

$$3x_1+x_2+5=0$$
$$4x_1+2x_3-1=0.$$

There is insufficient material in this book to enable the reader to solve questions 6 and 7. They are included for the interest of those who have read some further reference, such as Intrilligator (1971) Chapter 4.

6**. Solve the following problem using the *K–T* conditions:

$$\max\ x_1^2+2x_2^2$$
$$\text{s.t.}\quad x_1+x_2\leqslant 2+\delta,\quad x_1\geqslant 0,\quad x_2\geqslant 0$$
$$2x_1\leqslant 1$$

(*a*) where $\delta=0$
(*b*) where $\delta>0$.
(*c*) How does the value of the program depend on δ, for δ small? Interpret the result.

7**. A country which is a member of a trading community has produced quantities b_1 and b_2 of two agricultural goods for export. The demand functions for the products in the other countries are of the constant elasticity form: $x_1=p_1^{e_1}$, $x_2=p_2^{e_2}$, $e_i<-1$, where x_i is the quantity of the ith good exported. To protect farmers in other countries, community rules require that $a_1x_1+a_2x_2\leqslant c$, $a_i>0$, $c>0$. The country wishes to choose prices for its goods so as to maximize its revenue. Show that it may be profitable for the country to destroy some of an 'over-produced' good and charge a positive price for it. Interpret. How much would the country be willing to pay the central government in order to secure a unit increase in c? Solve explicitly if $b_1=2, b_2=3, a_1=\frac{1}{2}, a_2=\frac{1}{3}, e_1=-\frac{4}{3}, e_2=-2, c=\frac{3}{2}$. Suppose e_2 changes to $-\frac{3}{2}$. Solve and interpret.

18 Comparative statics

18.1 Introduction

This section is concerned with a set of techniques which can be of immense value to social scientists, if they are sensibly used, and if their limitations are understood. The discussion here is fairly brief since there are several texts giving a more complete analysis; general principles and a summary of the available formal theorems will be found in the final chapter of Quirk and Saposnik (1968); Smith (1982) gives applications in the field of micro and welfare economics and Kuska (1974) has a detailed discussion of the theory and practice of solving comparative statics problems.

In fact we need to introduce very few new concepts since most of them have been introduced with illustrative applications and in discussion of various pieces of theory. The reader might find it helpful to remind himself of the following material: Problem 2.3.4, Section 8.7, Problems 8.8.1 and 8.8.4, Section 13.5(*c*) and Problem 16.7.4. In each of these cases a problem was split into two parts. First we had to find an equilibrium value for each variable of the given system–an equilibrium level of income and so on. In some cases it was possible to calculate this explicitly; in others the best one could do was to make sufficient assumptions to guarantee that one existed. Second, we were asked to investigate the response of these equilibrium values to changes in one (or more) of the parameters of the system which had so far been taken as constants–rate of taxation, government expenditure, money supply and so on. If we already had an explicit solution to the first problem, then this was relatively simple to do; we could just differentiate the solution for the variable of interest with respect to the changing parameter. However, we illustrated in Section 13.5(*c*) that a good deal of information about those responses may be deducible even if the determination of the equilibria has to be left in implicit form. As we said in Sections 8.7 and 13.5(*c*), the technique is known as *comparative statics*, because one is comparing one long-run equilibrium situation with another, without considering the intermediate *dynamic* behaviour of the system.

18.2 A simple example

We illustrate the general principles with a very simple example, somewhat similar to the purchase tax example of Section 13.5(c). Suppose we have demand and supply functions:

$$d = f(p, \alpha)$$
$$s = g(p)$$

and an equation defining what we mean by an equilibrium:

$$d = s.$$

Here the variable α is to be taken as a fixed parameter, known as a *shift parameter*. One of the attractive things about the method is the freedom that one has in interpreting α. Thus, if we are considering the demand for ice-cream, α might represent hours of sunshine, in which case we might assume $\partial f/\partial\alpha > 0$, corresponding to a rightward shift in the demand curve–*ceteris paribus* (that is, at any constant price) more sunshine leads to a higher demand. On the other hand, α might be the price of a complementary good, in which case we would assume that $\partial f/\partial\alpha < 0$.

We have three equations in three *dependent*, or *endogenous*, variables which we would normally choose to be p, d and s. This leaves the single *independent*, or *exogenous*, variable, α. As is typical, however, the choice of endogenous variables is somewhat arbitrary, and must be made to suit the particular problem at hand. If, for instance, we were a government agency wishing to know which values of α were consistent with certain, specified equilibrium prices, then we would choose d, s and α as our endogenous variables and p as exogenous. Since we have three functionally independent equations we must choose exactly three endogenous variables, the remainder being exogenous. Notice particularly that this system contains *four* variables only; *variables* called 'f' and 'g' do *not* appear; these are the names of *functions*. This may seem obvious here, but in more complicated situations it is very easy to become confused, especially if one is indulging the common habit of using the same symbol as a variable name and as a function name; for instance, writing a consumption function

$$C = C(Y, r).$$

Having selected our endogenous variables, the next stage is to simplify things as much as possible by eliminating as many as convenient of those which are not of interest. In this case, if we only wish to analyse effects of changes in α on p then we can easily eliminate d and s to give the single relation:

$$f(p, \alpha) = g(p)$$

As in Section 13.5(c) we now have an implicit definition of p as a function of α, and we can find the derivative of this function (assuming the function to exist and to be differentiable) by performing the implicit differentiation:

$$\frac{\partial f(p,\alpha)}{\partial p}\frac{\mathrm{d}p}{\mathrm{d}\alpha}+\frac{\partial f(p,\alpha)}{\partial \alpha}=\frac{\mathrm{d}g(p)}{\mathrm{d}p}\frac{\mathrm{d}p}{\mathrm{d}\alpha}$$

and, solving for $\mathrm{d}p/\mathrm{d}\alpha$,

$$\frac{\mathrm{d}p}{\mathrm{d}\alpha}=\frac{\partial f/\partial\alpha}{\mathrm{d}g/\mathrm{d}p-\partial f/\partial p}$$

which, assuming the usual signs for the slopes of demand and supply curves will have the same sign as $\partial f/\partial\alpha$. So a small rightward shift in the demand curve will lead to an increase in price, unless $\mathrm{d}g/\mathrm{d}p$ is very large (supply infinitely elastic), in which case the increase will be vanishingly small.

18.3 A more complex, macro model

Let us now consider a more complicated system, the chief complication being that it is not possible to reduce it to a single equation by elimination of variables. In other words, we have genuine simultaneity, and it is not surprising that the methods of linear algebra are a great help. The sequence of steps used here is offered as a suggestion which usually works well. The reader might like to compare this model with those given in Sections 8.7 and 13.5(*d*), and with those analysed in the final appendix to H. G. Johnson (1971) and in the last two chapters of Smith (1982).

First we are given a production function,

$$Y=f(N)$$

giving the amount of output Y that can be obtained per unit time as a function of the labour employed N, tacitly assuming capital stock, technology, etc., to be constant. (These could be introduced as shift parameters.) Equilibrium in the goods market meaning that total desired demand is equal to desired supply is specified by

$$G+I(Y,r)=S(Y,r)$$

and in the money market by

$$\frac{M}{P}=L(Y,r)$$

where r is the interest rate, G is government expenditure, M the stock of money and P the price level. Finally we assume that the amount of labour employed is equal to what is supplied,

$$N=g(W)$$

and that what is supplied is equal to what is demanded,

$$g(W)=h\left(\frac{W}{P}\right)$$

where W is the money wage. The demand for labour is usually taken to be derived from the profit-maximizing behaviour of firms, which would lead them to employ to the point where the marginal product of labour was equal to the real wage $W/\dot{P}$ so that the functions f and h are related. In fact, h would be the inverse of the first derivative of f.

To summarize, the model is:

$$Y = f(N)$$
$$G + I(Y, r) = S(Y, r)$$
$$M/P = L(Y, r)$$
$$N = g(W)$$
$$g(W) = h(W/P).$$

We must now choose our five endogenous variables. This choice will usually be dictated by the problem at hand. Suppose we wish to evaluate the effect of changes in government expenditure G and the money supply M on the equilibrium level of output Y. This type of analysis would be helpful in deciding, say, the relative merits of fiscal and monetary changes in executing expansionary policy. In that case we should take as endogenous Y, r, N, P and W, leaving our two policy variables, G and M, as exogenous. Since a five equation system is rather large for convenient handling we now look for suitable endogenous variables to eliminate. N is an obvious candidate, and we are left with

$$Y = f\{g(W)\}$$
$$G + I(Y, r) = S(Y, r)$$
$$M/P = L(Y, r)$$
$$g(W) = h(W/P).$$

If at some stage we require the change in N we can always obtain it from the change in W by the relationship

$$\mathrm{d}N = \frac{\mathrm{d}g(W)}{\mathrm{d}W}\,\mathrm{d}W.$$

We could eliminate more variables, but it is doubtful whether it is worth it, since the differentiation which follows would become rather complex.

There are two alternative steps which we could take at this point. Possibly the more natural thing would be to differentiate each equation with respect to, say, G and then solve the resulting four simultaneous equations for the derivative of interest, say, $\mathrm{d}Y/\mathrm{d}G$. This would be similar to what we did in the previous section. However, we shall take the total differential of each equation (see Section 16.4), which has a slight advantage when there are more than two exogenous variables, which will become apparent later. So, we have

$$\mathrm{d}Y = \frac{\mathrm{d}f}{\mathrm{d}g} \cdot \frac{\mathrm{d}g}{\mathrm{d}W}\,\mathrm{d}W$$

$$dG + \frac{\partial I}{\partial Y} dY + \frac{\partial I}{\partial r} dr = \frac{\partial S}{\partial Y} dY + \frac{\partial S}{\partial r} dr$$

$$\frac{dM}{P} - \frac{M\,dP}{P^2} = \frac{\partial L}{\partial Y} dY + \frac{\partial L}{\partial r} dr$$

$$\frac{dg}{dW} dW = \frac{dh}{d(W/P)} \left(\frac{dW}{P} - \frac{W\,dP}{P^2} \right)$$

since the differential of M/P is $dM/P - M\,dP/P^2$, etc.

Now, if all changes are small, so that we remain in a neighbourhood of the equilibrium, it is a reasonable approximation to assume that all the derivatives in this system, evaluated at the original equilibrium point, are constants. If we make this assumption, we have a system of four *linear*, *simultaneous* equations determining the four variables dY, dr, dP and dW, where the coefficients are the (constant) derivatives. We may solve this system by any appropriate method, Cramer's rule being convenient.

To this end, we rearrange the equations so that all terms involving *changes* in the endogenous variables are on the left, and all others on the right (using standard abbreviations for derivatives):

$$dY - f'(g)\,g'(W)\,dW = 0$$

$$(S_Y - I_Y)\,dY + (S_r - I_r)\,dr = dG$$

$$L_Y\,dY + L_r\,dr + \frac{M}{P^2}\,dP = \frac{dM}{P}$$

$$\left\{ g'(W) - \frac{1}{P} h'\left(\frac{W}{P}\right) \right\} dW + \frac{W}{P^2} h'\left(\frac{W}{P}\right) dP = 0$$

or equivalently

$$\begin{bmatrix} 1 & 0 & 0 & -f'(g)\,g'(W) \\ (S_Y - I_Y) & (S_r - I_r) & 0 & 0 \\ L_Y & L_r & \dfrac{M}{P^2} & 0 \\ 0 & 0 & \dfrac{W}{P^2} h'\left(\dfrac{W}{P}\right) & g'(W) - \dfrac{1}{P} h'\left(\dfrac{W}{P}\right) \end{bmatrix} \begin{bmatrix} dY \\ dr \\ dP \\ dW \end{bmatrix} = \begin{bmatrix} 0 \\ dG \\ \dfrac{dM}{P} \\ 0 \end{bmatrix}.$$

Now we must choose which differential to solve for, and for illustration we take dY. Then, if we denote the matrix of the system by $\mathbf{A}$, and assuming $\mathbf{A}$ nonsingular, Cramer's rule (Section 8.6) gives

$$dY = \frac{1}{|\mathbf{A}|} \left[-dG \left\{ -f'(g)\,g'(W)\,L_r \frac{W}{P^2} h'\left(\frac{W}{P}\right) \right\} + \frac{dM}{P} \left\{ -f'(g)\,g'(W)\,(S_r - I_r) \frac{W}{P^2} h'\left(\frac{W}{P}\right) \right\} \right].$$

If we assume for the moment that the money supply is held constant, so that $dM = 0$, divide by dG, and take the limit as dG becomes small, we obtain

$$\frac{\partial Y}{\partial G} = \frac{1}{|\mathbf{A}|}\left\{f'(g)\, g'(W)\, L_r \frac{W}{P^2} h'\left(\frac{W}{P}\right)\right\}.$$

This is a true *partial* derivative, because the other exogenous variable is being held constant. Similarly we have

$$\frac{\partial Y}{\partial M} = \frac{-1}{|\mathbf{A}|P}\left\{f'(g)\, g'(W)\, (S_r - I_r) \frac{W}{P^2} h'\left(\frac{W}{P}\right)\right\}.$$

The slight advantage of carrying differentials of all the exogenous variables right through to this stage is now apparent: if we had just differentiated the whole system with respect to one of the exogenous variables, and then solved for the required partial derivative, we would have to go through the whole procedure again to obtain the partial derivative with respect to the second exogenous variable. Of course, if any exogenous variable is going to be held constant throughout, its differential is set to zero immediately to avoid evaluating cofactors unnecessarily. The analysis is completed by evaluating $|\mathbf{A}|$, which in this case is the reciprocal of the Keynesian multiplier. (Cf. Sections 8.7 and 14.2(*b*)). This evaluation is left as an exercise, the result being

$$|\mathbf{A}| = (S_r - I_r)\left[\frac{M}{P^2}\left\{g'(W) - \frac{1}{P}h'\left(\frac{W}{P}\right)\right\} - L_Y f'(g)\, g'(W) \frac{W}{P^2} h'\left(\frac{W}{P}\right)\right]$$
$$+ (S_Y - I_Y)\, L_r f'(g)\, g'(W) \frac{W}{P^2} h'\left(\frac{W}{P}\right).$$

If we know the exact form of the various functions involved in this solution then we have a complete expression for the rate of change of our endogenous variable with respect to an infinitesimal change in our exogenous variable. However, very often we do not have that information; we may, for example, only know the signs of the slopes of the functions. One of the interesting problems in this field is to discover the extent to which useful information about the solutions can be obtained from purely qualitative information about the functions. In some instances one can get a surprisingly long way, but there are few general theorems about this. The reader is referred to Quirk and Saposnik (1968) for a summary. In our example, if we make the 'usual' assumptions that

$$\frac{df}{dN} > 0, \quad \frac{\partial I}{\partial Y} > 0, \quad \frac{\partial I}{\partial r} < 0 \quad 1 > \frac{\partial S}{\partial Y} > 0, \quad \frac{\partial S}{\partial r} \geqslant 0,$$
$$\frac{\partial L}{\partial Y} > 0, \quad \frac{\partial L}{\partial r} < 0, \quad \frac{dg}{dW} > 0, \quad \frac{dh}{d(W/P)} < 0$$

then we find that as long as

$$(S_Y - I_Y) > 0$$

then the multiplier $|\mathbf{A}|$ is positive, and also

$$\frac{\partial Y}{\partial G} > 0, \qquad \frac{\partial Y}{\partial M} > 0$$

as a standard Keynesian analysis would lead one to expect. If the extra condition is not met then the result may, or may not, still hold; it depends upon the relative magnitudes of the various terms in the determinant.

One could proceed to use these expressions to advantage in discussions of the circumstances under which, say, fiscal policy would be more or less effective than monetary policy (although one would want to include taxation in the model first) and each result would have interpretations, both in terms of the nature of the *I–S* and *L–M* curves (see Section 13.5(*d*) also), and, more important, in terms of the nature of the underlying economic behaviour. Smith (1982) gives a discussion.

18.4 Comments

There are several minor devices and short cuts which can be used to speed up an analysis of this type, and they are quickly learnt with practice. Three general points are worth making.

The first is one we have made before: it is always worthwhile having a careful look at the equations of the system before one starts mechanically carrying out the procedure described in the previous section. This will often help one to predict the outcome and hence aid in the detection of errors. In fact it sometimes allows one to solve the problem completely, so saving a great deal of unnecessary work. For instance, suppose we slightly change our assumptions in the model so that the supply of labour depends on the real wage, rather than the money wage. Then we have

$$Y = f(N)$$

$$N = g\left(\frac{W}{P}\right)$$

$$g\left(\frac{W}{P}\right) = h\left(\frac{W}{P}\right)$$

together with the other equations and neither government expenditure nor the money supply can have any effect at all on employment or real output, since the requirement that the labour market be in equilibrium fixes both the real wage, W/P, and employment N (and hence real output Y) independently of anything. In fact changes in money supply could only lead to equiproportionate changes in the equilibrium price level. Had we missed this point and carried out the standard mechanical procedure, we would have found that the matrix in the numerator of Cramer's solution for $\mathrm{d}Y$ would be singular, one row being a scalar multiple of another, yielding zero for the change in Y.

Second, it is vital that the results are interpreted once they are obtained, if they are to be sensibly used. One can argue that a justification for the method is that it enables one to obtain precise results concerning a mathematical (and social) system which is too complicated to understand without using it. Hence it may not be possible or even necessary to obtain a *complete* interpretation of the results. However, one should attempt, at the very least, to get some feel for what is going on in the system. So, for example, when we observe that our solutions to the macro model imply that if L_r becomes very large, $\partial Y/\partial M \rightarrow 0$ whilst $\partial Y/\partial G \rightarrow$ a positive constant (to see this, divide top and bottom of $\partial Y/\partial G$ by L_r), so that fiscal policy would be much more effective than monetary policy, we interpret this as a 'liquidity trap' where a small fall in the rate of interest in response to an increase in the supply of money leads to a big increase in the speculative demand for money (because the interest rate has moved closer to its supposed bottom limit, increasing expectations of an increase in the near future, and hence expectation of a fall in asset prices, so that money becomes more attractive relative to assets). Relatively little of the extra money is available to finance transactions.

The third point is a mathematical observation. The differential of a function was introduced as the first (linear) term in the Taylor expansion of the function about a point (Section 16.4). Hence we see that when we are taking differentials of each equation in a system we are making the approximating assumption that every function is linear in the neighbourhood of the initial equilibrium point; in other words, we are using a plane, passing through the point, and tangential to the actual function. This enables us to apply the techniques of linear analysis, but it does mean that the results are only 'local'; that is, valid for small changes only. This technique is also used in the local stability analysis of *dynamic systems* (see Chapter 19).

18.5 A final example: properties of demand functions

This standard example is included to illustrate how qualitative information of another kind can be used to attribute signs to comparative static results. It should be noted that the results themselves can be more elegantly obtained by other methods. See Smith (1982).

In Section 17.6 we derived the following first-order conditions for the maximization of utility, subject to a budget constraint:

$$u_1 - \lambda p_1 = 0, \quad \text{where } u_1 = \frac{\partial u(x_1, x_2)}{\partial x_1}, \text{ etc.}$$

$$u_2 - \lambda p_2 = 0$$

$$m - p_1 x_1 - p_2 x_2 = 0$$

Now, these three equations are assumed to define implicitly the three endogenous variables x_1, x_2 and λ in terms of the exogenous variables p_1 and p_2, giving something of the form

$$x_1 = f_1(p_1, p_2), \quad x_2 = f_2(p_1, p_2)$$

the individual's demand functions. One can derive information about these functions by the comparative statics technique as follows.

Taking total differentials:

$$u_{11}\,\mathrm{d}x_1 + u_{12}\,\mathrm{d}x_2 - \lambda\,\mathrm{d}p_1 - p_1\,\mathrm{d}\lambda = 0, \quad \text{where } u_{12} = \frac{\partial^2 u(x_1, x_2)}{\partial x_1\,\partial x_2}, \text{ etc.}$$

$$u_{21}\,\mathrm{d}x_1 + u_{22}\,\mathrm{d}x_2 - \lambda\,\mathrm{d}p_2 - p_2\,\mathrm{d}\lambda = 0$$

$$\mathrm{d}m - p_1\,\mathrm{d}x_1 - p_2\,\mathrm{d}x_2 - x_1\,\mathrm{d}p_1 - x_2\,\mathrm{d}p_2 = 0$$

Rearranging, and putting into matrix form, we have:

$$\begin{bmatrix} 0 & p_1 & p_2 \\ p_1 & u_{11} & u_{12} \\ p_2 & u_{21} & u_{22} \end{bmatrix} \begin{bmatrix} -\mathrm{d}\lambda \\ \mathrm{d}x_1 \\ \mathrm{d}x_2 \end{bmatrix} = \begin{bmatrix} \mathrm{d}m - x_1\,\mathrm{d}p_1 - x_2\,\mathrm{d}p_2 \\ \lambda\,\mathrm{d}p_1 \\ \lambda\,\mathrm{d}p_2 \end{bmatrix}$$

Calling the matrix $\mathbf{H}$, and the cofactor of h_{ij}, H_{ij}, as in definition D6.3, we have

$$\mathrm{d}x_2 = \frac{1}{|\mathbf{H}|}\{(\mathrm{d}m - x_1\,\mathrm{d}p_1 - x_2\,\mathrm{d}p_2)H_{13} + \lambda H_{23}\,\mathrm{d}p_1 + \lambda H_{33}\,\mathrm{d}p_2\}$$

so that

$$\frac{\partial x_2}{\partial p_2} = \frac{1}{|\mathbf{H}|}(-x_2 H_{13} + \lambda H_{33})$$

To give a sign to this expression it is clearly going to be necessary to give a sign to $|\mathbf{H}|$. However, $\mathbf{H}$ is exactly the bordered Hessian matrix we would use in the test of the second-order conditions for utility maximization and, applying the rules of Section 17.7, $|\mathbf{H}| > 0$. Hence we use the assumption that the individual was originally maximizing his utility, to help predict his response to price changes.

To complete the analysis, we also have

$$\frac{\partial x_2}{\partial m} = \frac{H_{13}}{|\mathbf{H}|}$$

so

$$\frac{\partial x_2}{\partial p_2} = -x_2\frac{\partial x_2}{\partial m} + \lambda\frac{H_{33}}{|\mathbf{H}|}$$

Suppose now that when prices are changed, the individual's income is also changed so that he can obtain just the same level of utility as before, that is, so that

$$\mathrm{d}u = u_1\,\mathrm{d}x_1 + u_2\,\mathrm{d}x_2 = 0$$

We also know from the first-order conditions that

$$u_1 = \lambda p_1 \quad \text{and} \quad u_2 = \lambda p_2$$

so, substituting for u_1 and u_2,

$$\lambda p_1 \, dx_1 + \lambda p_2 \, dx_2 = 0$$

or

$$p_1 \, dx_1 + p_2 \, dx_2 = 0$$

Hence, from the differential of the budget constraint,

$$dm - x_1 \, dp_1 - x_2 \, dp_2 = 0$$

when income compensations are made. So, from the equation for dx_2,

$$\frac{\delta x_2}{\delta p_2} = \lambda \frac{H_{33}}{|\mathbf{H}|}$$

where $\delta x_2/\delta p_2$ means the change in x_2 in response to a change in p_2, when everything else is held constant *except m* which is also changed, in such a way as to allow the individual to remain on the same indifference curve. This is known as the *pure substitution* term, being the change attributable to changes in relative prices alone. Moreover, since

$$H_{33} = -p_1^2 < 0$$

and λ, the marginal utility of income (see Section 17.3), being positive, we see that the knowledge that $|\mathbf{H}| > 0$ implies that this term must be negative.

Finally then, we have

$$\frac{\partial x_2}{\partial p_2} = \frac{\delta x_2}{\delta p_2} - x_2 \frac{\partial x_2}{\partial m}$$

so that the slope of the demand curve is split into a *substitution effect* and an *income effect*. Certainly if

$$\frac{\partial x_2}{\partial m} > 0, \quad \text{then} \quad \frac{\partial x_2}{\partial p_2} < 0$$

and the demand curve has a negative slope. In the event that $\partial x_2/\partial m < 0$, that is x_2 is an *inferior good*, there is the possibility that the demand curve would slope upwards. The reader is referred to Henderson and Quandt (1971), Quirk and Saposnik (1968).

18.6 Problems

1. Following the method of Section 18.5, find expressions for $\partial x_1/\partial p_2$ and $\partial x_2/\partial p_1$, and show that the two cross-substitution terms are equal. (This is one of the interesting predictions of this theory of consumer behaviour.)

2. Consider the following model:

$$Y = f(N, t), \qquad \frac{\partial f}{\partial N} > 0, \qquad \frac{\partial f}{\partial t} > 0$$

$$\frac{W}{P}=\frac{\partial f(N,t)}{\partial N}, \quad \frac{\partial^2 f}{\partial N^2}<0$$

$$N=n(W), \quad \frac{dn(W)}{dW}>0$$

$$I(r)=S(Y), \quad \frac{dI(r)}{dr}<0, \quad \frac{dS(Y)}{dY}>0$$

$$\frac{M}{P}=L(r,Y), \quad \frac{\partial L(r,Y)}{\partial r}<0, \quad \frac{\partial L(r,Y)}{\partial Y}>0$$

where Y is output, N employment, W the money wage, P the price level, $n(W)$ the supply of labour, r the rate of interest, and M the quantity of money. t is a parameter taken to represent technical change. Investigate the proposition that technical progress will necessarily lead to a fall in the level of employment, by finding an expression for the effect of a small change in t on W (and hence on employment). You are free to specify the effect of technical progress on the marginal product of labour (that is $\partial^2 f(N,t)/\partial t\,\partial N$).

3. Assume the model:

$$C=C(Y) \qquad 0<\frac{dC}{dY}<1$$

$$I=I(r) \qquad \frac{dI}{dr}<0$$

$$Y=C+I$$

$$\frac{M}{P}=L(Y,b) \qquad 0<\frac{\partial L}{\partial Y}<1, \quad \frac{\partial L}{\partial b}<0$$

$$\frac{B}{(1+b)P}=G(Y,r,b) \quad 0<\frac{\partial G}{\partial Y}<1, \quad \frac{\partial G}{\partial r}<0, \quad \frac{\partial G}{\partial b}>0$$

where C is consumption, Y is income, I is investment, r is the rate of interest on bonds, M is the quantity of money, P is the price level, b is the Treasury bill rate, and B is the quantity of Treasury bills; $L(Y,b)$ is the demand function for real money balances, and $G(Y,r,b)$ is the demand function for real Treasury bills. M, P and B are assumed to be exogenous; the other variables are assumed to be endogenous.

Derive the expression for the effect on r of an increase in M. Is it possible to sign this derivative?

4. The following is a model of a country trading with the rest of the world which is considered as a single economy.

$$Y=C+I+G+X-M$$

$$C = f(Y), \qquad \frac{\partial f}{\partial Y} > 0$$

$$I = g(Y), \qquad \frac{\partial g}{\partial Y} > 0, \quad \frac{\partial f}{\partial Y} + \frac{\partial g}{\partial Y} < 1$$

$$X = h\left(Z, \frac{p}{p^*}\right), \qquad \frac{\partial h}{\partial Z} > 0, \quad \frac{\partial h}{\partial (p/p^*)} < 0$$

$$M = \phi\left(Y, \frac{p}{p^*}\right), \qquad \frac{\partial \phi}{\partial Y} > 0, \quad \frac{\partial \phi}{\partial (p/p^*)} > 0$$

$$B = pX - p^*M$$

$$p = \psi(w, p^*), \qquad \frac{\partial \psi}{\partial w} > 0, \quad \frac{\partial \psi}{\partial p^*} > 0$$

where for the home country Y is national income, C is consumption, I is investment, G is government expenditure, X is exports, M is imports, B is balance of payments, p is price level and w is wage rate. Z is 'rest of world' income and p^* is 'rest of world' price level in terms of prices in the home country.

Thus $p^* = \alpha q$ where q is 'rest of world' own price level and α is the exchange rate. q is assumed constant.

The endogenous variables are Y, C, I, X, M, B and p; the remainder are exogenous.

(*a*) Write down the differential structure of the system and derive the effect of an increase in government expenditure on the balance of payments.
(*b*) Find the effect of an increase in the wage rate on national income.
(*c*) Discuss the effect of a change in the exchange rate.

Note: One simplification which can be made to this system is the elimination of C, I, X and M.

19 Integration and differential equations

19.1 Introduction

The main aim of this book has been to give a working knowledge of the elements of linear algebra and the differential calculus together with a few applications. However, this short chapter is added because the *integral* calculus is quite easily understood once the differential calculus is known, and because it has many important applications in economic theory. Examples of these are: in the solution of differential equations (which are equations describing dynamic behaviour, rather similar to difference equations except that time is continuous, rather than being broken into discrete periods), in the theory of the statistical methods used in empirical work, and in the specification and solution of problems in dynamic optimization, such as problems of optimum investment planning for firms and of optimum growth rates for economies. The reader requiring a more thorough analysis will find plenty of good books on the subject. Part 5 of Chiang (1974) and Chapters 11 and 13 of Binmore (1983) are very readable.

The order in which the material is presented here is not the most common one. We start by defining the notion of the area under the graph of a function, and then show that the process of finding such an area can be interpreted as the *reverse* of the process of differentiating the function. A moment's thought will show this to be reasonable; the process of differentiation is the process of finding the rate of change of something with respect to its argument, and we are claiming that the rate of change of the area under a curve is the value of the function—the distance of the curve from the x-axis—at the point at which we are differentiating. We shall only consider functions of a single variable.

19.2 Area

We suppose that we have the problem of defining what we mean by the 'area' of the shaded region in Figure 19.1, that is, the area bounded by the graph of the function $f(x)$, the x-axis and the condition that $a \leqslant x \leqslant b$.

As so often, we start by making an approximation and then improving it. Let us *partition* the segment of the x-axis between a and b by $n+1$ arbitrary points, denoted by x_i, with $x_0 = a$ and $x_n = b$ (see Figure 19.2). Then, if we calculate the area of each rectangle shown on the diagram and add them together, this will give us an approximation (in this case, an overestimate) of the true area. The area of each rectangle is given by

$$f(x_i)(x_i - x_{i-1}), \quad i = 1, 2, \ldots, n,$$

and denoting the true area by $A(a, b)$ we have

$$A(a, b) \leqslant \sum_{i=1}^{n} f(x_i)(x_i - x_{i-1}).$$

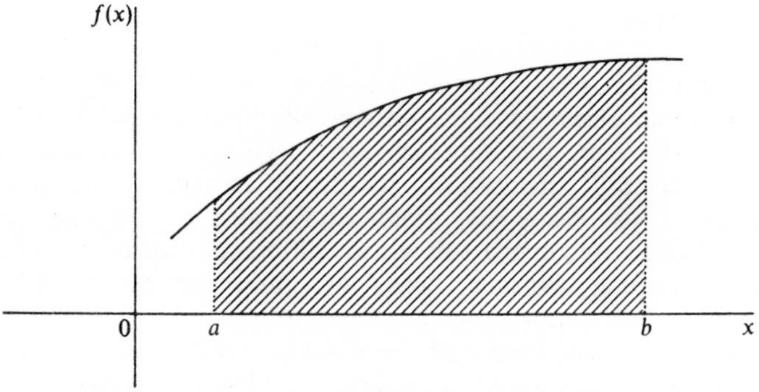

Figure 19.1

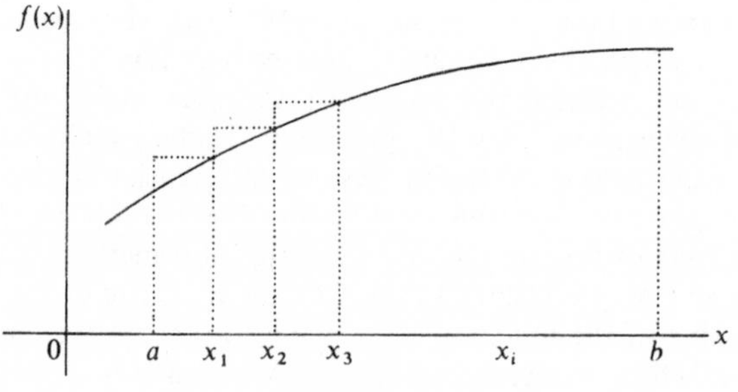

Figure 19.2

Clearly, the error will get smaller if more points are taken giving a finer grid. However, with a function less 'smooth' than the one drawn here, some schemes for making the grid finer might introduce a systematic error, and so we consider the limit of the above sum, taken over 'all possible partitions', to give the *upper sum*, $\bar{A}(a, b)$.

Instead of overestimating the area we can underestimate it, by taking rectangles *underneath* the curve, so that

$$A(a,b) \geqslant \sum_{i=1}^{n} f(x_{i-1})(x_i - x_{i-1})$$

and if we take the limit of this sum, over all possible partitions, then we obtain the *lower sum*, $\underline{A}(a, b)$. If and only if the upper and lower sums are equal then we have

$$\bar{A}(a,b) = \underline{A}(a,b) = A(a,b),$$

the true area, and we say that the function is *Riemann integrable* on the interval between a and b. To indicate that the distance between adjacent x_is has become vanishingly small, we replace $(x_i - x_{i-1})$ by $\mathrm{d}x$, and convert the summation sign to an elongated S, and write

$$A(a,b) = \int_a^b f(x)\,\mathrm{d}x.$$

As in differentiation, the $\mathrm{d}x$ indicates that the integration is being carried out with respect to the variable x. The result, for any specified function, depends only on the two end points, indicated by the *limits* (a and b) appended to the integral sign, and not on x. For this reason x is sometimes known as a *running variable*, *dummy variable* or *variable of integration*. Various types of integral, other than the Riemann integral, exist to deal with functions which are not Riemann integrable, but these will not concern us. (Note that the statement that the definitions given here for upper and lower sums are respectively over and underestimates of the true area depends upon the fact that the curves are drawn monotonic increasing. If this were not the case it is easy to see how a suitable definition could be constructed by dividing the domain into monotonic segments.)

The following program calculates the integral of any function in line 120 between the lower and upper limits that the user is asked to specify. The results called 'LOWER' and 'UPPER' are the two alternative measures defined above and calculated in lines 190 and 200. The integral is first estimated by assuming the whole area to be a rectangle. Then the x axis is partitioned into two, into four, into eight and so on. A third estimate is obtained by Simpson's rule. The AVERAGE in line 210 is the average of the values of the function evaluated at each end of each partition. The MIDPOINT in line 220 is the function evaluated at a point half-way between the end points of the partition. For each partition Simpson's rule takes the altitude of the function to be one third of the AVERAGE and two thirds of the MIDPOINT. Note how much more efficient Simpson's rule is than the other two techniques, in that it reaches a good approximation to the 'correct' answer much more quickly.

```
100 INPUT "LOWER LIMIT"; MIN
110 INPUT "UPPER LIMIT"; MAX
120 DEF FNF(X) = EXP(-0.1*X)*100
130 PRINT" LOWER      UPPER      SIMPSON"
140 INCREMENT = MAX - MIN
150 LOWER = 0
160 UPPER = 0
170 SIMPSN = 0 : REM NOTE NO O TO AVOID "ON"
180 FOR X = MIN + INCRMENT TO MAX STEP INCRMENT
190 LOWER = LOWER + FNF(X - INCRMENT)*INCRMENT
200 UPPER = UPPER + FNF(X)*INCRMENT
210 AVERAGE = 0.5* (FNF(X - INCRMENT) + FNF(X))
220 MDPNT = FNF(0.5*(X - INCRMENT) + 0.5*X)
230 S = 0.333333*AVERAGE + 0.666667*MDPNT
240 SIMPSN = SIMPSN + S*INCRMENT
250 NEXT X
260 PRINT LOWER, UPPER, SIMPSN
270 INCRMENT = INCRMENT/2
280 GOTO 150
```

19.3 Evaluation of integrals

In order to see how to evaluate these areas we must first show the relationship between integration and differentiation; and to do that we need the following result:

Theorem 19.1 If c is a point such that

$$a \leqslant c \leqslant b$$

then

$$\int_a^b f(x)\,dx = \int_a^c f(x)\,dx + \int_c^b f(x)\,dx.$$

In other words the area between a and b is the area between a and an intermediate point c, added to the area between c and b. This is quite obvious, but to prove it one could look at the properties of the summations used in defining the upper and lower sums.

We can show that the derivative of the area with respect to its upper (or lower) limit is the value of the function itself at the upper (or lower) limit:

Theorem 19.2

$$\frac{\partial A(a,b)}{\partial b} = f(b)$$

Proof.

$$A(a, b + \mathrm{d}b) = \int_a^{b+\mathrm{d}b} f(x)\,\mathrm{d}x$$

$$= \int_a^{b} f(x)\,\mathrm{d}x + \int_a^{b+\mathrm{d}b} f(x)\,\mathrm{d}x \text{ (by theorem 19.1)}$$

$$= A(a,b) + \int_a^{b+\mathrm{d}b} f(x)\,\mathrm{d}x.$$

Rewriting this

$$\frac{A(a, b+\mathrm{d}b) - A(a,b)}{\mathrm{d}b} = \frac{1}{\mathrm{d}b}\int_b^{b+\mathrm{d}b} f(x)\,\mathrm{d}x$$

$$= \frac{1}{\mathrm{d}b} f(b)\,\mathrm{d}b$$

if $\mathrm{d}b$ is small (this is a rectangle approximation again). Taking the limit as $\mathrm{d}b$ tends to zero gives the required result. ∎

We now show how this can be used to find the area (sketched in Figure 19.3) under the function $f(x) = x^3$, between the points a and b; that is

$$\int_a^b x^3\,\mathrm{d}x.$$

Now, by the previous theorem:

$$\frac{\partial A(a,b)}{\partial b} = b^3$$

and we wish to deduce what $A(a, b)$ must be. Actually, this is an example of what is known as a *differential equation*. We are given an equation which the derivative of a function must satisfy, and required to find out what the function itself must be. In this case we ask: Holding a constant (and therefore

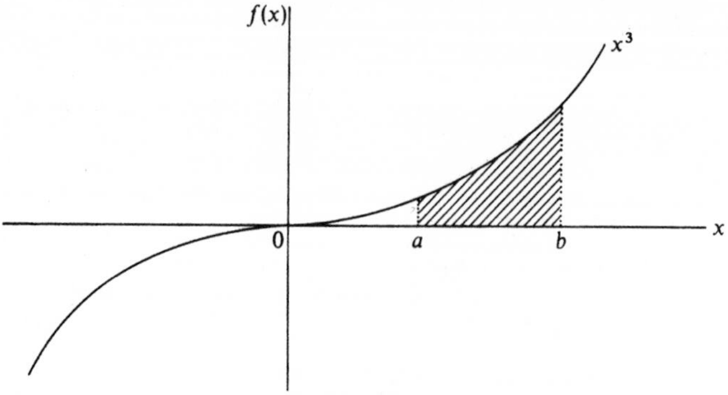

Figure 19.3

leaving it out of account), what function of b, when differentiated, yields b^3? Clearly, the answer is going to involve b^4, and a first guess might be $\frac{1}{4}b^4$. In fact, since the derivative of anything not dependent on b is zero, the complete answer is given by

$$A(a, b) = \tfrac{1}{4}b^4 + c$$

where c is the *constant of integration*. This can be evaluated, since the relationship must hold for all values of b. In particular, setting $b = a$ we have

$$A(a, a) = \tfrac{1}{4}a^4 + c$$

and since the 'area' between a and a is obviously zero,

$$c = -\tfrac{1}{4}a^4.$$

Our complete solution then reads:

$$\int_a^b x^3\, \mathrm{d}x = \tfrac{1}{4}b^4 - \tfrac{1}{4}a^4.$$

For example, if $a = 1$ and $b = 2$, then the area is

$$\tfrac{1}{4}.2^4 - \tfrac{1}{4}.1^4 = 4 - \tfrac{1}{4} = 3\tfrac{3}{4}.$$

Similarly, if $a = -1$ and $b = 0$, then the area is

$$\tfrac{1}{4}(0)^4 - \tfrac{1}{4}(-1)^4 = -\tfrac{1}{4}$$

which illustrates that the integral of a curve lying below the x-axis is negative. Finally, if $a = -1$, $b = +1$ then

$$\int_{-1}^{1} x^3\, \mathrm{d}x = \tfrac{1}{4}.1^4 - \tfrac{1}{4}(-1)^4 = 0.$$

This is because the curve is symmetrical about the vertical axis, apart from a sign change, so that the two areas cancel out.

The concept of a negative area may seem a little strange, but it is a consequence of the definitions of upper and lower sums, above. It is clear that if $f(x_i) < 0$ then the contribution of that term to the sum will be negative. Hence any area between a negative part of a function and the x-axis will be negative. So the integral of a function which cuts the axis in the interval of integration will be the 'net' area.

These results may be confirmed by using the above program for evaluating integrals.

19.4 The indefinite integral

The integral considered in the last section, where the limits are specified, is known as the *definite integral.* However, one can ask the slightly more general question: Given a function $f(x)$, what other function $F(x)$, when differentiated, gives $f(x)$? In other words: Can we find a function $F(x)$ such that

$$\frac{\mathrm{d}F(x)}{\mathrm{d}x} = f(x)?$$

If so, then we write

$$F(x) = \int f(x)\,\mathrm{d}x$$

and call $F(x)$ the *indefinite integral* of $f(x)$.

In our previous section, then, we had

$$\int x^3\,\mathrm{d}x = \tfrac{1}{4}x^4 + c$$

since, when differentiated with respect to x, the function on the right-hand side gives the function under the integral, known as the *integrand*, c being an arbitrary constant.

The relationship between the indefinite and the definite integral is now fairly clearly

$$A(a, b) = \int_a^b f(x)\,\mathrm{d}x$$

$$= F(b) - F(a)$$

which is often written

$$= [F(x)]_a^b,$$

being the difference between the indefinite integral evaluated at b and evaluated at a. Note that there is no question of evaluating the arbitrary constant of integration in this case; it cancels out in finding the definite integral. Since, in practice, the process of evaluating definite integrals involves first finding indefinite integrals, a few general rules for finding them follow, somewhat analogous to the rules of differentiation given in Section 13.4. One should, however, be aware that whereas it is fairly easy to differentiate any function, the same is by no means true of integration. There is a very considerable repertoire of standard tricks and procedures, which are to be found in many texts (such as O'Brien and Garcia, 1971 and Binmore, 1983) for finding integrals, but these can fail so that one is faced with devising some trick appropriate to the particular problem at hand, and possibly failing to find any solution. However, it is almost always very easy to write a computer program to evaluate a definite integral with extreme accuracy using numerical methods and, in fact, most installations have library programs available to do this. Even with relatively 'easy' problems, the choice of a technique which works is an art which has to be learnt with experience. Some standard rules are the following:

(1) $$\int x^n \,\mathrm{d}x = \frac{1}{(n+1)} x^{(n+1)} + c \ (n \neq -1)$$

(2) $$\int \frac{1}{x} \,\mathrm{d}x = \log x + c \ (x > 0)$$

(3) $\int \alpha f(x)\,\mathrm{d}x = \alpha \int f(x)\,\mathrm{d}x$, where α is any constant, so that multiplying the integrand by a constant multiplies the integral by that constant.

(4) $\int \{f(x) + g(x)\}\,\mathrm{d}x = \int f(x)\,\mathrm{d}x + \int g(x)\,\mathrm{d}x$, so that the integral of a sum is the sum of the integrals.

(5) $$\int \mathrm{e}^x \,\mathrm{d}x = \mathrm{e}^x + c.$$

Rules (3) and (4) mean that the operation of integration is a linear operation, as are the operations of multiplication of a vector by a matrix and of differentiation of functions. Hence, for example:

$$\int (x^5 + 3x + 1)\,\mathrm{d}x = \int x^5\,\mathrm{d}x + 3\int x\,\mathrm{d}x + \int \mathrm{d}x$$

$$= \tfrac{1}{6}x^6 + \tfrac{3}{2}x^2 + x + c.$$

These five rules (and some others) form the basis for the standard routines. For instance,

$$\int \frac{1}{(1+x^2)}\,\mathrm{d}x$$

is difficult to find, but

$$\int \frac{2x}{(1+x^2)}\,\mathrm{d}x$$

which looks similar, is very easy, because the top line is the derivative of the bottom, and we remember from Section 13.5(*a*) that such a function is the derivative of the logarithm of the bottom line; so the result is

$$\int \frac{2x}{(1+x^2)}\,\mathrm{d}x = \log(1+x^2) + c.$$

Using the same principle,

$$\int \frac{2x}{(3x^2+5)}\,\mathrm{d}x = \frac{1}{3}\int \frac{2x}{x^2+\frac{5}{3}}\,\mathrm{d}x = \frac{1}{3}\log\left(x^2+\tfrac{5}{3}\right) + c.$$

There are just two other techniques which must be mentioned here. The first is integration by substitution. Consider

$$\int (x^4+3)^8 \,.\, 9x^3\,\mathrm{d}x.$$

Conceivably one could expand this as a polynomial in x and integrate term by term. Suppose instead we define a new variable

$$y = x^4 + 3$$

so we have

$$\int y^8 \,.\, 9x^3\,\mathrm{d}x.$$

Here the variable of integration is still x and we try converting it to y by using the fact that

$$\mathrm{d}y = 4x^3\,\mathrm{d}x$$

or

$$\mathrm{d}x = \tfrac{1}{4}x^{-3}\,\mathrm{d}y$$

so, substituting for dx we have

$$\begin{aligned}\int y^8 \,.\, 9x^3 \,.\, \tfrac{1}{4}x^{-3}\,\mathrm{d}y &= \tfrac{9}{4}\int y^8\,\mathrm{d}y \\ &= \tfrac{9}{4}\,.\,\tfrac{1}{9}y^9 + c \\ &= \tfrac{1}{4}(x^4+3)^9 + c.\end{aligned}$$

It is clear that this works very well here, and the technique can be developed to a point of extreme sophistication.

Finally, a method of evaluating integrals of functions which are products, known as *integration by parts*. We know that

$$\frac{\mathrm{d}}{\mathrm{d}x}\{u(x)\,.\,v(x)\} = u(x)\frac{\mathrm{d}v(x)}{\mathrm{d}x} + v(x)\frac{\mathrm{d}u(x)}{\mathrm{d}x}.$$

Working 'backwards'

$$u(x)\,v(x)=\int u(x)\frac{dv(x)}{dx}\,dx+\int v(x)\frac{du(x)}{dx}\,dx-c$$

or

$$\int u(x)\frac{dv(x)}{dx}\,dx=u(x)\,v(x)-\int v(x)\frac{du(x)}{dx}\,dx+c.$$

This formula shows us how to use our knowledge of differentiation to help us to integrate; suppose we want to find

$$\int x\,e^x\,dx$$

then, if we put

$$u(x)=x,\quad \frac{dv}{dx}=e^x$$

we have

$$\frac{du(x)}{dx}=1,\ v(x)=e^x$$

and applying the formula

$$\int x\,e^x\,dx=x\,e^x-\int e^x\,dx+c$$

$$=x\,e^x-e^x+c$$

which can be verified by differentiation.

Examples of application of this material will be found in the following section.

19.5 Differential equations

As mentioned above, the theory of differential equations has a lot in common with the theory of difference equations which was discussed in Section 9.5. Differential equations are equations involving derivatives (rather than differences) of functions, from which one wants to deduce the functions themselves, or at least something about their nature. The independent variable (very often time) is continuous here, rather than being broken up into arbitrary intervals.

Let us consider an example. Suppose that we wish to calculate the repayment due on a loan which has been made at a compound interest rate of

$100r$ per cent unit of time. Now, if the loan was made at time 0, and we denote the amount due at time t by $x(t)$, then we know that

$$x(t) = (1+r)^t x(0)$$

where $x(0)$ was the amount of the original loan. However, as long as the sum is compounded at discrete intervals, there is always the problem of knowing what to do if the loan has to be repaid in between two of the intervals. The rule often adopted is that interest is only paid for each complete period for which it is borrowed. This problem can easily be overcome by using *continuous compounding*, which works as follows. Again, let $x(t)$ be the amount due at time t, and suppose that it is borrowed for a further short instant of time, $\mathrm{d}t$. Then we assume that the extra interest due is proportional to the amount already due, and to the extra time interval,

$$x(t+\mathrm{d}t) = x(t) + rx(t)\,\mathrm{d}t.$$

Rearranging,

$$\frac{x(t+\mathrm{d}t) - x(t)}{\mathrm{d}t} = rx(t)$$

and taking the limit as $\mathrm{d}t \to 0$ gives us

$$\frac{\mathrm{d}x(t)}{\mathrm{d}t} = rx(t).$$

This is an example of the simplest type of differential equation; linear homogeneous and of the first order (cf. Section 9.6(a)). To solve it we divide by $x(t)$

$$\frac{1}{x(t)}\frac{\mathrm{d}x(t)}{\mathrm{d}t} = r$$

and then observe that the top of the left-hand side is the derivative of the bottom, so, integrating both sides,

$$\log\{x(t)\} = \int r\,\mathrm{d}t + \log c$$

$$= rt + \log c$$

where we have called the constant $\log c$ for later convenience. Then,

$$\log\{x(t)\} - \log c = rt$$

or

$$\log\left\{\frac{x(t)}{c}\right\} = rt,$$

and taking antilogs

$$\frac{x(t)}{c} = e^{rt}$$

so

$$x(t) = c\, e^{rt}.$$

All that remains is to evaluate the constant c by putting $t = 0$,

$$x(0) = c\, e^{0}$$
$$= c.$$

So the complete solution is

$$x(t) = x(0)\, e^{rt}$$

and we see that the amount owing grows along an exponential curve. Solutions of this type are extremely common in all the sciences. They describe the growth of populations of living organisms (where r is the birth rate), the decay of radioactive materials (with r negative), the temperature of a body cooling in surroundings of constant temperature, the decline of a capital asset (where r is the constant depreciation rate), the growth of an economy (where r is the rate of growth).

Not all differential equations can be solved easily, and so it is useful to have a method of simulating them to obtain a numerical solution. The following program illustrates how this can be done. The first two lines establish the beginning and ending values of the independent variable t. Line 120 establishes a step size and line 130 the initial value of the dependent variable x. The first-order differential equation itself is specified in line 140 where the expression on the right is the first derivative of x with respect to t. The example given is the one of continuous compounding just discussed with $r = 1$.

```
100  INPUT "START"; MIN
110  INPUT "END"; MAX
120  INPUT "INCREMENT"; INCRMENT
130  INPUT "INITIAL VALUE OF X AT START"; X0
140  DEF FNF(T) = X
150  T = MIN
160  X = X0
170  XOLD = X0
180  PRINT " X                  T"
190  PRINT X,T
200  FOR T = MIN TO MAX - INCRMENT STEP INCRMENT
210  XMID = XOLD + FNF(T)*INCRMENT/2
220  X = XMID
230  X = XOLD + FNF(T+INCRMENT/2)*INCRMENT
240  PRINT X, T + INCRMENT
```

```
250  XOLD = X
260  NEXT T
```

The technique given here uses a first-order Taylor approximation in line 230 to calculate the new value for X as the old value of X plus the slope of X (i.e. the derivative as specified in line 140) multiplied by the increment. For greater accuracy it is desirable to use the slope at the centre point of the interval, rather than at the lower end point. Of course the true value for X at the centre point cannot be known, but it can itself be estimated by a first-order Taylor approximation, using the known slope at the lower end point. This is achieved in lines 210 and 220. Note that the code could be made more compact by eliminating the intermediate variables XMID and XOLD but it would become harder to understand. The accuracy of the final numerical solution is dependent on the step size. If you integrate the example given between 0 and 1 with an initial value of 1 the result should be the natural constant e. A suitable step size is 0·1 but you can try larger and smaller step sizes to investigate the trade-off between computing time and accuracy.

If the equation is nonhomogeneous, of the form

$$\frac{\mathrm{d}x}{\mathrm{d}t} = rx + b$$

then the device used in Section 9.5(b), of finding an equilibrium (or *stationary*) value x, such that

$$\frac{\mathrm{d}x(t)}{\mathrm{d}t} = 0$$

and then working in terms of deviations from this equilibrium value, will also work here.

As in Section 9.5(c), systems of *simultaneous* linear first-order differential equations can be solved by a suitable transformation which diagonalizes (or almost diagonalizes) the matrix of the system. This would have the form

$$\frac{\mathrm{d}\boldsymbol{x}(t)}{\mathrm{d}t} = \mathbf{A}\boldsymbol{x}(t) + \boldsymbol{b}$$

where now

$$\frac{\mathrm{d}\boldsymbol{x}(t)}{\mathrm{d}t} = \begin{bmatrix} \frac{\mathrm{d}x_1(t)}{\mathrm{d}t} \\ \frac{\mathrm{d}x_2(t)}{\mathrm{d}t} \\ \vdots \\ \frac{\mathrm{d}x_n(t)}{\mathrm{d}t} \end{bmatrix}, \quad \boldsymbol{x}(t) = \begin{bmatrix} x_1(t) \\ x_2(t) \\ \vdots \\ x_n(t) \end{bmatrix}, \quad \boldsymbol{b} = \begin{bmatrix} b_1 \\ b_2 \\ \vdots \\ b_n \end{bmatrix}$$

and a_{ij} represents the effect on the ith derivative of the level of the jth variable. An exactly parallel argument to Section 9.5(c) would show that, if the eigenvalues of **A** are distinct, the solution for $x_i(t)$ would have the form

$$x_i(t) = k_{i0} + k_{i1}\,e^{\lambda_1 t} + k_{i2}\,e^{\lambda_2 t} + \ldots + k_{in}\,e^{\lambda_n t}$$

where the k_{ij} are constants to be determined from the initial values of the x_is, and the λ_j are the eigenvalues of **A**.

A second-order, linear, homogeneous differential equation would have the form

$$\frac{d^2x(t)}{dt^2} + b\frac{dx(t)}{dt} + cx(t) = 0$$

and, analogously with the argument of Section 9.5(d), the solution is given by

$$x(t) = k_1\,e^{\lambda_1 t} + k_2\,e^{\lambda_2 t}$$

where λ_1 and λ_2 solve the auxiliary equation,

$$\lambda^2 + b\lambda + c = 0.$$

Of course, as before, λ_1 and λ_2 (or the eigenvalues in the solution to the first-order system) may be complex conjugates of the form (cf. Section 14.3)

$$\lambda_1 = a + ib$$

$$\lambda_2 = a - ib.$$

In that case we have

$$\begin{aligned} x(t) &= k_1\,e^{(a+ib)t} + k_2\,e^{(a-ib)t} \\ &= e^{at}(k_1\,e^{ibt} + k_2\,e^{-ibt}) \\ &= e^{at}\{(k_1 + k_2)\cos bt + i(k_1 - k_2)\sin bt\} \\ &= A\,e^{at}\cos(bt + \epsilon) \end{aligned}$$

as before, where the constants A and ϵ are to be determined from the initial conditions.

In each of these cases it will be seen that the conditions for stability, that is the condition for $x(t)$ to tend to zero (or some equilibrium, x^*) as $t \to \infty$ is the $e^{\lambda_j t} \to 0$ for all j if λ_j is real, and that $e^{a_j t} \to 0$ if $\lambda_j = a_j + ib_j$ is complex. In other words, it is necessary and sufficient for stability that the *real* parts of all eigenvalues be negative. In the case of difference equations the condition was that all eigenvalues lie within the unit circle.

As with integration, the techniques for solving nonlinear differential equations are diverse and complicated. The interested reader will find many good books devoted entirely to the subject.

We end this section with a note to indicate how the various methods discussed in this book can be used to carry out an approximate (or *local*) stability analysis of a system of nonlinear differential equations. This involves using Taylor's theorem to make linear approximations, to which the standard linear techniques can then be applied.

Suppose we have two simultaneous nonlinear differential equations,

$$\frac{dx_1(t)}{dt} = f\{x_1(t), x_2(t)\}, \qquad \frac{dx_2(t)}{dt} = g\{x_1(t), x_2(t)\}.$$

An example, which describes the population sizes of a predator and its prey, and which has also been used by R. M. Goodwin (1967) to describe a 'Marxian' competition between workers and capitalists, would be

$$\dot{x}_1 = x_1(\rho x_2 - \gamma)$$
$$\dot{x}_2 = x_2(\beta - \sigma x_1) \quad (\rho, \gamma, \beta, \sigma \text{ positive constants})$$

where

$$\dot{x}_1 = \frac{dx_1(t)}{dt} \quad \text{and} \quad \dot{x}_2 = \frac{dx_2(t)}{dt}.$$

The first stage in analysing such a problem is to find a pair of equilibrium or stationary points, x_1^* and x_2^* such that

$$f(x_1^*, x_2^*) = 0, \quad g(x_1^*, x_2^*) = 0$$

(which may not be easy, since f and g are nonlinear). Then we take the Taylor expansion of these two functions, about the point x_1^*, x_2^*, to give, approximaterly,

$$\dot{x}_1 = f_1(x^*)(x_1 - x_1^*) + f_2(x^*)(x_2 - x_2^*)$$
$$\dot{x}_2 = g_1(x^*)(x_1 - x_1^*) + g_2(x^*)(x_2 - x_2^*)$$

where

$$f_1(x^*) = \frac{\partial f(x_1^*, x_2^*)}{\partial x_1}, \quad \text{etc.}$$

and where these partial derivatives are regarded as constants (cf. the comparative statics technique of Section 18.3). Now let

$$z_1(t) = x_1(t) - x_1^* \quad \text{and} \quad z_2(t) = x_2(t) - x_2^*.$$

Then

$$\dot{z}_1(t) = \dot{x}_1(t) \quad \text{and} \quad \dot{z}_2(t) = \dot{x}_2(t)$$

since x_1^* and x_2^* are constants, and rewriting the system in terms of the zs:

$$\dot{z}_1 = f_1 z_1 + f_2 z_2$$
$$\dot{z}_2 = g_1 z_1 + g_2 z_2$$

or, in matrix notation,

$$\dot{z}(t) = \mathbf{A}z(t)$$

where

$$\mathbf{A} = \begin{bmatrix} f_1(x^*) & f_2(x^*) \\ g_1(x^*) & g_2(x^*) \end{bmatrix} \quad \text{and} \quad z(t) = \begin{bmatrix} z_1(t) \\ z_2(t) \end{bmatrix}.$$

This is now in the standard form of a *linear*, homogeneous, simultaneous system as described above, and it is stable if and only if the real part of every eigenvalue of **A** is negative.

This analysis is, of course, only local (unless the functions f and g are linear) because of the approximation involved in the Taylor expansion, and one can only say what will happen if the initial point is 'close' to the stationary point. However, it may be the best one can do, and in any case it can be very helpful. One can, of course, deduce more about the local properties of the system than just whether or not it is stable. If the eigenvalues are complex there will be a cycle about the equilibrium points, otherwise the motion will be a steady movement towards, or away from the equilibrium (see above). It happens that in the example given the roots are pure imaginary numbers, so we have cycles which neither grow nor decline.

Very little can be said about global behaviour on the basis of local analysis, except that local stability is a *necessary* condition for global stability. It is clearly not sufficient since, apart from anything else, the equilibria may not be unique, so if the system is displaced from one equilibrium to another, it cannot return to its initial state, whatever the local behaviour.

Stability analysis is a large and fascinating subject. The interested reader is referred to Appendix A of Intrilligator (1971), Goldberg (1958), Davis (1962) and especially to Brand (1966).

If analytical methods fail then the numerical methods illustrated in the last program may be extended to deal with simultaneous differential equations. The following simulates the predator and prey model. The parameters are set up so that the equilibrium values of the predators and the prey are both 100. If you start the populations off at any point other than the equilibrium then you should find that both populations execute a cycle with the remarkable property that sooner or later the pair of starting values will return (a suitable step size may be 0·1). For instance if both populations are started at 75 then they will both return to 75 after about 90·12 units of time. The further the starting values are away from the equilibria on the low (high) side, the further they will be away from them on the high (low) side at some future date. This model and its relatives has found many uses in ecology, biology, epidemiology and the social sciences.

```
90  GAMMA = 0.05 : REM 5% DEATH RATE OF PREDATORS
91  RHO = GAMMA/100 : REM EQUILIBRIUM PREY = 100
92  BETA = 0.1 : REM 10% BIRTH RATE OF PREY
93  SIGMA = BETA/100 : REM EQUILIB. PREDATORS = 100
100  INPUT "START"; MIN
```

```
110 INPUT "END"; MAX
120 INPUT "INCREMENT"; INCRMENT
130 INPUT "INITIAL VALUE OF X1 AT START"; X0(1)
135 INPUT "INITIAL VALUE OF X2 AT START"; X0(2)
140 DEF FNF1(T) = X(1)*(RHO*X(2) - GAMMA)
145 DEF FNF2(T) = X(2)*(BETA - SIGMA*X(1))
150 T = MIN
160 X(1) = X0(1)
165 X(2) = X0(2)
170 XOLD(1) = X0(1)
175 XOLD(2) = X0(2)
180 PRINT " PREDATOR      PREY      T"
190 PRINT X(1), X(2), T
200 FOR T = MIN TO MAX - INCRMENT STEP INCRMENT
210 XMID(1) = XOLD(1) + FNF1(T)*INCRMENT/2
220 X(1) = XMID(1)
230 X(1) = XOLD(1) + FNF1(T+INCRMENT/2)*INCRMENT
240 XMID(2) = XOLD(2) + FNF2(T)*INCRMENT/2
250 X(2) = XMID(2)
268 X(2) = XOLD(2) + FNF2(T+INCRMENT/2)*INCRMENT
270 PRINT X(1), X(2), T+INCRMENT
280 XOLD(1) = X(1)
290 XOLD(2) = X(2)
300 NEXT T
```

19.6 Applications

(*a*) *Present value.* The concept of the present value of a stream of future receipts or costs is an extremely important one in many fields of economics. Suppose, for instance, that we wish to decide whether or not to undertake a certain project which will yield a net return at the rate $\pi(t)$, where this is known for all future t up to T. This might be profit attributable to an investment, if the decision-maker is a firm, or a stream of social benefits (measured in money terms) resulting from some public project (such as an urban road). This stream of future earnings has to be compared with the cost of undertaking the investment, and this is usually done by calculating the present value of the stream. The contribution to this of the return earned between t and $t + \mathrm{d}t$, $\pi(t)$ is

$$e^{-rt}\pi(t)\,\mathrm{d}t$$

where r is the rate of interest, since this is the sum, which if invested 'now' (at time 0) at the compound rate of interest r, would yield returns at the rate $\pi(t)$ at time t. 'Adding up' all these contributions we get

$$\text{p.v.} = \int_0^T e^{-rt}\pi(t)\,\mathrm{d}t.$$

This sum can then be compared with the cost of the project, and a decision made. (Clearly, one of the critical problems, besides that of predicting $\pi(t)$, is that of deciding precisely what rate of interest one should use–a small change in that may make a big difference to the present value.) In particular, if $\pi(t)$ is a constant, π, we have

$$\begin{aligned}
\text{p.v.} &= \int_0^T e^{-rt}\pi \, dt \\
&= \pi \int_0^T e^{-rt} \, dt \\
&= \pi \left[\frac{-1}{r} e^{-rt} \right]_0^T \\
&= \frac{\pi}{r}(1 - e^{-rt}).
\end{aligned}$$

(*b*) *Dynamic optimization.* The ideas of present value are exploited in a very interesting class of problems. Imagine, for instance, an individual born with an initial level of assets £$A(0)$, earning a constant wage of £w per unit time, wishing to leave bequests of £$A(T)$ at his death (which he assumes will occur at time T), and who gets satisfaction at the rate $u\{c(t)\}$ if he consumes at the rate £$c(t)$ per unit time t. We suppose that he wishes to allocate his consumption over his lifetime, so as so satisfy his budget constraint (given that he can always borrow or lend as much as he wishes at the rate of interest r, as long as he has net assets of $A(T)$ left at T), whilst maximizing

$$\int_0^T e^{-\delta t} u\{c(t)\} \, dt$$

which is the 'present value' of his future utility 'discounted' at the rate δ, the *subjective rate of discount*, which measures the degree of his myopia, the rate at which he gives less weight to satisfaction enjoyed in the distant future relative to that enjoyed in the near future. The constraint can be written as a differential equation,

$$\frac{dA(t)}{dt} = w + rA(t) - c(t), \quad A(0) \text{ and } A(T) \text{ given}$$

which says that the rate of change of his assets is equal to his earned plus his unearned incomes, net of consumption.

A very similar problem occurs in the theory of planning. Suppose we take the same objective function, which is to be maximized by a planning authority, where $c(t)$ is now national consumption, and δ is the rate at which the utility of future generations is being discounted. The problem then is to decide how much of the national output should be consumed at each point of time, and how much should be invested so as to add to the capital stock, which will produce more output in the future. This will produce an optimum growth path for the economy.

Assuming constant returns to scale, output per man can be written in terms of capital per man as $f(k)$. Investment per man is output per man net of consumption per man and net of the output which is required to provide capital to go with the additions to the population:

$$\frac{\mathrm{d}k(t)}{\mathrm{d}t} = f(k(t)) - nk(t) - c(t).$$

The objective given above has to be maximized subject to this differential equation as a constraint. Note that the choice quantity is a *function*, $c(t)$. This is a problem in *control theory*. The following is a brief and heuristic account of how this kind of problem may be approached. The formal proofs will be found in Intriligator (1971).

One can think of the differential equation in k as providing one constraint at each instant in time, so it is natural to define a Lagrangean multiplier for each instant in time. We form the 'Lagrangean' function

$$\int_0^\infty \mathrm{e}^{-\delta t} u(c(t))\,\mathrm{d}t + \int_0^\infty \mathrm{e}^{-\delta t}\lambda(t)\left[f(k(t)) - c(t) - nk(t) - \frac{\mathrm{d}k(t)}{\mathrm{d}t}\right]\mathrm{d}t.$$

(The multiplier is taken to be $\mathrm{e}^{-\delta t}\lambda(t)$ rather than $\lambda(t)$ for simplicity later.) This is to be maximized with respect to $c(t)$ and $k(t)$.

In order to eliminate the awkward term

$$\int_0^\infty \mathrm{e}^{-\delta t}\lambda(t)\frac{\mathrm{d}k(t)}{\mathrm{d}t}\,\mathrm{d}t$$

we integrate it by parts to give

$$\int_0^\infty \mathrm{e}^{-\delta t}\{u(c(t)) + \lambda(t)[f(k(t)) - c(t) - nk(t)]\}\,\mathrm{d}t - [\mathrm{e}^{-\delta t}\lambda(t)\,k(t)]_0^\infty$$

$$+ \int_0^\infty \mathrm{e}^{-\delta t}k(t)\left[\frac{\mathrm{d}\lambda(t)}{\mathrm{d}t} - \delta\lambda(t)\right]\mathrm{d}t.$$

Assuming that

$$\lim_{t\to\infty} \mathrm{e}^{-\delta t}\lambda(t)\,k(t) = 0$$

(this is known as a *transversality condition*), this is equivalent to

$$\int_0^\infty e^{-\delta t}\left\{u(c(t)) + \lambda(t)[f(k(t)) - c(t) - \lambda(t)\,k(t) - \delta k(t)] + k(t)\frac{d\lambda(t)}{dt}\right\} dt.$$

This will be maximized if the term in { } is maximized for each instant, t. This gives the first-order conditions

$$\frac{\partial\{\ \}}{\partial c(t)} = \frac{du(c(t))}{dc(t)} - \lambda(t) = 0$$

$$\frac{\partial\{\ \}}{\partial k(t)} = \lambda(t)\left[\frac{df(k(t))}{dk(t)} - (\lambda + \sigma)\right] + \frac{d\lambda(t)}{dt} = 0$$

or

$$\lambda(t) = \frac{du(c(t))}{dc(t)}$$

and

$$\frac{d\lambda(t)}{dt} = -\lambda(t)\left[\frac{df(k(t))}{dk(t)} - (\lambda + \delta)\right].$$

The necessary conditions therefore take the form of a differential equation in the Lagrangean multiplier, which is simultaneous with the constraining differential equation in capital per man, together with a condition which relates the Lagrangean multiplier to consumption through the marginal utility of consumption.

We can illustrate the workings of these conditions if we make the special assumptions

$$f(k) = Ak^\alpha \quad \text{and } u(c) = -\frac{1}{\nu}c^{-\nu}.$$

Note that this utility function is negative but monotonically increasing in consumption.

After eliminating $\lambda(t)$ and rearranging, the two differential equations can then be written as

$$\frac{dk(t)}{dt} = Ak(t)^\alpha - nk(t) - c(t)$$

and

$$\frac{dc(t)}{dt} = -c(t)[A\alpha k(t)^{\alpha-1} - (n + \delta)].$$

We can use the above technique for numerical simulation of simultaneous differential equations to investigate the properties of this system. You will find the two differential equations in lines 134 and 136 of the following program.

```
100  ALPHA = 0.25 : REM POWER IN COBB-DOUGLAS PROD. FN.
102  A = 73 : REM CONSTANT IN PRODUCTION FUNCTION.
104  N = 0.1 : REM RATE OF POPN. GRO. + DEPRECIATION
106  DELTA = 0.1 : REM RATE OF DISCOUNT
108  NU = 2 : REM COEF. IN UTILITY FUNCTION
110  NPV = 0
112  MIN = 0
114  MAX = 100
116  INCRMENT = 0.1
118  Z = ((N + DELTA)/(ALPHA*A)↑(1/(ALPHA − 1))
120  PRINT"EQUILIBRIUM CAPITAL STOCK = "; Z
122  Z = A *(Z↑ALPHA) − N * Z
124  PRINT"EQUILIBRIUM CONSUMPTION = "; Z
126  INPUT "INITIAL CAPITAL STOCK"; X0(1)
128  PRINT"INITIAL RATE OF OUTPUT = "; A*X0(1)↑ALPHA
130  INPUT "INITIAL VALUE OF CONSUMPTION"; C
132  X0(2) = C↑(−(1+NU))
134  DEF FNF1(T) = A*X(1)↑ALPHA − N*X(1) − C
136  DEF FNF2(T) = −X(2)*(A*ALPHA*X(1)↑(ALPHA−1) − (N +
     DELTA))
138  T = MIN
140  X(1) = X0(1)
142  X(2) = X0(2)
144  XOLD(1) = X0(1)
146  XOLD(2) = X0(2)
148  PRINT
150  PRINT"CAPITAL    CONSUM    PRES VALUE    T"
152  PRINT
154  PRINT X(1), C, T
200  FOR T = MIN TO MAX − INCRMENT STEP INCRMENT
210  XMID(1) = XOLD(1) + FNF1(T)*INCRMENT/2
220  X(1) = XMID(1)
230  X(1) = XOLD(1) + FNF1(T + INCRMENT/2)*INCRMENT
240  XMID(2) = XOLD(2) + FNF2(T)*INCRMENT/2
250  X(2) = XMID(2)
260  X(2) = XOLD(2) + FNF2(T + INCRMENT/2)*INCRMENT
265  C = X(2)↑(−1/(1+NU))
266  NPV = NPV − (EXP(−DELTA*T)*(C↑(−NU))/NU)*INCRMENT
270  PRINT X(1); C; NPV; T+INCRMENT
280  XOLD(1) = X(1)
290  XOLD(2) = X(2)
300  NEXT T
```

In order to interpret the output of this program refer to Figure 19.4. This is known as the phase diagram for the differential equations. Each path marked with an arrow-head represents the development of the two variables over time for any pair of starting values for c and k through which it passes. The two heavy lines represent loci of points such that either c or k is not changing: at the intersection is changing and we have a long-term equilibrium.

This equilibrium is the first thing which the program calculates. You are then asked to specify a value for the initial capital stock per man, corresponding to a point like $k(0)$ in Figure 19.4 (try 200). Then you must specify an initial level of consumption, $c(0)$. This fixes an initial point in the phase diagram and the program will then calculate the subsequent development of the system. If you choose a level of consumption that is too low then consumption will fall to zero in finite time leaving a large accumulated capital stock. This cannot be sensible. If initial consumption is too high then all the capital stock will be 'eaten up' in finite time. This can only be optimal if the time horizon is finite. The solution to the problem with an infinite horizon must therefore be the path which leads to the equilibrium. The program calculates the 'net present value' of the utility of each consumption path so you can compare the benefits of the alternative paths.

Notice that if the horizon is finite then the optimum path spends a lot of its time 'close' to the equilibrium; the longer the horizon, the closer is the path to the equilibrium and the longer it spends within a given neighbourhood of it. This is known as the *turnpike* property in the economic growth literature.

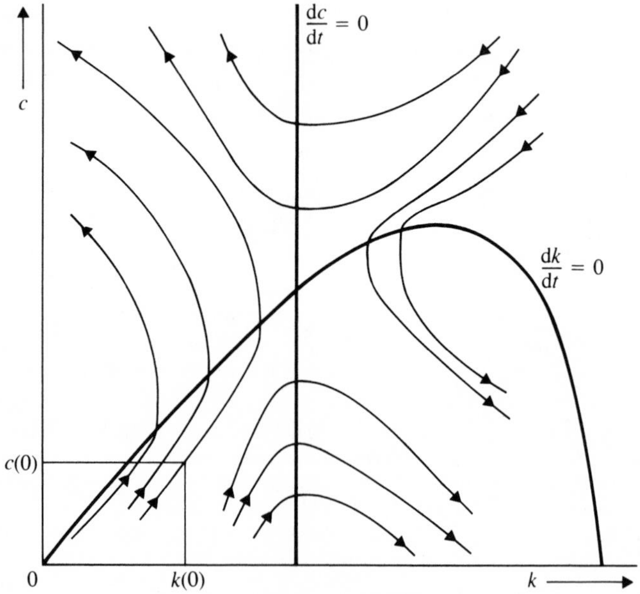

Figure 19.4

The general procedure for solving simple problems in optimum control may be summarized as follows. The problem is to maximize

$$\int_0^\infty f(x, u)\,\mathrm{d}t$$

with respect to $u(t)$, given $x(0)$ and subject to

$$\frac{\mathrm{d}x}{\mathrm{d}t} = g(x, u).$$

u is known as the *control* variable and x is the *state* variable. Define the *Hamiltonian* as

$$H(x, u, \lambda, t) = f(x, u) + \lambda(t)\,g(x, u).$$

This is the analogue of the Lagrangean function.

Then maximize $H(x, u, \lambda, t)$ with respect to u,

$$\frac{\partial H}{\partial u} = \frac{\partial f}{\partial u} + \lambda \frac{\partial g}{\partial u} = 0,$$

and put

$$\frac{\mathrm{d}\lambda}{\mathrm{d}t} = -\frac{\partial H}{\partial x}$$

$$= -\frac{\partial f}{\partial x} - \lambda \frac{\partial g}{\partial x}.$$

These are the necessary conditions for a solution.

This sketch gives the barest outline of a subject which is interesting, important and very complex. It has many applications in economics, and Intriligator (1971) gives a good introduction.

Bibliography

Apostol, T. (1957), *Mathematical Analysis* (Reading Mass.: Addison-Wesley)
Binmore, K. G. (1983), *Calculus* (Cambridge: Cambridge University Press)
Brand, L. (1966), *Differential and Difference Equations* (New York: Wiley)
Chiang, A. C. (1974), *Fundamental Methods of Mathematical Economics* second edition (New York: McGraw-Hill)
Courant, R. and John, F. (1965), *Introduction to Calculus and Analysis*, Volume 1 (New York: Wiley)
Davis, H. T. (1962), *Introduction to Nonlinear Differential and Integral Equations* (New York: Dover)
Dorfman, R., Samuelson, P. and Solow, R. (1958), *Linear Programming and Economic Analysis* (New York: McGraw-Hill)
Gale, D. (1960), *The Theory of Linear Economic Models* (New York: McGraw-Hill)
Glaister, S. (1981), *Fundamentals of Transport Economics* (Oxford: Blackwell)
Glaister, S. (1984), 'The Allocation of Urban Public Transport Subsidy', in *Privatisation and the Welfare State*, LeGrand and Robinson (eds) (London: Allen and Unwin)
Goldberg, S. (1958), *Introduction to Difference Equations* (New York: Wiley)
Goodwin, R. M. (1967), in *Socialism, Capitalism and Economic Growth*, Feinstein (ed), (London: Cambridge University Press)
Hadley, G. (1961), *Linear Algebra* (Reading, Mass: Addison-Wesley)
Henderson, J. M. and Quandt, R. E. (1971), *Microeconomic Theory*, second edition (New York: McGraw-Hill)
Intriligator, M. D. (1971), *Mathematical Optimisation and Economic Theory* (Englewood Cliffs, New Jersey: Prentice-Hall)
Johnson, H. G. (1971), *Macroeconomics and Monetary Theory* (London: Gray-Mills)
Kemeny, J. G. and Kurtz, T. E. (1971), *BASIC Programming* (Wiley: New York)
Karlin, S. (1959), *Mathematical Methods and Theory in Games, Programming and Economics* (Reading, Mass.: Addison-Wesley)
Kuska, E. A. (1974), *Maximization, Minimization and Comparative Statistics* (London: Weidenfeld and Nicolson)
Lancaster, K. (1968), *Mathematical Economics* (New York: Macmillan)
Land, A. and Powell, S. (1973), *FORTRAN Codes for Mathematical Programming* (Chichester: John Wiley)
Mills, G. (1969), *Introduction to Linear Algebra for Social Scientists* (London: Allen and Unwin)
O'Brien, R. J. and Garcia, G. G. (1971), *Mathematics for Economists and Social Scientists* (London: Macmillan)
Quirk, J. and Saposnik, R. (1968), *Introduction to General Equilibrium Theory and Welfare Economics* (New York: McGraw-Hill)
Rogers, B. (1980), 'Fast Fourier Transforms', *Practical Computing* December
Smith, A. (1982), *A Mathematical Introduction to Economics* (Oxford: Blackwell)
Yamane, T. (1962), *Mathematics for Economists* (Englewood Cliffs, New Jersey: Prentice-Hall)

Answers to odd-numbered problems

2.3.1 The problem is to find two values (numbers) which, when given to the variables x_1 and x_2, make both the equations simultaneously true statements. In case (*a*), the first equation says that x_1 and x_2 must be any two numbers which add to 3. To put it another way

$$x_1 = 3 - x_2.$$

Now, using this fact, we can 'eliminate' x_1 in the second equation to give

$$4(3 - x_2) - 2x_2 = 0$$

or

$$12 - 4x_2 - 2x_2 = 0$$

or

$$12 - 6x_2 = 0$$

so that

$$6x_2 = 12 \quad \text{or} \quad x_2 = 2.$$

Hence $x_1 = 1$, and it is easy to verify that these values do satisfy both equations.

Similarly, the solution to (*b*) is $x_1 = -4, x_2 = 11$.

2.3.3 Let x_1 be the total number of units of coal, and x_2 the total number of units of electricity produced per unit time. These amounts must equal what is used up by the two industries in production (intermediate demand) plus what is to be left for consumption (final demand). In other words:

$$x_1 = \tfrac{1}{6}x_1 + \tfrac{1}{2}x_2 + 10$$
$$x_2 = \tfrac{1}{3}x_1 + \tfrac{1}{12}x_2 + 10.$$

Multiplying both equations by 12 and rearranging,

$$-10x_1 + 6x_2 + 120 = 0$$
$$4x_1 - 11x_2 + 120 = 0$$

and solving, as in 2.3.1 above, yields $x_1 = \frac{1020}{43}, x_2 = \frac{840}{43}$.

Further analysis of this model is given in Sections 4.3, 9.1 and 9.4.

3.8.1 The result is

$$\begin{bmatrix} 3+2-\ 5 \\ 6+0-\ 6 \\ 9+8-17 \end{bmatrix} = \begin{bmatrix} 0 \\ 0 \\ 0 \end{bmatrix}.$$

(So that the three given vectors are in fact linearly dependent. See Section 5.2.)

3.8.3 The norm of the vector is

$$\begin{aligned} \sqrt{\{2^2+3^2+(-1)^2\}} &= \sqrt{(4+9+1)} \\ &= \sqrt{14}. \end{aligned}$$

If we now divide each element of the original vector by $\sqrt{14}$ to give

$$\begin{bmatrix} 2/\sqrt{14} \\ 3/\sqrt{14} \\ -1/\sqrt{14} \end{bmatrix}$$

then you can easily show that this has a norm (length) of 1.

3.8.5 By definition,

$$\begin{aligned} \|\lambda \boldsymbol{x}\| &= \sqrt{\{\Sigma(\lambda x_i)^2\}} \\ &= \sqrt{(\Sigma \lambda^2 x_i^2)} \\ &= \sqrt{(\lambda^2 \Sigma x_i^2)} \\ &= \sqrt{\lambda^2}.\sqrt{(\Sigma x_i^2)} \end{aligned}$$

and, taking the positive square root,

$$= |\lambda| \sqrt{(\Sigma x_i^2)} = |\lambda| \, \|\boldsymbol{x}\|$$

3.8.7 *Hint:* Generalize the trick used in the answer to question 3.

4.7.1 $$\mathbf{AB} = \begin{bmatrix} 8 & 10 \\ 12 & 11 \end{bmatrix}, \quad \text{but } \mathbf{BA} = \begin{bmatrix} -1 & 6 \\ 2 & 20 \end{bmatrix}.$$

4.7.3 $$\mathbf{AB} = \mathbf{BA} = \begin{bmatrix} 1 & 0 & 0 \\ 0 & 1 & 0 \\ 0 & 0 & 1 \end{bmatrix} = \mathbf{I}.$$

Observe that the coefficients of the $\boldsymbol{x}$s in the system of equations are those of the matrix **A**. Hence, putting the system into matrix notation, and pre-multiplying both sides by **B**:

$$\mathbf{BA}\boldsymbol{x} = \mathbf{B}\begin{bmatrix} 6 \\ 6 \\ -5 \end{bmatrix}, \quad \text{or } \boldsymbol{x} = \mathbf{B}\begin{bmatrix} 6 \\ 6 \\ -5 \end{bmatrix},$$

so the solution is

$$\begin{bmatrix} x_1 \\ x_2 \\ x_3 \end{bmatrix} = \begin{bmatrix} 3 \\ 2 \\ 1 \end{bmatrix}.$$

The matrix **B** is known as the *inverse* of **A**, and conversely, **A** is the inverse of **B**. (See Chapter 7.)

4.7.5 We want **B** such that

$$\begin{bmatrix} 2 & 1 \\ 5 & 3 \end{bmatrix}\begin{bmatrix} b_{11} & b_{12} \\ b_{21} & b_{22} \end{bmatrix} = \begin{bmatrix} 1 & 0 \\ 0 & 1 \end{bmatrix}$$

This gives four equations, the first of which is

$$2b_{11} + b_{21} = 1.$$

These can be solved to give

$$\mathbf{B} = \begin{bmatrix} 3 & -1 \\ -5 & 2 \end{bmatrix}.$$

B is the inverse of **A** (cf. question 3).

4.7.7 If the price vector is $\boldsymbol{p}$ and the matrix is **A**, then $\boldsymbol{p}'\mathbf{A}$ is a row vector giving profits for each factory. Postmultiplying by the vector $\mathbf{1}' = (1, 1, 1, 1, 1)$ will sum these profits. The matrix formula is therefore

$$\boldsymbol{p}'\mathbf{A1}$$

and the answer is 6.

5.4.1 (*a*) Independent. (*b*) Dependent; the second is -8 times the first. (*c*) Independent. (*d*) Dependent; the third is the second minus the first. (*e*) Dependent; the last is the sum of the first two.

5.4.3

$$\begin{bmatrix} 2 \\ 4 \end{bmatrix} = 2\begin{bmatrix} 2 \\ 5 \end{bmatrix} + (-2)\begin{bmatrix} 1 \\ 3 \end{bmatrix}$$

(cf. Problem 5.4.5).

$$\begin{bmatrix} 2 \\ 4 \end{bmatrix} = 2\begin{bmatrix} 1 \\ 0 \end{bmatrix} + 4\begin{bmatrix} 0 \\ 1 \end{bmatrix}.$$

5.4.5 (*a*) The problem is to find λ such that

$$(1-\lambda)\begin{bmatrix} 2 \\ 2 \\ 4 \end{bmatrix} + \lambda\begin{bmatrix} 5 \\ 0 \\ 3 \end{bmatrix} = \begin{bmatrix} \frac{7}{2} \\ 1 \\ \frac{7}{2} \end{bmatrix}$$

where λ is the amount of additive used. Clearly, the solution is

$$\lambda = \tfrac{1}{2}.$$

(*b*)

$$\begin{bmatrix} 4 \\ \frac{1}{3} \\ \frac{10}{3} \end{bmatrix}$$

is linearly independent of the other two vectors and so there can be no solution.

6.3.1 (*a*) $(2.0.3)+(1.-5.-2)+(3.0.1)-(3.0.-2)-(1.0.3)$

$$-(2.-5.1)=0+10+0-0-0+10$$

$$=20.$$

(*b*) $-2(-5-0)-1(-10-0)+3(0-0)=10+10$

$$=20.$$

(*c*) $-0.(?)+0.(?)+5(2+2)=20.$

Note that (*c*) is much the quickest. The value in the first row and third column has no effect.

6.3.3 (*a*) 2. (*b*) −9. (*c*) −110. (*d*) 0; third column is twice first added to second.

6.3.5 Expanding along the first row, we want values of λ such that

$$(-3-\lambda)\{(4-\lambda)(6-\lambda)-3\}=0.$$

$$\lambda=-3$$

is clearly one solution. Others will be obtained by setting

$$(4-\lambda)(6-\lambda)-3=0$$

and by inspection we see that values which satisfy this condition are

$$\lambda=3 \quad \text{and} \quad \lambda=7.$$

So there are three values of λ which make this determinant zero, −3, 3 and 7. These are known as solutions to the characteristic equation, or *eigenvalues*. For more on this topic, see Chapter 9.

7.3.1 We require a matrix **C** such that

$$(\mathbf{AB})\mathbf{C}=\mathbf{I}.$$

Premultiplying by $\mathbf{A}^{-1}$,

$$\mathbf{BC}=\mathbf{A}^{-1}\mathbf{I}$$

and premultiplying by $\mathbf{B}^{-1}$

$$\mathbf{C}=\mathbf{B}^{-1}\mathbf{A}^{-1}\mathbf{I}=\mathbf{B}^{-1}\mathbf{A}^{-1}.$$

7.3.3 (*a*) $\frac{1}{54}\begin{bmatrix} 12 & 12 & 6 \\ -9 & -9 & 9 \\ 4 & -14 & 2 \end{bmatrix}$ (*b*) $\begin{bmatrix} -\frac{2}{3} & \frac{1}{3} & -1 \\ \frac{2}{3} & -\frac{1}{3} & 0 \\ 1 & 0 & 1 \end{bmatrix}$.

(*c*) No inverse; linearly dependent rows.

(*d*)

$$\tfrac{1}{12}\begin{bmatrix} 2 & 3 & -1 & -12 \\ -4 & 6 & 2 & -24 \\ 6 & -9 & 3 & 36 \\ 0 & 0 & 0 & 12 \end{bmatrix}.$$

8.8.1

$$S - bp = a$$
$$D - dp = c$$
$$S - D = 0$$

or

$$\begin{bmatrix} 1 & 0 & -b \\ 0 & 1 & -d \\ 1 & -1 & 0 \end{bmatrix}\begin{bmatrix} S \\ D \\ p \end{bmatrix} = \begin{bmatrix} a \\ c \\ 0 \end{bmatrix}$$

so

$$p = \frac{1}{(b-d)}\begin{vmatrix} 1 & 0 & a \\ 0 & 1 & c \\ 1 & -1 & 0 \end{vmatrix}$$
$$= \frac{(c-a)}{(b-d)}$$

8.8.3 (*a*) Each equation just says that

$$x_1 + x_2 + x_3 = 6.$$

The rank of **A** is 1, as is the rank of $[\mathbf{A}, b]$, so the system is consistent, and any numbers summing to 6 will solve. More generally:

$$x_1 = 6 - x_2 - x_3.$$

(*b*) rank $(\mathbf{A}) = 2$, but rank $([\mathbf{A}, b]) = 3$, so the system is inconsistent.
(*c*) $x_1 = 3, x_2 = 2, x_3 = 1$. Unique solution.

8.8.5 (*a*) $x_1 = 2$, $x_2 = 4$, $x_3 = 6$. (*b*) inconsistent. (*c*) rank $(\mathbf{A}) =$ rank $([\mathbf{A}, b]) = 2$

$$x_1 = 2x_3 - 10, \quad x_2 = 5x_3 - 26.$$

9.7.1 The characteristic polynomial is

$$(1-\lambda)\{(1-\lambda)(1-\lambda) - 4\} = 0.$$

One solution is immediately $\lambda = 1$. Others are $\lambda = 3, \lambda = -1$.

$$\mathbf{D} = \begin{bmatrix} 3 & 1 & 1 \\ 20 & 2 & -2 \\ -4 & 0 & 0 \end{bmatrix}$$

(any scalar multiple of each column will do).

9.7.3 (*a*) $\lambda = 2$, 1 or -1. An eigenvector corresponding to $\lambda = 2$ is $(2, -3, 1)'$.

(*b*) $\lambda = 5$, 2, or 1. An eigenvector corresponding to $\lambda = 5$ is $(11, 3, 3)'$. Note that all elements in this case have the same sign; a general property of the eigenvector associated with the largest eigenvalue of a matrix of positive elements. This eigenvalue will itself always be positive.

10.3.1 (*a*) The principal minors are respectively 1, 1, 5 and so the matrix is positive definite.

(*b*) The minors are 1, 0, 0, and so the matrix is positive semidefinite.

10.3.3 The principal minors are 1, 2, 1 and so the matrix is positive definite. The eigenvalues are $1, 2+\sqrt{3}$ and $2-\sqrt{3}$, all positive, confirming the result.

11.4.1 $\{0\}; \emptyset; \{\text{All values of } x\}; \{\text{All values of } x, \text{except } 0\}; \{0\}; \{x | x \geqslant 0\}; \emptyset$

11.4.3 (*a*) 0 and 1; closed. (*b*) 0 and 1; open. (*c*) 0 and 1; neither. (*d*) 1, 2, . . .; closed. (*e*) $\{x \mid \|x\| = 1\}$ (sphere of radius 1); open. (*f*) $1, \frac{1}{2}, \frac{1}{3}, \ldots, 0$; neither. (All points in this set are boundary points, but it does not contain 0, which is also a boundary point.)

11.4.5

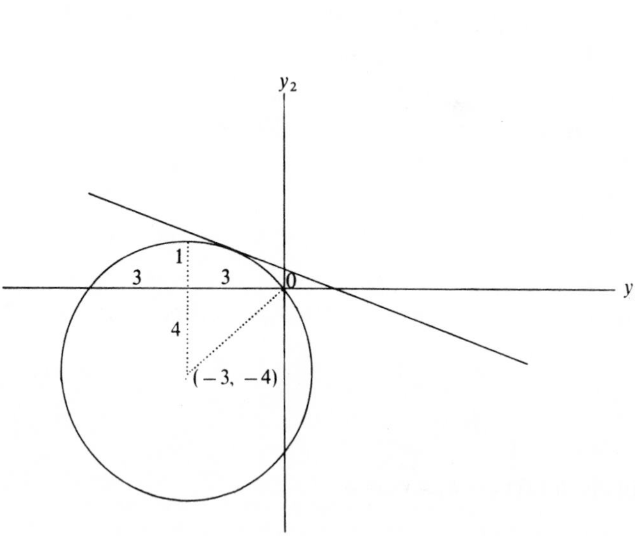

The set is the closed disc, radius 5, centre $(-3, -4)$ (which passes through the origin).

	Feasible	Boundary points	Efficient
(*a*)	No	No	–
(*b*)	Yes	Yes	Yes
(*c*)	Yes	No	No
(*d*)	Yes	Yes	Yes
(*e*)	Yes	Yes	Yes
(*f*)	Yes	Yes	Yes
(*g*)	Yes	Yes	No

Note that to be efficient a point must be a boundary point. (At an interior point one can have more output with the same input; clearly inefficient.) But a boundary point is not necessarily efficient (compare (*g*) and (*f*)). (*g*) would never be chosen when (*f*) is available, since in both cases 1 unit of good 1 is produced but (*g*) uses 7 units of good 2, whilst (*f*) only uses 1.

The price ratio of $\frac{1}{2}$ implies profit lines with a slope of $-\frac{1}{2}$. The solution is $y_1 = -3 + \sqrt{5}, y_2 = 2\sqrt{5} - 4$.

11.4.7 (*a*) In general

$$B' = \{\boldsymbol{x} \mid \boldsymbol{p}'.\boldsymbol{x} \leqslant m, \boldsymbol{p} \geqslant \boldsymbol{o}\}.$$

Take $\boldsymbol{x}_1 \in B'$ and $\boldsymbol{x}_2 \in B'$. Then

$$\boldsymbol{p}'.\boldsymbol{x}_1 \leqslant m \quad \text{and} \quad \boldsymbol{p}'.\boldsymbol{x}_2 \leqslant m.$$

So

$$\lambda \boldsymbol{p}'.\boldsymbol{x}_1 \leqslant \lambda m \quad \text{and} \quad (1-\lambda)\,\boldsymbol{p}'.\boldsymbol{x}_2 \leqslant (1-\lambda)\,m$$

and adding

$$\lambda \boldsymbol{p}'.\boldsymbol{x}_1 + (1-\lambda)\,\boldsymbol{p}'.\boldsymbol{x}_2 \leqslant \lambda m + (1-\lambda)\,m.$$

Or

$$\boldsymbol{p}'.\{\lambda \boldsymbol{x}_1 + (1-\lambda)\,\boldsymbol{x}_2\} \leqslant m$$

so

$$\lambda \boldsymbol{x}_1 + (1-\lambda)\,\boldsymbol{x}_2 \in B'$$

and B' is convex.

(*b*) Similarly, let $\mathbf{A}\boldsymbol{x}_1 = \boldsymbol{b}, \mathbf{A}\boldsymbol{x}_2 = \boldsymbol{b}$.

Then

$$\lambda \mathbf{A}\boldsymbol{x}_1 + (1-\lambda)\,\mathbf{A}\boldsymbol{x}_2 = \lambda \boldsymbol{b} + (1-\lambda)\,\boldsymbol{b}$$

or

$$\mathbf{A}\{\lambda \boldsymbol{x}_1 + (1-\lambda)\,\boldsymbol{x}_2\} = \boldsymbol{b}$$

so

$$\lambda \boldsymbol{x}_1 + (1-\lambda)\boldsymbol{x}_2$$

is also a solution, and the set of solutions is convex.

13.6.1 $(a)\ 4x^3$ $(b)\ 6x^5$ $(c)\ (n+1)x^n$ $(d)\ \dfrac{n}{m}x^{((n/m)-1)} = \dfrac{n}{m}x^{((n-m)/m)}$

$(e)\ -\frac{3}{2}x^{-\frac{5}{2}}$ $(f)\ 30x^4$ $(g)\ -x^{-(a+b)}$ $(h)\ 14x^6+5x^4$

$(i)\ (5x^4+2x)(x^3+x)+(x^5+x^2)(3x^2+1)$

$(j)\ 3(x+1)^2$ $(k)\ -x^{-2}-3x^{-4}$

$(l)\ \dfrac{3(4x^2+3)-(3x+2)8x}{(4x^2+3)^2}$ $(m)\ 18x\,e^{9x^2}$

$(n)\ e^{9x^2}(18x^4+3x^2) = 3x^2 e^{9x^2}(6x^2+1)$

$(o)\ 3e^{-3x}(1+e^{-3x})^{-2}$

(p) *Not* $2xa^{2x-1}$; that would be the derivative with respect to a. The correct result is $2a^{2x}\log a$.

13.6.3 $(a)\ \frac{2}{3}$ $(b)\ \dfrac{-y}{(x+2y)}$ $(c)\ -1$.

14.4.1 $(a)\ 2\sin x\cos x$ $(b)\ -6x\sin 3x^2$ $(c)\ e^x\sin x^3 + 3x^2 e^x\cos x^3$

$(d)\ 6x[1+\{\tan(3x^2)\}^2]$.

14.4.3 The characteristic equation is

$$(1-\lambda)\{(1-\lambda)(2-\lambda)+7\} = 0.$$

One solution is $\lambda = 1$. The others must solve

$$(1-\lambda)(2-\lambda)+7 = 0$$

or

$$\lambda^2 - 3\lambda + 9 = 0.$$

Using the standard formula (Section 9.2), the solutions are

$$\lambda_1 = \tfrac{1}{2}\{3+\sqrt{(9-36)}\} \quad \text{and} \quad \lambda_2 = \tfrac{1}{2}\{3-\sqrt{(9-36)}\}$$

or

$$\lambda_1 = \tfrac{1}{2}(3+\sqrt{-27}) \quad \text{and} \quad \lambda_2 = \tfrac{1}{2}(3-\sqrt{-27})$$

or

$$\lambda_1 = \tfrac{3}{2} + i\tfrac{3}{2}\sqrt{3} \quad \text{and} \quad \lambda_2 = \tfrac{3}{2} - i\tfrac{3}{2}\sqrt{3}$$

so that the roots are complex conjugates, with modulus

$$\sqrt{\{(\tfrac{3}{2})^2 + (\tfrac{3}{2}\sqrt{3})^2\}} = \sqrt{(\tfrac{9}{4}+\tfrac{27}{4})} = 3$$

and argument given by

$$\tan\theta = \frac{\frac{3}{2}\sqrt{3}}{3/2} = \sqrt{3}.$$

This is an example of a nonsymmetric matrix, having complex eigenvalues (and complex eigenvectors).

15.4.1 (*a*) 0; positive. (*b*) 0; same sign as a.

(*c*) 0; same sign as b; $-b/a$; opposite sign to b.

(*d*) No such values of x exist.

(*e*) As in (*d*); neither of these functions has a maximum or a minimum.

16.7.1 (*a*) A global minimum of $-\frac{100}{3}$ at $x_1 = -\frac{10}{3}$, $x_2 = -\frac{10}{3}$; no global maximum.

(*b*) A local minimum of 0 at $x_1 = \frac{1}{4}$, $x_2 = \frac{1}{2}$; a point of inflexion at $x_1 = 0$, $x_2 = 0$. No global maxima or minima.

(*c*) A saddle point at $x_1 = 1, x_2 = 4$. No maxima or minima.

16.7.3 (*a*) $\dfrac{\partial f}{\partial r}\,\mathrm{d}r + \dfrac{\partial f}{\partial m}\,\mathrm{d}m$

(*b*) $\dfrac{\partial f}{\partial r}\,\mathrm{d}r + \dfrac{\partial f}{\partial (M/P)}\,\mathrm{d}(M/P) = \dfrac{\partial f}{\partial r}\,\mathrm{d}r + \dfrac{\partial f}{\partial (M/P)}\left(\dfrac{P\,\mathrm{d}M - M\,\mathrm{d}P}{P^2}\right)$

(*c*) $\mathrm{e}^r g\{r, h(r)\}\,\mathrm{d}r + \mathrm{e}^r \dfrac{\partial g}{\partial r}\,\mathrm{d}r + \mathrm{e}^r \dfrac{\partial g}{\partial h}\dfrac{\mathrm{d}h}{\mathrm{d}r}\,\mathrm{d}r$

$$= \left[g\{r, h(r)\} + \frac{\partial g}{\partial r} + \frac{\mathrm{d}g}{\mathrm{d}h}\frac{\partial h}{\partial r}\right]\mathrm{e}^r\,\mathrm{d}r.$$

16.7.5
$$\begin{aligned} F(\lambda K, \lambda L) &= [a(\lambda K)^{-\beta} + b(\lambda L)^{-\beta}]^{-1/\beta} \quad (\lambda > 0) \\ &= [\lambda^{-\beta}(aK^{-\beta} + bL^{-\beta})]^{-1/\beta} = \lambda\,.\,F(K, L) \end{aligned}$$

$F_K = aK^{-(\beta+1)}(aK^{-\beta} + bL^{-\beta})^{-(1/\beta)-1}$,

$F_L = bL^{-(\beta+1)}(aK^{-\beta} + bL^{-\beta})^{-(1/\beta)-1}$

$F_K.K + F_L.L = (aK^{-\beta} + bL^{-\beta})\,(aK^{-\beta} + bL^{-\beta})^{-(1/\beta)-1} = F(K, L).$

17.8.1 Minimum (since functions are convex) of $\frac{1}{5}$ at $x_1 = \frac{1}{5}, x_2 = \frac{2}{5}, x_3 = 0$, $\lambda = -\frac{2}{5}$. (Note that the unconstrained minimum would be 0 at $x_1 = x_2 = x_3 = 0$.)

17.8.3 (*a*) By symmetry, $x_1 = x_2$, hence

$$x_1 + 1 = x_2 + 1 = \sqrt{4} = \pm 2$$

Taking the positive value (since the log is not defined for negative values),

$$x_1 = x_2 = 1.$$

(*b*) Minimum of $2-12\sqrt{5}$ at $x_1=2-12/\sqrt{5}, x_2=1-6/\sqrt{5}, \lambda=+\sqrt{5}/6$ and maximum of $2+12\sqrt{5}$ at $x_1=2+12/\sqrt{5}$, $x_2=1+6/\sqrt{5}$ and $\lambda=-\sqrt{5}/6$. Think carefully about the geometry of these problems. For instance, in (*b*) we have found points on the boundary of a circle in the x_1-x_2 plane, radius 6, centre $x_1=2, x_2=1$, which maximizes and minimizes a positively sloped plane.

17.8.5 A minimum of 10225/289 at $x_1=-\frac{21}{17}$, $x_2=-\frac{22}{17}$, $x_3=\frac{101}{34}$, $\lambda_1=\frac{56}{17}, \lambda_2=-1$.

18.6.1 $$\frac{\partial x_i}{\partial p_j}=\frac{\delta x_i}{\delta p_j}-x_j\frac{\partial x_i}{\partial m}$$

$$\frac{\delta x_1}{\delta p_2}=\frac{\lambda \mathbf{H}_{32}}{|\mathbf{H}|}=\frac{\lambda \mathbf{H}_{23}}{|\mathbf{H}|}=\frac{\delta x_2}{\delta p_1} \text{ by symmetry of } \mathbf{H}.$$

18.6.3 $$\frac{\partial r}{\partial M}=\frac{-1}{|\mathbf{A}|P}\left\{(1-C_Y)\left(G_b+\frac{B}{(1+b)^2P}\right)\right\}<0,$$

where

$$|\mathbf{A}|=\left\{(1-C_Y)\,L_b\,G_r-I_r\left[L_Y\left(G_b+\frac{B}{(1+b)^2P}\right)-L_bG_Y\right]\right\}>0.$$

Review problems

1. Define the term *linear independence* of a set of vectors, and also the term *a basis for* E^n. Prove that the representation of any vector with respect to a given basis is unique.

   One of the following three sets of vectors forms a basis for E^3. Identify it (giving your reasoning) and write the vector

$$\boldsymbol{x}=\begin{bmatrix}-3\\-2\\3\end{bmatrix}$$

   with respect to it.

   (*a*) $\begin{bmatrix}0\\-1\\2\end{bmatrix}\begin{bmatrix}3\\1\\1\end{bmatrix}$ (*b*) $\begin{bmatrix}0\\-1\\2\end{bmatrix},\begin{bmatrix}3\\1\\3\end{bmatrix},\begin{bmatrix}3\\1\\1\end{bmatrix}$ (*c*) $\begin{bmatrix}0\\-1\\2\end{bmatrix},\begin{bmatrix}3\\0\\3\end{bmatrix},\begin{bmatrix}3\\1\\1\end{bmatrix}$

   Explain the relevance of these concepts to the solution of systems of linear equations.

2. Solve the following systems of equations, briefly describing the theory underlying the techniques you use.

   (*a*)
$$\begin{aligned}2x_1+3x_2-x_3&=3\\-x_1+4x_2+x_3&=-2\\x_1\qquad+2x_3&=-1\end{aligned}$$

   (*b*)
$$\begin{aligned}2x_1+2x_2+2x_3&=4\\-x_1-3x_2+5x_3&=-4\\3x_1+5x_2-3x_3&=8\\x_1+x_2+x_3&=2\end{aligned}$$

   (*c*)
$$\begin{aligned}3x_1+5x_2+4x_3\qquad&=0\\x_1+2x_2+2x_3-3x_4&=0\\x_1\qquad-2x_3+14x_3&=0\end{aligned}$$

   (*d*)
$$\begin{aligned}5x_1+4x_2\qquad&=1\\2x_1+2x_2-3x_3&=-6\\-2x_2+14x_3&=30\\3x_1+2x_2+3x_3&=7\end{aligned}$$

(*e*)
$$\begin{aligned} x_1 + x_2 + x_3 &= 2 \\ x_1 + 2x_2 + 2x_3 &= 3 \\ x_1 + x_2 + 2x_3 &= 1 \end{aligned}$$

(*f*)
$$\begin{aligned} x_1 + x_2 + x_3 &= 2 \\ x_1 + 2x_2 + 2x_3 &= 3 \\ x_1 + x_2 + x_3 &= 1 \end{aligned}$$

(*g*)
$$\begin{aligned} x_1 + x_2 + x_3 - x_4 &= 2 \\ x_1 + 2x_2 + 2x_3 - x_4 &= 3 \\ x_1 + x_2 + x_3 - x_4 &= 2 \end{aligned}$$

(*h*)
$$\begin{aligned} 2x_1 + x_2 + x_3 - x_4 &= 0 \\ 3x_1 - x_2 + x_3 + 2x_4 &= 0 \\ -x_1 + 2x_2 + x_3 + 3x_4 &= 0 \\ 6x_1 - 2x_2 + 2x_3 + 4x_4 &= 0 \end{aligned}$$

(*i*)
$$\begin{aligned} 2x_1 + x_2 &= -1 \\ 3x_1 - x_2 &= 6 \\ -x_1 + 2x_2 &= -7 \end{aligned}$$

(*j*)
$$\begin{aligned} 2x_1 + x_2 + x_3 &= -2 \\ 3x_1 - x_2 + x_3 &= 5 \\ -x_1 + 2x_2 + x_3 &= -8 \end{aligned}$$

3. (*a*) Define the adjoint matrix and the inverse matrix of a square matrix, and state the necessary and sufficient conditions for the inverse to be well defined.
   (*b*) If $\boldsymbol{A}$ is a square matrix derive the conditions under which the equations $\boldsymbol{Ax} = \boldsymbol{0}$ will have a nonzero solution vector, $\boldsymbol{x}$.
   (*c*) Show that the matrix

$$\begin{bmatrix} 1 & 0 & 0 & 1 \\ 1 & 2 & 0 & 0 \\ 2 & 0 & 0 & 1 \\ 0 & 0 & 1 & 1 \end{bmatrix}$$

   is of full rank and calculate its inverse.

4. Define the terms eigenvalue and eigenvector. Prove the following propositions:

   (*a*) If $\boldsymbol{A}$ is a matrix with the property that

$$\boldsymbol{AA} = \boldsymbol{A}$$

   then its eigenvalues can only take the values 0 or 1.
   (*b*) If $\boldsymbol{x}$ is an eigenvector of a nonsingular matrix then it is also an eigenvector of its inverse.

   Find the eigenvalues of the matrix

$$\begin{bmatrix} 2 & 0 & 1 \\ 0 & 3 & 0 \\ 1 & 0 & 2 \end{bmatrix}$$

   and all the associated eigenvectors, normalized so as to have unit length. What can you say about the definiteness of this matrix?

5. Define the terms eigenvalue and eigenvector of a square matrix and describe the theory of a technique for finding them, illustrating your

answer by calculating all the eigenvalues of the matrix

$$\begin{bmatrix} 2 & 1 & 0 \\ 1 & 2 & 0 \\ 0 & 0 & 2 \end{bmatrix},$$

and finding an eigenvector associated with the largest eigenvalue. State the relationship between the eigenvalues and the determinant of a matrix and verify that it holds in this case. What do the eigenvalues you have found tell you about the definiteness of the above matrix?

6. Establish the relationship between the eigenvalues and eigenvectors of the nth power of a square matrix (that is, the matrix multiplied by itself n times) and those of the matrix itself. Diagonalize the matrix

$$\begin{bmatrix} 2 & 0 & 0 \\ 1 & 2 & 3 \\ -3 & -1 & -2 \end{bmatrix}.$$

Briefly describe any applications of the theory of matrix diagonalization.

7. (*a*) State Taylor's theorem for a function of one variable and use it to obtain the expansion of the function

$$f(x) = xe^x$$

(*b*) The function

$$f(x_1, x_2) = x_1^\alpha (x_2 - 1)^\beta$$

when constrained by

$$x_1^\beta - (x_2 - 1)^2 = -1$$

has a maximum and a minimum. Obtain expressions for the values of x_1 and x_2 at these points, and in the special case $\alpha = \beta = 1$ determine which is which by reference to the second order conditions.

8. (*a*) Use Taylor theorem to expand

$$f(x) = \log(1 + x)$$

about the point $x_0 = 0$. For what values of x is this expansion valid?

(*b*) Solve the problem of minimizing

$$2x_1 + x_2^2 + x_2 x_3 + x_3^2$$

subject to the constraint

$$(x_1 + x_2 + x_3)^2 = 1.$$

9. Describe the Lagrangean method of solving optimization problems when there are two constraints (including a statement of the second-order conditions). What interpretation can be given to the values of the Lagrangean multipliers at the optimum?

Find the extreme point of

$$f(x_1, x_2, x_3) = x_1 x_2^2 x_3^3$$

subject to the constraint that

$$x_1 + x_2 + x_3 = 12$$

and determine its nature.

10. Define the derivative of a function $f(x)$ at a point x_0 and use it to find the derivative of

$$f(x) = \frac{4}{x} + 2x^2$$

at a point $x_0 \neq 0$. What happens at $x_0 = 0$?

Extend the definition to include the partial derivative of a function of several variables.

Find the stationary point of

$$f(x_1, x_2, x_3) = x_1^2 + 2x_2^2 - x_3^2 + \tfrac{1}{2}x_1 x_2 - x_2 x_3 - x_2 - 20$$

subject to

$$x_1 - x_2 + 3x_3 = 1$$
$$x_1 \qquad + 2x_3 = 4.$$

11. Solve the following problems:

(*a*) minimize $x_1^2 + x_1 x_2 + (2x_2 - 1)^2$

(*b*) minimize $x_1^2 + x_1 x_2 + (2x_2 - 1)^2$, subject to the constraint $x_1^2 + x_2^2 = 1$.

In each case calculate the minimized value of the function and use the second order conditions to confirm that you have found a minimum. Comment on the relationship between the solutions to the two problems.

12. Consider the following model of the market of a product sold by a monopolist who advertises:

$$D = a + bP + cA \qquad a > 0, b < 0, c > 0$$
$$A = d + eS \qquad d > 0, 1 > e > 0$$
$$S = f + g(P - T) \qquad f > 0, g > 0$$
$$S = D,$$

where D is demand, P is price paid by consumers, A is advertising expenditures, S is supply and T is purchase tax (paid by the firm). The second equation says that the firm uses the 'rule of thumb' of fixing its advertising expenditure as a linear function of the number of units supplied. Use Cramer's rule to find the expression for the equilibrium level of advertising. How will this change if the government changes the level of purchase tax?

13. Consider the following model of the market for beef:

$$D = f(P_b)$$
$$S = g(P_b, P_f, \sigma_b)$$
$$P_f = h(W, \sigma_f)$$
$$e = P_b S,$$

where D and S are the demand and supply of beef, P_b is the price of beef, P_f is the price of feed for livestock, σ_b and σ_f are government subsidies on the beef and feed markets, W is the world price of grain and e is the (gross) earnings of beef producers.

Assuming equilibrium in the beef market, derive and compare expressions for the response of earnings to changes in the two government subsidies. Convert these into elasticity form and check the directions of these responses.

14. Consider the following model of crime deterrence:

$$p = \pi(f)$$
$$n = \nu(p, s, b)$$
$$\phi(f) + pn\sigma(s) = k$$

where

p	is the probability that a criminal will be caught and imprisoned (assume one crime per criminal in a unit of time)
f	is the size of the police force
n	is the number of crimes committed
s	is the severity of punishment (say, number of years sentence)
b	is the average booty ('winnings') of a crime
$\phi(f)$	is the cost of maintaining the police force at size f
$\sigma(s)$	is the cost of imposing a sentence s
k	is a constant sum of money available for expenditure on crime prevention

Find expressions for the effects of changes in severity of punishment and of average booty on the number of crimes committed. Make sufficient suitable assumptions (with justifications) to allow you to sign at least one of these. Comment on the relative efficiencies of changing sentences and changing security (i.e. changing b) in the light of this model.

15. Building societies are institutions who borrow from the general public and lend to those who wish to buy houses, using the rate of interest m (the mortgage rate) in both operations. Consider the following simple model:

$$D = f(m, a, Y) \qquad f_m < 0, f_a > 0, f_Y > 0$$
$$S = g(p, r) \qquad g_p > 0, g_r > 0$$

$$D = S$$

$$a = h(m, r) \qquad h_m > 0, h_r < 0$$

$$S(Y) = I(r) \qquad S_Y > 0, I_r < 0$$

$$M = L(Y, r) \qquad L_Y > 0, L_r < 0,$$

where

D is the demand for houses for home ownership,
S is the supply of houses for home ownership,
m is the mortgage rate,
a is the availability of funds,
Y is national income,
r is the market rate of interest on assets other than building society deposits,
p is the price of houses,
M is the real money supply.

The last two equations are the elementary *I–S* and *L–M* relationships.

(*a*) By simple substitutions reduce the system to three or four equations.
(*b*) Derive expressions for the response of house prices to a change in the money supply. Sign these responses if possible and discuss appropriate government policy if the sole aim is to reduce house prices, assuming the government can, if it wishes, put pressure on building societies to change m.

16. The following is a linear model of commuter behaviour in a city where the only modes of transport are bus and car:

$$b = \beta_1 A - \beta_2 f_b \qquad \beta_1 > 0 \quad \beta_2 > 0$$

$$c = \gamma_1 A - \gamma_2 f_c \qquad \gamma_1 > 0 \quad \gamma_2 > 0 \quad \beta_1 + \gamma_1 < 1$$

$$A = b + c$$

$$f_b = p_b + \tau_b(b + \alpha c) \qquad p_b > 0 \quad \tau_b > 0 \quad \alpha > 1$$

$$f_c = p_c + \tau_c(b + \alpha c) + t \qquad p_c > 0 \quad \tau_c > 0,$$

where b and c are the numbers of bus and car users, A is the 'attraction' of the city centre (which is proportional to the total number of city workers through the third equation), f_b and f_c are the respective total costs of bus and car use which (through the last two equations) are composed of money costs p_b and p_c, and time costs. Time costs depend on the total amount of road traffic (because of congestion) and $\alpha > 1$ represents the fact that a car user causes relatively more congestion than a bus user. t is a tax levied on car users.

(*a*) Eliminate A by substitution and rearrange the remaining four equations so that the four endogenous variables b, c, f_b and f_c

appear on the left, and the exogenous variables p_b, p_c and t appear on the right.

(*b*) Convert into matrix notation and use Cramer's rule to solve for the number of bus travellers.

(*c*) Hence, show that an increase in the (money) bus fare, p_b, will lead to fewer bus users. What is the effect of an increase in the car tax, t, on the number of bus users?

(*d*) Discuss the economics of these results.

Index

Bold numbers refer to sections or whole chapters